NOT FOR AMERICA

ALONE

Men of Zeal: The Iran-Contra Hearings (with William Cohen)
World on Fire: Saving an Endangered Earth

NOT FOR
AMERICA
ALONE

The Triumph of Democracy and the Fall of Communism

GEORGE J. MITCHELL

KODANSHA INTERNATIONAL
New York • Tokyo • London

Kodansha America, Inc.
114 Fifth Avenue, New York, New York 10011, U.S.A.

Kodansha International Ltd.
17-14 Otowa 1-chome, Bunkyo-ku, Tokyo 112, Japan

Published in 1997 by Kodansha America, Inc.

Library of Congress Cataloging-in-Publication Data

Mitchell, George J. (George John), 1933–
    Not for America alone: the triumph of democracy and the fall of
communism / George J. Mitchell.
        p.   cm.
    Includes bibliographical references and index.
    ISBN 1-56836-083-5 (hardcover : alk. paper)
    1. Communism–History.   2. Cold War.   3. Decommunization.   4. Post-
communism.   5. Democracy–United States.   I. Title.
HX36.M488   1997   96-50332
335.43–dc21

Book design by Debbie Glasserman

Printed in the United States of America
97 98 99 00   RRD/H   10 9 8 7 6 5 4 3 2 1

To My Parents

We defend and we build a way of life, not for America alone, but for all mankind.

–Franklin Delano Roosevelt

Contents

THE WRITING OF A BOOK on history is a rewarding experience. It requires extensive research and forces the making of many judgments. As a result, I have learned a lot, about the subject and about myself, from this book.

The judgments in it are mine. Therefore, any errors in judgment—or in fact—are mine. But the effort to create this book was not mine alone. Several people helped make it possible.

The two who did the most were Jack Waugh and Anita Jensen. As I have noted elsewhere, Jack is a brilliant researcher and writer, and a successful author in his own right. He is also a friend, whose opinion I value. Anita is a remarkable person. Of Latvian heritage, born in Germany amid the chaos of World War II, reared and educated in Australia, she has become extremely knowledgeable about American institutions and recent American history. She was a member of my staff in the U.S. Senate, where I relied heavily on her talents. I still do.

Others provided valuable assistance. Mike Hamilburg is more a friend than an agent. His guidance made this book possible. One of the many good things Mike has done for me was introduce me to Philip Turner, the editor-in-chief at Kodansha America. Philip always had time and sound advice for me.

Philip did me the favor of asking Elinor Nauen to review the manuscript. She was full of enthusiasm and good ideas.

Mikhail Gorbachev was generous with his time. I talked with him several times, including a lengthy interview in San Francisco in 1995.

Finally, I thank my wife, Heather. She provided continuing support and encouragement, which helped me complete a project that stretched over too many years.

This book is dedicated to my parents. Their influence on me increases over time; this is especially true of my mother. She had no formal education; she could not read or write English and she spoke with an accent and in fractured sentences. But she was wise, strong, generous, and inspiring. She has been gone for nine years but is still with me. She always will be.

Washington, D.C.
November 1996

NOT FOR AMERICA

ALONE

IN APRIL 1990, a group of U. S. senators met with Mikhail Gorbachev in a room next to his office in the Kremlin. For two hours we discussed the political, economic, and social revolution sweeping his country. He struck me as a man with problems of a magnitude to make my own difficulties as majority leader of the U.S. Senate seem trifling in comparison. He was playing the central role in the most important political drama of this century, a drama that was not only profoundly changing his own country, but the world as well. He was on center stage. And he seemed to me at once determined and uncertain—determined to proceed, uncertain as to how. He told us: "We cannot go on living as we did before. We must forge ahead. We have left the old behind, but we have not yet reached the new."

His general direction seemed clear to him; the precise course did not. His plans for his nation's economy were vague, at times contradictory. He said, "We must have radical reform of the economy." Then he said, "But we must do it carefully, phase by phase." It seemed to me that not only had "the new" not been reached, it had yet to be defined.

As with all revolutionaries, Gorbachev was following a hard

and peril-ridden path. In the minds of those in his society whom he scorned as "hard-liners," he was a disaster. In their view he was dealing away the fruits of victory so dearly won by Russian blood in World War II. The Soviet Union could no longer rely on the buffer states of East Germany, Czechoslovakia, Poland, Rumania, and Hungary to shield it from a hostile Western world. The realignment that the Russians most feared, that of a unified, powerful Germany, was suddenly about to become a reality. Moreover, the infection of freedom had reached into the very heart of the Soviet Union itself. From the Baltic in the north, through the Ukraine in the west, to Georgia, Armenia, and Azerbaijan in the south, the clamor for independence within the Soviet Union's own republics had grown irresistible. The hard-liners wished to return to the old ways, to shut this bold experiment down before it was too late.

But it was already too late.

Gorbachev has since given way to Boris Yeltsin, but the revolution he launched marches on. A return to the old ways is impossible. The Russian people have tasted freedom. They no longer live with the old fears. They are on a new course, wherever it may lead. As Gorbachev himself said in a more recent meeting: "I must say I think that the current brand of Communists, the Communist leaders and the various Communist parties that now exist in Russia, have decided that they would like to turn the clock back, that they want a kind of political revanche. That is bound to fail. They could try to get together with some members of the military, with members of some other circle and use a dramatic situation in our economy and our society to take power. But that, too, is doomed to fail."

As I left the earlier meeting with Gorbachev, the stocky, compactly built Soviet leader stood with his feet apart, looking very much like an aging boxer ready to counterpunch at the first sign of a clenched fist. Although he had already been through much—in five years he had changed history—the hardest struggle was still ahead. He looked me straight in the eye and smiled ever so slightly.

"Will Gorbachev succeed?" he asked rhetorically. "I know there's a lot of speculation about that." He didn't answer the question directly. But in his words, his bearing, and his actions, the answer was clear. He did not intend to fail.

But to me it was clear that he could not succeed. In our meeting and in his public statements, he had expressed his intention to complete the needed reforms within the structure of communism. He did not want to end communism. He wanted to change it.

Later that day, as I walked across Red Square, past the imposing complex of buildings that housed the center of the Soviet empire, I thought about what Gorbachev had said. It seemed to me that he was right about the need for reform, but wrong about the capacity of communism to accommodate that reform. I believed that communism was failing precisely because of its rigidity, and that meaningful reform could occur only if communism were first swept away. Communism was decaying, and its inability to compete was increasingly obvious, especially to those who lived within its grip.

The contrast was stark: Democracy was alive and growing. When capitalism confronted a crisis in the Great Depression, American democracy had the flexibility to permit necessary changes. Under the leadership of an energetic and pragmatic president, Franklin Delano Roosevelt, the United States struggled through several years of extraordinary social upheaval, including helping to fight and win the greatest war in human history. Following that war, a resurgent democracy and healthy, vibrant capitalism made possible unprecedented economic growth and an ever rising standard of living.

The spring sun was setting on Red Square as I walked away. Right now, I thought, the sun is rising in the United States. That's the way it is with the two systems.

What was there about communism—its origins, its principles, its practices—that caused it to fail? What is there about democracy that enabled it to succeed? What lessons can we in the United States learn from our long competition with communism?

As I got to the waiting car, I looked back at the Kremlin one last time. Then and there, I decided to try to answer those questions in this book.

There is a second, more personal reason that I wrote this book.

Democracy's triumph over communism requires an understanding of the American system, in which individual liberty is the highest value. Here each person counts. Because it is so personal, it is a system that can best be understood through each individual's experience.

So my understanding of American democracy is defined by my life as an American.

What I am and what I believe are inseparable from what my parents were and what they believed. As with most Americans, their stories began in distant lands.

MARY

My mother was born on October 12, 1902, in Bkassine, a small village in the mountains of south central Lebanon. Her father, Ameen Saad, apparently was a person of some stature, since he owned land and employed others to work his fields. Ameen and his wife Hilda already had three children, all girls—Marium, Rose, and Tamem—when Hilda again became pregnant. Ameen desperately wanted a boy. Disappointed with the birth of his fourth daughter, he called it quits. So he named his fourth daughter Mintaha—in Arabic, "the end."

Hilda died soon thereafter and Ameen took a second wife. The oldest daughter, Marium, married a man named Thomas Boles and had a daughter, Eugenie. Tom and Marium decided to emigrate to the United States, and, as was common at the time, they left their daughter behind until they could establish themselves and send for her. Rose then left to attend school in Europe; she would eventually emigrate to the United States and settle in Bangor, Maine. Then Tamem married and moved to Beirut, where she remained, the only one of the four sisters not to emigrate to

America. Mintaha was now alone at home with her father and stepmother.

In 1920, Tom and Marium Boles, by now settled in Waterville, Maine, sent for their daughter. Eugenie was nine years old and could not make the trip alone, so Mintaha was chosen to accompany her. She was eighteen years old and had never before left Lebanon. She could not speak or understand a word of English.

They traveled first to France. Then on June 5, 1920, Mintaha and Eugenie boarded the SS *Leopoldina* in Le Havre, arriving in New York eleven days later, 2 of the 1,169 immigrants on board, part of the human tide filling the American continent. Although they could not have known it at the time, they were on one of the last of the large immigrant ships. Within a few years the first laws sharply restricting immigration were enacted.

Mintaha never again lived in Lebanon. Once in America, she stayed.

It was—and is—common for immigrants to modify or change their names to sound more American. So, soon after she came to Maine, Mintaha became Mary.

Shortly after arriving in Waterville and moving in with her sister and brother-in-law, Mary learned the trade she would ply for over thirty years. The textile mills were running around the clock, spinning out yards of cotton and woolen goods. In the previous half century they had become, in the aggregate, the largest employer in the state, hiring thousands of immigrants.

Mary started in the Wyandotte mill in Waterville. By all accounts, she became a skilled weaver. For three decades she worked the night shift, from eleven o'clock in the evening until seven in the morning. The textile mills of the time were noisy, the clatter of the looms so deafening that conversation was impossible. The air inside the mill was hot and heavy, filled with suffocating lint that filled the workers' lungs, hair, nostrils, and ears and covered their clothing. The floors were slick with many years' accumulation of lubricating oil, forcing the workers to shuffle around, their feet always in contact with the floor so as not to slip. It was (and still is, although conditions in modern mills are much improved, particularly the reduction of lint) hot, hard, demanding work. Mary did it for more than thirty years so her children would never have to.

GEORGE

My father was born Joseph Kilroy on September 2, 1900, in Boston, the son of Irish immigrants. He never knew his parents and was raised in an orphanage in Boston.

It was a common practice at the time for the nuns who operated the orphanage to take the children on weekends to Catholic churches throughout northern New England. After Mass the children would be lined up in the front of the church. Any person attending Mass who wanted to adopt a child could do so simply by taking one by the hand and walking out. In that way, when he was four years old, Joe was adopted by an elderly couple from Bangor, John and Mary Mitchell.

The Mitchells had emigrated from their native Lebanon to Egypt, where they lived for several years before coming to the United States. Once here they assumed the surname of Mitchell. So when they walked out of church with him on that Sunday in 1904, Joe Kilroy became George Mitchell.

Soon after, the family moved to Waterville, fifty-five miles southwest of Bangor, where they operated a small store. George attended a parochial elementary school for a few years. Many of the students were of French ancestry, and he soon learned that language.

In his early teens he went to the Portland area, where he worked as a laborer on the railroad. From there he traveled to northern Maine to find work as a logger. Despite his lack of formal education—he attended school only through the fifth or sixth grade—my father was an avid reader. A friend of his once told my sister about one of their early trips into the woods. It was a cold winter. They took the train to Farmington, about forty miles to the northwest. From the station they walked several miles through the snow into the woods to a logging camp. For the whole trip, young George struggled with two large suitcases. One of them was especially heavy, because, as his friend learned when they unpacked, it was full of books.

The loggers slept in a big one-room building that held about sixty men. There was a large opening in the ceiling near the center of the building, for ventilation. Because my father was one of the youngest men, he got the least desirable bunk: an upper, right under what his friend called "the big hole in the ceiling." There he spent a miserable winter, working all day, cold and coughing all night. No wonder he enjoyed so much being a janitor in his later years. At least he was inside, keeping warm.

GEORGE AND MARY

When she arrived in the United States in 1920, Mary moved in with her sister and brother-in-law, who lived on the same street as the Mitchells. Sometime between 1920 and 1924, George and Mary met, fell in love, and married. I was born on August 20, 1933, the fourth of their five children.

Although she worked at several mills in the area, much of my mother's time was spent at the Wyandotte mill, a short walk from our house. She would be home in the morning to get us off to school and be ready with supper when we returned home. After putting us to bed in the evening, she would leave for work. She slept briefly during the day, but to her children she seemed tireless.

My father worked too, of course. But in the manner of the time, his working day ended when he got home. For my mother, home was another workplace—she cooked, cleaned, did the wash, the daily shopping, and many other chores. She often must have been exhausted, and surely she complained in private. But none of that was visible to her children. To us she was always there, always strong, always ready, always supportive.

My mother could not read or write English, and spoke it with an accent, mispronouncing words and fracturing sentences. But when any of us kidded her about it, she would laughingly mispronounce the words even more, for comic effect. She loved to cook and did so constantly. I can still recall the warm smell of freshly baked bread. It filled the house constantly, sweeter than the most expensive perfume.

She was totally devoted to her husband. But her dependence on him did not become evident until after his death. It soon became clear that life had been taken from her, too. She began to shrink, physically and mentally. She became irritable and unpredictable. Worst of all, my mother, who had been so open, warm, and trusting, became mistrustful. Within a few years she had to enter a nursing home. There, despite good and warm care, she declined rapidly. Seeing her near the end—pale, eyes shut tight, murmuring incoherently—was the most painful experience of my life, far more painful than her death. Gradually, that image fades and I recall the strong, laughing woman of my youth, looking across the table at me and saying, "You want to grow up strong and smart? Drink your milk and do your homework!"

For many years my father worked at the bottled-gas division of the local utility company. In 1950 the utility discontinued the bottled-gas business and my father lost his job. This crisis nearly destroyed him and his family.

He was fifty years old, and for nearly a year he was out of work. My mother's income barely supported us. As the year stretched on, my father's mood darkened. I was sixteen years old when it happened, in my last year in high school; that September, I entered Bowdoin College. I didn't appreciate at the time what my father was going through. We argued often, to my mother's dismay. Try as he might, he couldn't get a job. And each failure drove the downward cycle of despair. Finally, just as his self-esteem had all but vanished, he found a job as a janitor at Colby College in Waterville. For him, and for the family, it was a reprieve, a new life.

To this day I have difficulty restraining my anger when I hear someone engage in blanket condemnation of the unemployed. Having lived through the tragedy of unemployment, I know that not everyone who is out of work wants to be. Yet, without precisely saying so, that is the message of many who seek to exploit the issue. The more conscienceless among them equate all of the unemployed with welfare cheats. Whenever I hear such remarks, I angrily think (and often, if the situation permits, say): My father wasn't like that; he wanted to work, and I'm sure that many who are out of work are like him; they are human beings, many of them perhaps living through the despair that gripped my father.

Fortunately, Colby College needed a janitor. It didn't seem like much of a job, but it suited my father. He loved books and learning, so just being at and around an institution of higher learning all day was a pleasure for him. In addition, his intelligence soon became obvious, and he was quickly promoted to being in charge of all the janitors and maids and then of much of the grounds crew as well. As a result, he thoroughly enjoyed the last fifteen years of his working life, even though he earned very little during those years.

I learned from my father's experience that there is dignity in every human being and in every form of work. My father took pride in his work as a janitor and as a groundskeeper. He brought excellence to his work. In turn, this work gave him back his dignity and self-esteem. It saved his life.

Gradually, his despair gave way to optimism. The difficult times were fewer and fewer, and finally disappeared. He again laughed and joked and took an interest in what and how I was doing. I felt as though we had come out of a long dark tunnel into bright sunshine.

Although he was not a learned man, when my father became interested in a subject, he pursued it avidly. Perhaps because he could rarely travel, he was fascinated by geography. I can still recall sitting with him, poring over maps of the world.

Because of him I became interested in the subject. After he retired from Colby, and for the next seven years until his death, whenever I returned to Waterville to visit, I prepared a geography quiz for him. I studied maps and atlases, trying to stump him. But I never did. I remember clearly the quiz I gave him on my last visit before his sudden death in July of 1972. I asked him three questions, of increasing difficulty: Which country has the most cities with a population of more than 1 million? How many such cities are there in that country? Name them. Without hesitation he answered: China (obviously); fourteen (not so obvious); and then, methodically, with brief pauses, Peking, Shanghai, Canton, Chunking, Mukden, and so on down the list. Perfect! I told him I'd stump him the next time. We both laughed.

I never saw him again.

MY PARENTS KNEW little of history or political science. But they understood the meaning of America because they valued freedom and opportunity.

They conveyed their values to their children by example more than by words. Though it was not often expressed aloud, their message was clear. Their values were simple, universal in reach, and enduring in strength: faith, family, work, and country.

My mother's faith was total and unquestioning, an integral part of her life. After she stopped working, she attended church every day. Her faith involved more than ritual. For her, religion meant more than just listening to the gospel or reciting it. It meant living its message in daily life. And she did.

My parents' commitment to family was deep and unwavering. Nothing came before their children. Ever. My father's goal in life was to see that all of his children graduated from college. And I'm proud to say that we all did.

As far back as I can remember, everyone in our family worked: delivering newspapers, mowing lawns, washing cars, sweeping floors, shoveling snow, in textile mills and paper mills, self-employed and for others. We never talked about it. It was expected and we just did it. I worked my way through college by working as a truck driver, an advertising salesman, a dormitory proctor, and a fraternity steward. I then worked full-time as an insurance adjuster while attending law school at night. To me, this was not remarkable. It was the way of life I learned from my parents. My father believed that success was certain for anyone who got a good education, worked hard, and lived in our open society. Conversely, to him the obstacles to success were a lack of education, an unwillingness to work hard, or the misfortune of living in someplace other than America. He believed, deeply and totally, that there is no limit to how far and high one can go in America. And he was right.

We Americans are the most fortunate people ever to have lived, citizens of the most free, the most open, the most just society in history. Most of us are Americans by accident of birth. But America was built by immigrants who became citizens by choice. Some came to escape religious persecution or political oppression, some to join families already here. Most came to seek a better life in a land of freedom and opportunity.

Before I entered the Senate, I had the privilege of serving as a federal district court judge. Occasionally, I presided over naturalization ceremonies, where immigrants are sworn in as citizens. I've never done anything more meaningful or enjoyable.

In these ceremonies the new citizens-to-be gathered before me in a federal courtroom. They had come from every part of the world and had gone through all the required procedures. Now I administered to them the oath of allegiance to the United States and made them Americans.

After every ceremony I spoke with each of the new citizens. Their devotion to, and enthusiasm for, the country of their choice was inspiring. I asked them why they came, how they came, what they hoped to find here. Their answers were as different as their countries of origin. But through them all ran a common theme, best expressed by a young man from Asia who, when I asked why he came, answered slowly, in halting English, "I came because here in America everybody has a chance." That young man, who had been an American for only a few minutes, summed up the meaning of our country in one sentence. America is freedom and opportunity.

Throughout history, in society after society, the status quo has hardened into place as the temporary convenience of one generation became the fixed privilege of the next. That tendency stems from the natural desire of people to preserve what they possess.

The search for security and predictability is never-ending. And societies must provide some security and predictability, for in their absence, civilized life is impossible.

But they also enhance a tendency toward possession, power, and status. Thus it is understandable and inevitable that the wealthy will seek to preserve their wealth, the powerful to continue their power, and those with high status to maintain that status. In each case they will try to institutionalize and make permanent their privilege, to pass it on to their heirs if possible. To accomplish this, at various times in countless societies, traditions and categories (or classes, or castes) have been established on the basis of birth, religion, occupation, wealth, or skin color.

Usually, the power of government has been used to protect the privileged. And the result has been a more rigid, less flexible, less dynamic society. Mighty civilizations have come into being, grown strong and productive, built great cities and produced powerful works of architecture, art, and literature, only to become, over time, calcified by the accretion of tradition, privilege, heredity, and social structure. The civilizations of Sumer and Aqqad, of Egypt and Ch'in China, of Rome and Byzantium, all succumbed to enemies which, in earlier and more vibrant times, they would have conquered and assimilated.

Measured across the sweep of human history, the American experiment is young. But in its short history, what is unique and promising about America is that here the government has often been a force for change; not always, but more so than in other societies. The American people have acted, through their government, to steadily expand their liberties and rights, to resist the natural tendencies to preserve and pass on wealth, status, and power.

For example, in the beginning, the right to vote was granted only to adult white men who owned property. Seventy-five years later, in the wake of a bloody civil war, the right to vote and the protections of law were extended to all adult men. Sixty years later the same rights were extended to women. Another half century later the nation agreed that those old enough to fight its wars were also old enough to vote.

It was through the power of government, acting for the common good, that Americans expanded the concept of civil rights, from the abolition of slavery to the integration of the military and ultimately of the whole society.

It was through the power of government, acting for the common good, that Americans enhanced the rights of women, freeing them from the discrimination to which they were for so long (and in many parts of the world, still are) subjected.

It was through the power of government, acting for the common good, that Americans made human rights a central consideration in international affairs. It is the right thing to do. And it is in our interest, because only in a world that shares a common understanding of the inalienable rights of the individual can the ideals of American democracy be safeguarded.

Unlike Soviet Russia and most governments throughout history, the power of government in America has been deployed to break down barriers of discrimination, not build them; to open the doors of opportunity, not close them. It is a crowning achievement that, more than most and more often than not, the American government has worked to protect and enhance the most important thing about our civilization: the freedom of each individual to choose freely what to be and do, to the limits of human initiative, energy, and talent.

To maintain that freedom is the ultimate American challenge.

Part 1

THE RISE

AND FALL

Chapter 1

THE RED TERROR

DOCTOR

IN THE SPRING OF 1990, I stopped in Berlin for meetings with the mayor and other German officials before going on to Moscow to meet with Gorbachev and top Soviets. I had the chance to go to the center of Berlin, where I stood before the remnants of the infamous wall that had divided that city for nearly thirty years.

Enterprising young Germans offered hammers and picks for a small fee to visitors who wanted to chisel out their personal chunk of the wall. Couples strolled peacefully across the broad field of grass that for so long was a free-fire zone separating East from West.

Amid the carnival atmosphere I wondered what Karl Marx would have thought about the fact that his life's work found its most tangible expression in a barbed-wire-topped concrete wall, defended by machine guns, erected to keep workers from fleeing the workers' paradise. It's ironic, I thought, that it should end here, not far from where it began.

One hundred forty-three years earlier, in the last days of 1847, an intense young man, not yet thirty, sat at his desk in Brussels. His goal was large: he wanted to change the world. He dipped his steel-tipped pen into India ink and wrote with a fury to match his ambition. The words he wrote would change the course of history.

"A spectre is haunting Europe," Karl Marx wrote, "the spectre of communism." He knew exactly what he wanted to say; he had been shaping these ideas for the past half decade. But it had to be put just right this time, for this was to be the manifesto that synthesized the very core of his thinking. It had to have force. He wanted to move people.

"The history of all hitherto existing society is the history of class struggles," he wrote next—an idea from which everything else would follow.

His friend and coauthor, Friedrich Engels, had written a first draft. But it had been in the form of questions and answers—much too soft to suit Marx. It didn't have the impact this work required. So he was rewriting it, giving it emotion. It was already late; they had missed the first deadline. It was all so clear to Marx. In the economic order that had been building for more than fifty years since the beginning of the industrial revolution, two classes had been at war in the world. The capitalists, the bourgeoisie—how he hated that word; he spit it out on the page—had seized and monopolized the total product of all labor for their own exclusive, selfish use. To do that they had subjugated the other class, the workers—the proletariat—in the most cruel, inhumane, and unnatural way. Such subjugation went against natural needs, against what men as social human beings require to develop themselves freely and fully. By accumulating the means of production exclusively into their own hands, and all its product in the form of capital, they had deprived the majority of the producers—the workers themselves—of the fruit of their own labors, the sweat of their own brows. Because of this, industrial society was now divided into the exploiter and the exploited. Alienation had replaced cooperation for common ends.

Marx believed there was only one way to change that: revolution. It had to happen, it was inevitable. The masses would—must—rise up, throw off the bourgeois rule, end this final form of exploitation, and create a truly classless society at last. There would be only a Communist society, then, in which there would be no more class warfare, only the harmonious cooperation that all human beings crave. It would be the revolution to end all revolutions.

It would happen, he believed, in two stages in every country. A bourgeois revolution would first overthrow the remnants of the feudal order and establish a bourgeois democracy and capitalism, with its attendant phenomenon—a subjugated industrial proletariat. The proletariat, created and organized by the bourgeois for its own selfish ends, would then rise up like Frankenstein's avenging monster and carry the process to its ultimate conclusion—the final revolution, the overthrow of the capitalist system and the establishment of socialism.

Marx saw revolutions as "the locomotives of history." And this particular locomotive now screaming down the track was coming no matter what the bourgeoisie thought or did. It would without question run them over. "What the bourgeoisie . . . produces, above all," he was now writing, "are its own gravediggers. Its fall and the victory of the proletariat are equally inevitable."

He was nearly finished now, writing the final paragraph. "Let the ruling classes tremble at the Communist revolution," he wrote. "The proletarians have nothing to lose but their chains. They have a world to win. Working men of all countries, unite!"

There it was, his manifesto, his call to revolution. He had put it succinctly, in just a few pages, and he had said it well.

Actually, he had done much more than that. It was, as Isaiah Berlin would say, the greatest of all socialist pamphlets, eloquent and powerful, a document of prodigious dramatic force with "the lyrical quality of a great revolutionary hymn." Berlin saw it, as have most of us since, as the fuse that ignited "the great ideological storms that have altered the lives of virtually all mankind."

Karl Marx's temperament, that of a theoretician, ill fitted him for the life of the bomb-throwing revolutionary. Nor did he ever live that life. He may have thought and written dangerously, as one of his biographers has said, but he didn't live that way, choosing to remain always the "verbal revolutionary." He plotted his revolutions on paper, never approaching the barricades.

Even if Marx never personally stormed a rampart, there was

not a more fierce and effective insurrectionist or one more often exiled as dangerous to the government in power. He was heart and soul a revolutionary, and had been since his university days.

Marx abhorred political romanticism, emotionalism, and humanitarian appeals of every kind. There is not much mention in the *Manifesto,* or anywhere else in Marx's prodigious output, of moral progress, eternal justice, the equality of men, the rights of individuals and nations, the liberty of conscience, the fight for civilization, and other such high-minded ideals so dear to us. To Marx all that was cant, and he had no sympathy with it.

Indeed, Marx fancied himself the rigorous, severely factual social scientist. He was, Berlin tells us, "repelled as much by the rhetoric and emotionalism of the intellectuals as by the stupidity and complacency of the bourgeoisie."

In February 1848 the London Communist League, which had commissioned the *Manifesto,* published it in Marx's native German, encased in a yellow jacket. The world would never be the same again. It is with the *Manifesto* and its creator that the story of the remarkable events of our own century must begin.

TRIER WAS GERMANY'S oldest city and one of its most beautiful. Nestled in the Rhineland's rich Mosel Valley, it was a city of spires, home to more churches than any other German town of its size. In the early 1800s it was a village of 12,000 inhabitants, a remnant of another time, little touched by the social or economic upheavals then reshaping much of the civilized world.

There Karl Marx was born in 1818, the second of eight children, to prosperous middle-class parents. Descended from generations of rabbis on both sides of his family, it was no surprise that his bent was toward scholarship.

Marx went away to university in 1835, first to Bonn, then to Berlin, ostensibly to study law, but at Berlin he was soon diverted to the extracurricular pursuit of political theory and philosophy. Formal studies were neglected. His father, who thought he saw in his young son the spark of something unique, concluded sadly that Karl's academic life had degenerated into "a sort of gloomy drifting around in all branches of knowledge, dark brooding by a dull oil-lamp."

After Marx got his doctorate from the University of Jena—which he never attended—he married Jenny von Westphalen, a tall auburn-haired, green-eyed beauty four years his senior. She was to remain throughout their life together his "dearest treasure." In forty years of marriage he would put her through all shades of turmoil, joy, exile, poverty, despair, and revolutionary dreams. And she would love him as much as he loved her.

The newlyweds emigrated almost immediately to Paris. Marx had become a journalist, the editor of a radical weekly with seditious leanings, and it had become almost impossible for him to speak out openly in Germany. It was 1843 and Paris was a hotbed of intellectual and revolutionary ferment—a perfect fit for Marx. The city teemed with poets, painters, musicians, writers, reformers, and theorists, many of them exiles from across Europe. Marx dove into this milieu, and in it he began to shape and refine his theories of political and economic revolution. When the magazine he came to Paris to edit folded after one issue, he caught on as editor of an incendiary weekly review called *Vorwärts!* (Forward!).

Paris had also attracted Friedrich Engels, the young son of a wealthy manufacturer—a bourgeois capitalist—with factories in Germany and in England. Engels was a respected member of the Manchester Stock Exchange, but wholly faithless to his class, enthusiastically sharing Marx's loathing of bourgeois capitalism. Even as they met for the first time, over lunch at Paris's famous Café de la Régence in August 1844, Engels was about to begin writing a fiery indictment of capitalist subjugation of the English working class. The book, *The Condition of the Working Class in England,* published early the next year, was a masterpiece of reporting. Engels was a first-rate observer and a skilled writer. His descriptions of the life of workers in England, where he represented his father's firm, were devastating. Marx would read and reread them often over the years to remind himself of the plight of the proletariat.

These two young German revolutionaries were soulmates from

the start, sharing their insurrectionary visions. Marx was the scholar, the thinker digging deep and drawing out original interpretations from history, slow but steady with a pen. Engels was not so deep, but he was quick with the written word. Engels became Marx's alter ego, his chief of staff, his coauthor, his best friend, and his financial underpinning through the years, unwavering in his devotion. Together they were what one observer called "the personification in our time of the ideal friendship portrayed by the poets of antiquity." It was said that "their brains . . . worked in unison." When they were apart, they wrote one another almost daily. Marx would talk to Engels's letters as if they were Engels himself: "No, that's not the way it is," he would reason with the letter; or, "You're right there."

Where Marx was exiled, Engels would follow. And in early 1845, Marx was exiled from Paris for his radical writings, leaving for Brussels in February, where he lived for the next three years.

There he tied his hopes to a new party which, to distinguish itself from the more moderate socialists, had adopted the name of Communists. It was a party not of intellectuals, like Marx, but of factory workers and small artisans, self-educated men enraged by wrongs and easily persuaded of the need for revolution to abolish privilege and private property. They became Marx's people, his proletariat. He created a small revolutionary organization consisting of his wife, Engels, a handful of other radical writers, and two typesetters, and called it the Communist League. Marx had concluded by then that communism could only be won by a rising up of the proletariat, and he had dedicated his life to organizing and disciplining it to that end.

In Brussels, Marx wrote the *Communist Manifesto,* and in March 1848 it was published in London. A week later a revolution came—in Paris. It wasn't the revolution Marx envisioned, and the *Manifesto* had nothing to do with inciting it. Indeed, his short work would have little to do with inciting anything in its first decades. It was little known as the Paris revolutionaries stormed the barricades in 1848. It would not be much known outside of Germany until the 1870s.

But there in 1848, happening before their eyes, was what the *Manifesto* preached—a people's revolution. Europe was ablaze at last, with an uprising—what Engels was to call "the first great battle between Proletariat and Bourgeoisie." It was a revolution that wouldn't last, however; it was over and being reversed by June. But it did bring Marx back to Paris briefly—in the nick of time, for the *Manifesto* had gotten him kicked out of Belgium. Soon he was back in Germany to edit an even more inflammatory and insurrectionist journal. By the following July he was again thrown out of Germany. Suddenly, England appeared to be the only congenial place left for him. Marx arrived in London in August 1849, with Jenny and their children following a month later. He expected to be in England but a few months, until he could get another publication together or until the next insurrection, anticipated at any moment. But he remained in London for the rest of his life, waiting for the revolution that never came.

The failure of the Paris uprising in 1848 was a disappointment to Marx. It had not been "the iron broom of revolution" he had hoped it would be. But that did not shake his basic theoretical structure. He simply made adjustments and revisions. He could see that it wasn't going to be as simple as a quick coup d'état followed by proletariat control and a withering away of all class struggle. A small elite band of leaders alone could not seize power and pull off a successful revolution. The proletarian masses must be made conscious of their role, educated to their destiny, prepared by the leaders. That could take time, but unless it was done, nothing permanent would ever be won.

Permanence was important to Marx. In March 1850, he and Engels outlined for the German Communists, in their *Address of the Central Authority to the League* (sometimes called *Address of the Central Committee to the Communist League*), how the revolution, when it did come, should be consolidated. When the uprising against the old order began, cooperation with the bourgeoisie would at first be necessary. But from that point the proletariat must move quickly and ruthlessly to take the revolution one final step, out of the hands of the bourgeois reformers—who would use it only for their own ends—and make it permanent for the masses.

As he settled into exile in London, all that Marx saw missing from this scenario was the right kind of revolution. None was in sight; in fact, there was a general collapse of militant radicalism everywhere. But one, he thought, must surely be imminent, certain to come in the train of some catastrophic economic slump that could not long be delayed. He continued to wait, longing to scent "the morning air of revolution," passing years looking for, hoping for, and predicting the "colossal eruption of the revolutionary crater." It would one day come, but not as he had envisioned, not in his lifetime, and not where he thought it would happen.

Marx's reputation shut him off from most respectable employment. Desperate, he applied at one point for a position as a booking clerk in a railway office. His worn clothes, unkempt appearance, and finally his illegible handwriting did him in. He would in time be known throughout the world, but now he was down and out in London, living hand to mouth, moving his growing family from one squalid flat to another, pawning his clothes and hiding pantless from creditors in the upstairs rooms. His friend Wilhelm Liebknecht figured that Marx's rate of pay, if computed on the amount of years and hours he spent producing his masterwork, *Capital,* put him well beneath the salary level of the worst-paid day laborer in Germany.

Engels helped, sending Marx as much money as he could, or raising it among their friends. But the poverty–"all this hellish muck," Marx called it–ground on. Three of his and Jenny's children died, in part because of their living conditions. Marx himself, of rugged constitution, began to be stalked by chronic illness– boils, carbuncles, hepatitis, liver and gall disorders, headaches, inflammation of the eyes, neuralgia, catarrh, and rheumatic pains. At times, that he was able to work at all was miraculous. But he did, going to the British Museum the instant it opened and staying until the moment it closed, doing "this continual journalistic hack-work" by day and working on the more serious stuff deep into the night, often in intense pain. "Whatever happens," he growled in a letter to Engels, "I hope the bourgeoisie, as long as they exist, will have cause to remember my carbuncles."

Ordinarily, Marx did not complain; he simply lived and worked, always with a single-minded obsession. "If one approaches him," wrote a friend, "one is greeted with economic expressions instead of salutations." Marx's mother said: "If only Karl had *made* capital, instead of just *writing* about it."

In these poverty-wrenched years in London, Marx was indeed writing about it, publishing the first volume of *Capital* in 1867. He came to call it "the damned book," and in the end would only finish the first volume. Second and third volumes would be completed by Engels after his death, and a fourth by the German Marxist Karl Kautsky from the voluminous notes Marx left behind. If the *Manifesto* was, as Liebknecht says, "the cornerstone of the modern labor movement," then *Capital* was its foundation. Engels would call volume one "the Workers' Bible."

By then Marx's fortunes were beginning to turn. A new and militant party of German socialist workers had risen out of the ruins of the revolution of 1848, and they continued to consult him. He had inspired their movement and laid its foundation, and all questions of theory and practice were referred to him. He was admired, feared, suspected, and obeyed. But he was also in London and out of socialism's mainstream, and he was loath to lend his name to any organization that he and Engels hadn't personally created. An exception was finally made, however, in 1864 when French and English labor representatives met in London and formed the International Working Men's Association, later known as the First International. For the first time, Marx was pulled into world socialism, a movement built on his own ideas. Finally, he would be actively engaged.

The French and English labor leaders had come to London for the great Exhibition of Modern Industry. Meeting casually, they made a landmark decision—to constitute an international federation of workers pledged not to reform but to destroy the prevailing economic system and substitute a socialist society—Marx's *Communist Manifesto* incarnate. Marx, of course, was invited in, and he came to the first organizing meeting of the executive committee as the representative of the German artisans in London. He saw this federation as a movement to propagate the ideas of the *Manifesto* and to prepare the way for the revolution to come.

By the second meeting he was in charge. He drafted the International's constitution and wrote its inaugural address. Like the *Manifesto,* the inaugural was boldly drawn, making many of the same points and ending with the same rallying cry: "Workers of the world unite!"

Thus launched, with Marx's stamp all over it, the International grew rapidly. Soon there were branches in many nations. Governments grew uneasy and began talking of arrests and proscriptions. With Engels, Marx took charge of the central office and of strategy. Everything passed through his hands and went where he directed it. With this activity, his spirits soared.

It was too good to last. Marx was hard to work with and soon faced breakaway movements. Following the Franco-Prussian War in 1870 and another aborted revolutionary uprising in France, which the International neither created nor inspired, the organization slid into decline. In 1876 it expired.

Even though it didn't last, the International did more than anything else to secure Marx's fame and influence in world socialism—that and the publication of the first volume of *Capital* in 1867. With *Capital* he had given the international socialist movement a definitive intellectual foundation in place of a scattered mass of vaguely defined and conflicting ideas. The work was translated into Russian, English, and French, and discussed worldwide. Marx was without question the supreme moral and intellectual authority of international socialism.

He had in fact a mixed image. To many government officials, he was the *chef pétroleur*–head troublemaker–of that "insane Commune movement" and every other odious revolutionary movement in Europe. They saw him as the fanatical dictator of a world conspiracy against the moral order, against the peace, happiness, and prosperity of mankind, and the evil genius of the working class, plotting to overthrow and destroy the peace and morality of civilized society, systematically exploiting the worst passions of the mob, befouling worker relations with employers to create universal chaos in which everyone would lose and all would be made level—rich and poor, bad and good, the industrious and the idle, the just and the unjust. Red had become the symbol of communism, and he had become the "Red Terror Doctor."

To revolutionaries and idealists, however, Marx was the untiring strategist and tactician of laboring classes everywhere, the infallible authority on all theoretical questions, the creator of an irresistible movement to overthrow injustice and inequality. He was the angry modern Moses bearing the tablets of the new law, leader and savior of the oppressed. With Engels, his Aaron, by his side, he stood ready to enlighten and lead the benighted, half-comprehending masses.

But it was nearly over for Marx. He was now in his last decade, old beyond his years, ravaged by his chronic illnesses. The worst of his poverty had been lifted by the 1870s, mainly with permanent financial help from Engels. But his creative powers had faded. He had added nothing new to *Capital.* The rest of his life would be devoted to theoretical studies and vain attempts to restore his failing health. He would maintain a vigorous correspondence with socialists everywhere, and many would make pilgrimages to see him. But to the end there would be no revolution. Insurrection seemed dead everywhere, embers glowing faintly only in Russia and Spain.

By the early eighties, with his end near, the only European country that remained virtually impervious to Marx's teachings was the one he lived in. England's prolonged prosperity had drained away the workers' revolutionary energy. Marx thought it would be a while before they would shake off "their bourgeois infection."

In December 1881 his beloved Jenny died of cancer. Her last words: "Karl, my strength is broken." Little more than a year later, on March 14, 1883, ill with an abscess on his lung, Marx fell asleep in the armchair in his study and quietly died.

That day Engels wrote Liebknecht, "The greatest brain of the second half of our century has ceased to think." It is through him, Engels wrote, "that we all are what we are; and it is through his theoretical and practical activity that the movement is what it is today."

In America the next day the *New Yorker Volkszeitung* wrote: "In the anesthetizing clatter of the machines, in the comfortless darkness of mine shafts, in the scorching heat of the blast furnaces, in all the 'master countries' where there are workers who have not forgotten how to think under the deadly pressure of exploitation, and who with all their hearts and with iron will, struggle for a better future, today will be a day of sadness. . . . He discovered the cure for misery. He taught how to destroy the slavery which is the basis of other slavery."

At Marx's funeral, Engels said: "His mission in life was to contribute in one way or another to the overthrow of capitalist society . . . to contribute to the liberation of the present-day proletariat which he was the first to make conscious of its own position and its needs, of the conditions under which it could win its freedom. Fighting was his element. And he fought with a passion, a tenacity and a success which few could rival . . . and consequently was the best-hated and most calumniated man of his time . . . he died, beloved, revered and mourned by millions of revolutionary fellow workers from the mines of Siberia to the coasts of California, in all points of Europe and America . . . his name and his work will endure through the ages."

IT WAS NOT UNTIL THE 1880s, the decade of his death, that Marx's ideas began to make much progress. He would never know that socialist parties in every nation of the world would come to acknowledge him as their master. He would never know the power that his name would evoke. He would never know that for generations of workers worldwide the name Marx would become the symbol of hope for a life free of want and anxiety, that he had made them believe that it was not only possible, but certain. He would never know that movements built on his theories would nearly dominate the coming century. He would also never know what confusion, schisms, and anguish, what terror and murder, they would trigger.

The arguments broke out from the moment the German Social Democratic Party, the first to adopt Marx's philosophy, was founded at Gotha in 1875. The internal debates have not ceased to this day. The *Communist Manifesto* was clear enough. To get to a socialist society, the bourgeois capitalist society must be overthrown. But when that appeared to Marx in the light of experience to be unrealistic—at least right then—he fashioned an alternative approach: while the proletariat was being prepared for the revolution, it would be well to cooperate temporarily with the bourgeoisie, to encourage trade union activity, pass social legislation, and generally work for the betterment of the masses. He became in effect the prophet of democratic as well as insurrectionist socialism. And with that he set the stage for an endless variety of socialisms, from social democracy to revolutionary communism—all coexisting fitfully under Marxism, the philosophical umbrella he himself had unfurled.

Socialist thought broke into two competing camps. One, the pure Marxists, continued to believe that revolution was the only answer. The other, called revisionists, came to believe that evolution would reach the same end and make revolution unnecessary, that the same result was possible through parliamentary participation and maneuvering. There might not be a need to overthrow the existing system; it might instead simply be changed.

Engels, ironically, became the first revisionist after Marx's death. In his declining years, as socialist parties in various nations began to make electoral strides, Engels began to say that exploitation of the proletariat by the bourgeoisie might be lifted peaceably, parliamentarily. Socialism could gradually permeate capitalism and take it over, changing society and becoming the governing idea. Revolution would be unnecessary; the bourgeois state would simply wither away.

There was ample justification for such views. Things were happening everywhere to moderate militant Marxism—things Marx himself had not foreseen. Capitalism was not in trouble everywhere. The misery of the proletariat was not deepening as he had predicted; indeed, the worker's lot was improving in many nations.

In some countries revolution was not a likelihood—in America, for one. Capitalism was prospering in the New World, and so was the "proletariat." The democratic, representative system was open to reform; the social structure could be changed by an election at any time if a majority demanded it.

Indeed, as time passed, social revolution, if it was to come at all, seemed likely only in Eastern Europe—perhaps in Russia. In Western Europe, socialism was becoming daily less revolutionary and more reformist. Two factors Marx hadn't reckoned on—economic imperialism and national, rather than class, loyalties—were emerging, changing everything. Peaceful conquest seemed the workers' best hope. The relationship to pure Marxism, *Communist Manifesto*—style, was becoming more tenuous and difficult to find as the nineteenth century passed into the twentieth. Socialists in Western Europe, though still giving lip service to revolution, were opting for evolution.

Russia, however, was another matter, a special case. Marx had always hated Russia. He was as anti-Russian through most of his lifetime as any twentieth-century anti-Communist ever was—for many of the same reasons. He viewed tsarist Russia as the world's detestable champion of reaction—able and willing to crush all attempts at liberty within and without its borders. In the train of the 1848 uprisings in France, he had urged an immediate German war with Russia to forestall its interference with the democratic revolutions then under way. Of Russian politics, he said: "Its methods, tactics, manoeuvres may change, but the guiding star of its politics—world rule—is unchangeable."

It could have been Ronald Reagan speaking in the 1980s.

The Russian radicals, however, loved Marx. They had read his two great works with the same sense of exhilaration as those who had read Rousseau in the century before. They found much in his writings that applied exceptionally well to their own condition. Nowhere was the instrument of labor more effectively used to subjugate, exploit, and impoverish the worker than in Russia.

On learning that the first translation of *Capital* was to be in Russian, Marx couldn't suppress a rueful smile: "It is an irony of fate that the Russians, whom I have fought constantly for the past twenty-five years, not only in German but also in French and English, have always been my 'patrons.' "

There was a basic problem in Russia that did not lend itself to the kind of revolution Marx had in mind. Russia had very little proletariat to engineer a revolt and very little capitalism to revolt against. It was a peasant country, and Marx didn't believe that any society could become socialist while still peasant-dominated. It must first pass through a capitalist phase, which Russia had not yet even entered. It must become a mature bourgeois society with a well-developed and exploited proletariat to have his kind of revolution.

Nevertheless, toward the end of his life Marx came to believe that of all countries, Russia was the most likely to have a revolution. It might not be his kind, but it would be a revolution nonetheless. And that was better than nothing. At least the tsar would be overthrown and couldn't then interfere with other, more acceptable revolutions elsewhere in Europe. He believed as early as the 1870s that revolution was inevitable in Russia, and said that a war between Germany and the tsar would trigger it– "act as the midwife," as he put it. The elements were all there for "a fine explosion," he said. "Unless Mother Nature is particularly unkind to us then we will still experience this joy."

Mother Nature would not be kind to Marx, for he would die and not experience the joy. But thirty-four years later Germany and the tsar were at war as Marx had foreseen, and there were men in Russia hungering for revolution and waiting to seize the hour.

WHAT ARE WE to say of Marx today?

He once wrote, "The philosophers have only interpreted the world in different ways; the point is to change it." But Marx and Engels were an odd pair of world-changers. Neither of them had any aptitude whatever as party leaders; they lacked an important requirement: the art of handling people skillfully. But together they distilled the accumulated knowledge of centuries and gave it a unique revolutionary spin all their own. As Engels said, "Just as Darwin discovered the law of evolution in organic nature, so Marx discovered the law of evolution in human history."

Historian Harold Laski believed that no thinker of the nineteenth century drove home with such force the idea that the collective energies of men ought to be devoted to the common good, not just the good of a dominant class.

But Marx failed to recognize the extent to which all human beings act in their self-interest. Thus his analysis was flawed at its core. And his predictions were, as is now clear, far off the mark. That is because, committed as he was to historical inevitability, he could not foresee the adaptability of democratic capitalism; his hatred of capitalism blinded him to its capacity for change.

Marx did catch the hopes of the downtrodden. Alfred G. Meyer, a twentieth-century scholar, has written that Marx's thinking expressed "the yearning of backward societies for a place in the sun, of underprivileged minorities for equal treatment, of manual workers for a place of respect in their social system." It brought to the underprivileged "the hope and the conviction that they will catch up with, and overtake, those who are on top today; that the last shall be the first, and not in a paradise beyond, but on this earth and in the near future." Those are common aspirations.

But the method Marx advocated to achieve those aspirations—violent revolution—and his intolerant adherence to ideology led inevitably to the corruption of idealism that has so marked Marxism in practice. That brutal misapplication of ideals has caused untold misery in the world, right up to our time. Marx himself, toward the end of his life, said, "I am no Marxist."

Chapter 2

THE DAZZLING

BOLSHEVIK SUN

THE WORLD WAR WAS INTO ITS THIRD YEAR, all Europe was reeling, and Vladimir Ilyich Lenin was on his way to Petrograd's Finland Station with revolution on his mind.

Lenin was frantic to be in Russia. The revolution he had been waiting for all his adult life—working for, agitating for, living in exile for—had happened. And he had not even been there. The hated tsarist regime had collapsed swiftly. In four dramatic days in February 1917 the monarchy had tumbled and Nicholas II, the last of the Romanov line, had abdicated.

It was sudden and unplanned. It caught everybody by surprise, even the revolutionaries themselves, those who had been expecting it would someday come. It was an upsurge from below, an uprising by mutineering Russian army soldiers.

After three centuries of absolute rule the Romanov autocracy crumbled overnight, and there were few mourners. But there was nothing to replace it. A provisional government made up mainly of moderate socialists was quickly cobbled together. But Lenin saw it as a pitiful replacement—a "half-power," a shadow authority that couldn't last. He had a better idea.

Lenin, the leader of the small radical socialist offshoot called the Bolsheviks, was unhappy with the conduct of the Bolsheviks already in Petrograd (today's St. Petersburg). Like him, most of them had played no part in the February uprising; like him, they had been either in exile or in prison. When the first of them arrived on the scene—among them a Georgian Bolshevik named Joseph Stalin, fresh from exile in Siberia—they were hesitant, uncertain what to do. In Lenin's view they had done all the wrong things. Searching for a place in the emerging order, they had adopted a conciliatory posture toward the provisional government and the moderate socialist leadership. That must be stopped. Lenin had to get to Russia. And for nearly two long agonizing months he worried that it might not happen.

The stocky, balding, Tatar-eyed Marxist from the banks of the Volga River saw more clearly than anyone in Russia what was happening. It was just as Karl Marx had foreseen. In the whirlpool of war, the tsarist monarchy would totter and fall. When that hour came, the true socialist revolutionaries must seize power. As his railroad car rolled toward the Finland Station, Lenin knew the hour was at hand.

For Lenin the war had come as a godsend, even though it was killing Russians by the millions. Four of every ten Allied soldiers falling at the front were Russians. The war would kill 2.5 million of them before it would end. Lenin knew what it was doing to Russia, but still he welcomed it. He saw then what historians would see later, that the war would be the seedbed for revolution—"the forcing-house," as one writer put it. Lenin believed the war would transmute into an epidemic of civil wars that would turn all Europe to socialism. It would happen first in Russia, then spread throughout the continent.

In 1911, Lenin had told the socialist journalist Max Beer that "such a war as you see looming on the skyline will be the prologue of a tremendous revolutionary drama. . . . In our Russian history of the nineteenth century, war always brought deep changes and upheavals. I feel something is going to happen."

Russia's enemies in this war were not Lenin's enemies, Russia's friends were not his friends. His enemies were the tsar and the capitalist imperialists who exploited workers in every nation.

Imperialism was something new in the Marxist lexicon—Marx himself had little to say about it. But Lenin, thirty-four years after Marx's death, was saying a great deal about it. To him imperialism was the most advanced phase of capitalism—its "monopoly stage." Since Marx died, capitalism had grown stronger, not weaker as he had predicted. The lot of the worker had grown more prosperous, not more miserable. To Lenin that could only be explained by imperialism. Western capitalism had simply gone international, enabling the capitalists to exploit a colonial proletariat rather than their own workers. For Lenin the war was an imperialist-engineered struggle to expand capitalism to monopoly proportions worldwide. But it was capitalism's last gasp, he believed, to be followed by the longed-for wave of revolutions in the West. And it was all beginning in his own Russia.

That is what Lenin believed as his railcar raced out of Finland toward Petrograd. He had nearly given up the dream. When the world war raged on into 1917, he had nearly lost heart. As he waited in exile in Switzerland, watching and writing, he began to doubt if the revolution would happen in his lifetime. Like Marx, he might never see it.

It was a wonder the monarchy had survived so long. Twelve years before, in 1905, the tsar had gone to war with Japan over control of Manchuria and had been badly beaten. That defeat, together with widespread famine, had shaken the autocracy to its foundations. It shook then, but didn't collapse. The present revolution was triggered by the same two causes—an enervating and bloody war Russia was losing, and widespread famine. But this time the regime, twelve years more corrupt, could not survive.

There had been harbingers. As early as the summer of 1915, strikes and food riots erupted in the textile towns and in Moscow. One Russian had written then: "The strain is so great that any carelessly thrown match may kindle a terrible fire. And God save us from seeing this fire. This would not be a revolution but a terrible Russian riot, senseless and pitiless. It would be an orgy of the mob."

Within two years the match was struck. The revolution arrived, and Lenin believed it might become permanent if its leadership now fell into the right hands—Bolshevik hands, especially his. This war, this famine, might doom the monarchy once and for all and raise up a socialist dictatorship in Russia.

When the revolution swept Petrograd, Lenin was in Zurich, his optimism at low ebb. The news came as his wife was finishing the dishes and he was preparing to leave for the library. "Haven't you heard the news?" a friend threw open the door and exclaimed. "There's a revolution in Russia!"

Lenin burned to be there. But how, with no legal means of transportation available to him? The Allies would not let him through their lines, not the known firebrand who advocated turning the world war into an epidemic of civil wars. The only likely passage was through the territory of Russia's enemy, Germany, which could be counted on to be more sympathetic to an uprising against the tsar.

So he bargained with the Germans. They agreed to grant him rail passage in a sealed car through Germany to Sweden. From there he would pass through Finland to Russia.

"We will take the first train," the impatient Lenin told his wife, Nadezhda Krupskaya, the moment he and the Germans agreed. The first train departed in two hours, and they were on it.

When they arrived at the Russian border station at Belo-Ostrov, it was the first time in more than ten years that Lenin had been home. An advance contingent of Bolsheviks from Petrograd came aboard to greet their leader, and as the train sped on, he wagged an admonishing finger in their faces and assaulted them with questions.

The train pulled into Finland Station on April 3—Easter Sunday—at eleven o'clock at night. People filled the entire square, rendering movement nearly impossible. The Bolsheviks were putting on a show for their leader. Red flags hung everywhere. Trams could scarcely make their way through the crush. Throbbing motorcars edged slowly around the crowds. Here and there an armored car shouldered ominously through the throng, and a mounted searchlight thrust its way in. Banners and triumphal arches gilded in red and gold spanned the train platform, which was lined with soldiers ready to present arms. Welcoming inscriptions and revolutionary slogans were everywhere. Inside the tsar's waiting room a representative of the provisional government shifted uneasily.

As Lenin stepped from the train, the band struck up the "Marseillaise"; the "Internationale" was not yet in its repertoire. The crowd pushed Lenin before it into the waiting room. There the representative of the provisional government greeted him with the hope that he would join them in governing Russia. Ignoring him and his hope, Lenin hailed the coming civil war throughout Europe. Suddenly before them, as one of the provisional government's sympathizers put it, was this "dazzling Bolshevik sun," and "before the eyes of all of us, completely swallowed up by the routine drudgery of the revolution, there was presented a bright, blinding exotic beacon, obliterating everything we lived by."

Outside in the square, Lenin mounted an armored car and addressed the crowd: "Soldiers, sailors, and workers: The dawn of the world-wide Socialist Revolution has risen . . . our Russian Revolution marks its beginning and has opened a new era."

In the days to come he would reject the idea of any support for the provisional government and of Bolshevik participation in its revolution. He sensed immediately the new government's weakness, and systematically set about to engineer its overthrow.

This stern, relentless disciple of Karl Marx was not to be taken lightly. No other man in Russia at that moment—perhaps no other man in history—combined to so extraordinary a degree the traits of a true revolutionary leader. Lenin brought together in one mind and body absolute dogmatic faith in a cause, bold sweep of imagination, shrewd common sense, tight control over a band of dedicated followers, unshakable toughness, and total ruthlessness.

He was born Vladimir Ilyich Ulyanov in 1870 in the village of Simbirsk on the banks of the Volga—a little town set among orchards and fields of sweet-smelling grass. He was descended from German and Swedish merchants and landholders on his mother's side, from whom he inherited his iron will and relentless sense of purpose; and from Chuvash tribesmen from the east on his father's side, from whom he got his lawlessness and his slanting eyes.

Like Marx, Lenin was born to bourgeois parents. His father was a scholarly man, a professional educator and loyal servant of the tsar. He would have been mortified if he had lived to learn that all his surviving children had become dedicated revolutionaries.

Lenin didn't start out as a revolutionary. He began as a lawyer. In part, the decision for insurrection was made for him. His favorite, older brother, Alexander, was the first in the family to become a revolutionary—with an attempted assassination of the tsar himself. The attempt failed, and Alexander was hanged in 1887. Young Vladimir found himself at the University of Kazan in the Tatar heartland on the Volga, trying to be as inconspicuous as possible. With his neat dress and demeanor, he appeared anything but the revolutionary. But he couldn't avoid guilt by association. Detectives noticed him at a meeting protesting the dismissal of all professors of liberal tendencies and remembered his dead, incendiary brother. That was the end of university for Vladimir. He was briefly imprisoned, then expelled and never readmitted. He would get his law degree in 1890 from Petrograd, in absentia and by examination.

In the spring of 1893 he was twenty-three and prematurely bald, with a neatly trimmed beard and mustache. He was practicing law in Petrograd and was a dedicated revolutionary. In the autumn of 1888 he had read *Capital*. His sister Anna remembered the epiphany vividly. Lenin was in the kitchen, surrounded by newspapers and gesturing violently. He had found a new religion. At the time he knew little of the proletariat—there were few in that class in Russia—but he agreed with Marx's theories that the proletariat was the rightful heir to surplus value, not the capitalists into whose hands it had exclusively fallen. He would find, as his early Marxist mentor and friend, Georgi Plekhanov, already had, that Marx's teaching was "the modern 'algebra of the revolution.' An understanding of it is essential to all who want to carry on an intelligent fight against the existing order of things."

In Petrograd, Lenin began to practice law less and study revolution more. He became a leader in insurrectionist socialist circles, an acid-tongued apostle of Marx at his most revolutionary. Soon he was totally absorbed in figuring out how Marx's theories might be applied to Russia. And he became one of the hunted. Thoughts such as he was thinking, causes such as he was embracing, got people thrown into prison in tsarist Russia. Lenin became expert at finding new ways to hide, dodging up dark streets, inventing codes and stratagems and disguises to throw off the tsar's network of police spies. It was to become his way of life for the next two decades.

MARX SAW MONARCHIES as transitional institutions between the old feudal classes and the nascent bourgeoisie, which in turn would exploit, then give way to the proletariat. The Russian Marxists, like Marxists everywhere, split into evolutionary and revolutionary schools of thought. Lenin was clearly in the latter camp from the start. He believed that Marxist moderates such as the German Social Democrats and their Russian counterparts, the Mensheviks, had "turned Marx's teaching into an academy, while to me it is an arsenal replete with arms for the revolution."

Socialism did not take root in Russia until the 1880s–and then not within the peasant class, which comprised 75 percent of the population, but in the intelligentsia, which represented only 10 percent. The first socialists came from the cultured nobility, later from sons of the clergy, lesser government officials, and the lower middle classes. Often having little in common, they were held together by the idea of a new socialist order for their homeland. Dostoyevsky called them "the great wanderer of the Russian land," who had acquired the power of living by ideas alone. Marxism, either evolutionary or revolutionary, became their creed. Dreaming of a socialist Russia became their specialty.

For years they got nowhere. Ironically, virtually the first Marxist in the world was a Russian, N. I. Saznov, a steppe landowner who lived in Paris. He became a Marxist at the end of the 1840s when the ink was scarcely dry on the *Communist Manifesto*. This amazed Marx at the time–he such a confirmed Russian-hater and his first disciple a Russian landowner! Russian Marxism grew little over the next thirty years. Given the circumstances—an indifferent peasantry, too few bourgeois, virtually no proletariat—revolution in Russia seemed to face a long wait. If it was going to happen at all, a few steps had to be skipped. Marx simply had to be interpreted as a blueprint for revolution. That is what Lenin came to believe.

In those early days of socialism the tsardom itself was a considerable obstacle. Far from collapsing, it seemed to be prospering. Imperial Russia seemed secure, peaceful, and unassailable. Socialism seemed stalled. The assassination plot that got Lenin's brother hung in 1887 was a small blot on an otherwise serene canvas. The 1880s therefore became for Marxists the decade of "quiet," the era of "small deeds," a time of "inner soul-cleansing" and "step-by-step" progress.

In 1890 everything changed. A deep and protracted famine swept Russia. The imperial government reeled into a crisis that its clumsy bureaucratic apparatus proved ill equipped to handle. The famine brought with it a flurry of revolutionary activity, and for the first time, a perceptible swing to Marxism. Strikes in the Petrograd textile industry in the mid-1890s suggested that a revolution might indeed be possible. The Russian masses for the first time seemed aroused. The Marxists at long last had a foothold.

What they didn't have was unity. The Russian Social Democratic Party was not founded until 1898. By the turn of the century its members, nearly all in exile, were fighting one another. Soon there were Mensheviks touting evolution and Bolsheviks, with Lenin leading the cry, clamoring for revolution. Lenin believed Mensheviks talked revolution but did not intend to live it or produce it. He thought the party should be purged of all but a dedicated core of Marxists who wanted to act, not just talk. His idea was for a revolution run exclusively by a tight coterie of professionals—socialist editor Max Eastman called them "scientific revolutionary engineers." In 1903 there were few of them. They called themselves Bolsheviks (after the common Russian word *bolshe,* meaning "bigger, more," as opposed to *menshe,* meaning "less, smaller") for the first time that year. They were but a score in number, hardly living up to their new name, hardly enough to overturn anything, much less a three-hundred-year-old autocracy.

Lenin's Marx was the Marx of the *Communist Manifesto* and the March 1850 *Address of the Central Authority to the League*. A waiting game was not for him. If Russia had no bourgeois intermediaries to pull off the revolution, nor a proletariat to then displace them, he would do without both. By 1905, after an abortive uprising following the Russo-Japanese War, he was convinced it was possible, and he believed it could be made to happen by his small claque of revolutionary engineers. He set his sights on what he called an uninterrupted revolution and what Marx and Engels had called a permanent revolution.

The Mensheviks were appalled. They deplored both him and his interpretation of Marx. Taking Marx at his word—that the world ought to be changed, not merely interpreted differently— Lenin openly and angrily split with the Mensheviks. By 1905 he was preaching "everywhere and most decisively schism, schism, schism," and holding separate Bolshevik congresses. For the next dozen years, wherever he was, in exile or prison, he was thinking and plotting revolution twenty-four hours a day.

When the first opportunity for revolution came in 1905, Lenin was not ready. Tsar Nicholas had taken Russia into a war with Japan over Manchuria, and it had not gone well. On the battlefront the tsar's troops met with one setback after another, each lowering the prestige of the government another notch in the eyes of the educated classes and stirring the malice of the masses. On the home front there was widespread famine and discontent. When protestors marched on the tsar's Winter Palace on an icy, wind-blown Sunday in early January, the police made the streets run red with blood.

The key had been turned in the lock, however. The tsar, under the pressure of war and famine, was forced to grant rights and make concessions, and a Soviet of Workers' and Soldiers' Deputies was organized for the first time. But nothing much changed for the better, and in October the strikes began, first on the railroads, then spreading to other industries across the country, until Russia's economic life virtually stalled. In December the government cracked down, and the uprising crumbled, then collapsed.

Lenin was in Geneva as this first opportunity unfolded in 1905, living from one newspaper account to the next. In October, as the strikes were beginning, he returned to Petrograd but found himself out of sync with events. What was going on did not square with his own plans for revolution. He was constantly shadowed by the secret police. In December, before the last death rattle of the aborted revolution, he slipped across the Finnish border into more years of dispiriting exile. They would last until he rode the train back to Russia twelve years later. He would later call 1905 the "dress rehearsal" for 1917, because it embraced many of the same elements: an unsuccessful war; a mutinous army; a turbulent workforce; a land-hungry peasantry; and a restless, disaffected set of minor nationalities.

Early in 1995, I visited the place where Lenin had lived and worked. The rooms were small and sparsely furnished—a desk and chair in one room, a small metal-frame bed in another, a few other plain pieces of furniture. I was struck by this spare place, by the realization that from here one man had organized a system that came to control one of the largest countries in the world and for seven decades threatened and repressed billions of people in other lands.

That Lenin was oblivious to perquisites and luxuries was evident at a glance. He was interested only in power. To hold and wield it was his obsession, his life. He was indifferent to what was said or written about him personally, avoiding anything that might smack of a personality cult. He allowed his name to appear in news reports only when it was useful or necessary to the party.

Although he lived modestly, he thought violently. His mind swam with strategies, murder, assassination, and all the explosive details of armed revolution. The first thing he wrote in Petrograd was his "April Theses." Delivered the day after he arrived at Finland Station, they were his marching orders to his Bolshevik cadre. There was to be "no support to the Provisional Government . . . no parliamentary republic . . . but a republic of Soviets of Workers', Farmhands' and Peasants' Deputies in the whole country . . . confiscation of all landlords' estates, nationalization of all land . . . establishment of a single national bank . . . elimination of the army, police, official class . . . pay to all officials not above the average earnings of a skilled worker." And Russia was to be pulled out of the war immediately.

These ideas were quixotic, coming from a man who had no real power and few followers—only big hopes and big plans. They completely shattered any idea of a union between the Bolsheviks and the Mensheviks, who controlled the provisional government. They also alienated most of the Social Democratic intelligentsia, whom Lenin hated anyhow, and all but unnerved the Bolsheviks, who were, at the time, merely "a miserable little company." But it sounded about right to many workers in the factories, peasants on the farms, and demoralized Russian soldiers at the front. It would sound better and better to them as the weeks went by.

"But this is nonsense," said one Menshevik when he read the theses, "insane nonsense." Many believed that with this Lenin had written himself out of Russian Marxism and out of the revolution. They thought he would have a struggle bending even the Bolsheviks to his will.

Until another revolutionary named Trotsky, who was not yet a Bolshevik—indeed he had been a maverick-minded leader of the Mensheviks—also arrived in Russia, from exile in Canada. Unlike the other socialists, he agreed with Lenin.

Eventually, they would split sharply over the interpretation of Marxist doctrine, with Trotsky tilting toward the Mensheviks and alienating himself from Lenin, who came to regard him as a Judas. But on May 17, 1917, when Trotsky arrived in Petrograd, they found they thought alike. Both believed there must be a violent worldwide working-class revolution as an answer to the imperialist world war. Both believed the provisional government must give way to a hardfisted regime based on worker organizations called soviets. "All power to the Soviets; no support to the

Provisional Government," Trotsky exclaimed as he entered Petrograd—precisely what Lenin had said when he arrived six weeks earlier.

Trotsky was the most original of the Russian socialist thinkers. He had long believed, even before Lenin, that there could be a Russian revolution without the classic Marxist ingredients. He believed, before Lenin, that the only way such a revolution could be made permanent was for there to be similar socialist uprisings all across Europe; a Russian revolution could not survive alone surrounded by hostile foreign powers.

Now he was in Petrograd, and Lenin found his enormous talents—his powers of persuasion, gift for agitation, limitless energy, insight, erudition, and executive ability—to be priceless assets. For his part, Trotsky saw that he must convert to Bolshevism, and he did so.

Even as these two were joining forces, the provisional government under Aleksander Kerensky was having its problems, the least of which were the Bolsheviks. The army was sliding toward mutiny, the peasants were seizing their landlords' estates, and rebellious workers were taking over factories.

The Russian army, whose rank and file were mainly peasants, had become "an enormous, exhausted, badly clothed, badly fed, embittered mob . . . united by thirst for peace and general disillusionment." The chaos of breakdown and insubordination swept the army through the spring and summer, with more and more of its soldiers throwing in with the Bolsheviks. By October, the Kerensky government had "irrevocably lost the soul of the soldier," and faced the greatest mutiny in military history.

Mutiny in the army was to go hand in hand with peasant revolt in the villages. Like the mutiny, which was a spontaneous uprising of privates, corporals, and sergeants, the revolt on the farms was an extemporaneous, leaderless spasm of outrage. Peasants crying for peace and land, armed with axes and pitchforks, marched on the landlord's estate, wrested it from him, and burned his house and sheds. By autumn the peasant movement had become more and more brutal. The peasants were carrying out the Bolshevik program without having been recruited.

The twin uprisings on the battlefront and on the homefront, both peaking in the autumn, paralyzed the provisional government. Even so, it would be the third leg of this devastating triad—the radicalization of the rebellious city workers—that finally eviscerated Kerensky's government and opened the way for Lenin's Bolsheviks. The worker uprising proceeded by stages. At first there was a period of intensive organizing with minor conflicts over hours and wages. Then came more frequent and bitter strikes, demands for worker control, and arrests of unpopular managers, owners, and foremen. Plants that owners wished to close were forcibly kept open. Power gradually, inexorably, began to collect in the soviets. And the soviets began falling more and more under Bolshevik sway. There followed the same general breakdown in discipline in the factory as on the battlefront.

When Lenin arrived at the Finland Station, the Bolsheviks could count 80,000 members scattered throughout the soviets nationwide. By August they numbered 200,000. In September, Trotsky engineered a victory that tipped the Petrograd soviet into Bolshevik hands; by early October he was its president. The Moscow soviet went Bolshevik at about the same time, putting the two strongest soviets in the country under Bolshevik control.

But in midsummer Lenin miscalculated. He was in Finland when word of a developing coup in Petrograd reached him. Lenin said to one of his closest cohorts, Grigori Zinoviev, "Maybe we should do it now."

They tried, but the conditions were not yet ripe. The effort was improvised and halfhearted, forced on the Bolsheviks rather than initiated by them. Dogged again by failure, Lenin slipped into hiding, followed by charges that he was a German agent. He would stay undercover for the next four months, moving from one sympathetic hiding place to the next in Russia and Finland. Trotsky and other Bolshevik leaders were arrested and imprisoned.

The Bolshevik rank and file, however, remained at liberty, continuing to work the soviets, building support. As the summer wore on, Lenin felt out of touch and frustrated. He "saw clearly the moment approaching when everything would be at the knife's edge," Trotsky said. It became even clearer when Army General

Lavr Kornilov led an abortive counterrevolution against the provisional government in August. The government put it down, but at an almost unpayable price. The failed coup knocked the underpinning of confidence completely from under the feeble Kerensky government. It stirred the army rank and file, peasants, and workers to even more intense agitation. The Bolsheviks began winning support wholesale. Lenin saw immediately that Kornilov's defeat was his opportunity, that the failure to create a dictatorship of the right opened wide the way to a dictatorship of the left.

He began writing urgently, spraying letters and pamphlets in every direction. Like bullets they flew from his pen: "The Bolsheviki Must Take Power"; "Marxism and Insurrection"; "Can the Bolsheviki Hold State Power?"; "The Crisis Is Ripe." "In this matter it is now impossible to be premature," he wrote. "We stand in the vestibule of the worldwide proletarian revolution." He prodded the Petrograd and Moscow parties with rising urgency in October. "To wait is a crime," he cried. "The Bolsheviki . . . must take power immediately. . . ." An American journalist on the scene, John Reed, described "Lenin's great voice roaring, 'Insurrection! . . . We cannot wait any longer!' "

Lenin was now ready—more than ready—to seize power. He had his blueprint in Marx and Engels's March 1850 *Address of the Central Authority to the League,* a compendium of Communist tactics for a bourgeois-democratic revolution—from the united front strategy to the overthrow of the existing power to the subsequent backstabbing required to make it a permanent revolution and proletarian dictatorship. Most Marxists, including Marx tacitly and Engels explicitly, had long before abandoned the strategy because it presupposed a pattern of events that experience showed to be no longer plausible in any advanced country. But Russia wasn't an advanced country. In Lenin's view the *Address* was the pendant to the *Communist Manifesto*. It made the revolutionary strategy even plainer. He intended to implement it in Russia when the time came.

And the time was at hand. It was October, an awful month for weather in Petrograd. Bitter damp winds blew in from the Gulf of Finland, and chill fog rolled through the streets. Food became scarce, and women, many with babies in their arms, stood in long lines in the chill rain to get their quotas of milk, bread, sugar, and tobacco.

In this darkening climate, with mood to match, the forces favoring a Bolshevik takeover raced toward a climax. The outcry from the front for peace, from the farms for land, and from the factories for control of industry was rising to a shriek. Lenin's relentless calls for action had gradually penetrated the layers of inertia and hesitation. The provisional government had lost control everywhere. Lenin moved cautiously under cover from Viborg, in Petrograd's outskirts, into the city itself.

On the night of October 23, by the old Russian calendar the country was then living by, the government turned to deal with the crisis that was about to engulf it. Kerensky saw clearly that the Bolsheviks were a deadly threat, openly plotting his overthrow. That night the government realized its survival required action. The next morning it attempted to close two Bolshevik newspapers, arrest the Bolshevik leadership, and bring loyal troops into the capital. None of it succeeded.

The Bolsheviks instantly countered, throwing a protective shield of Red Guards, a makeshift little army of drilled factory workers, around the newspapers. Plans were made to storm the Winter Palace, the provisional government's headquarters, that night, the twenty-fourth. Trotsky, again out of prison, strode to the podium at the Petrograd soviet and called the provisional regime "a semi-government that awaits a sweep of the broom of history."

As Trotsky spoke, Lenin paced impatiently in an apartment where he was in hiding. He felt isolated. The revolution was proceeding without him. It was Zurich all over again. Just as he had to get to Russia nine months before, now he must get to the Smolny Institute, where his Bolsheviks were masterminding the uprising. Wearing a wig, with a crumpled handkerchief over his face to hide his identity, he slipped out into the raw, windy night and caught a streetcar.

Smolny was a former school for the daughters of the Russian

nobility. Situated in the heart of Petrograd, it was two hundred yards long and three stories high. Its barrackslike facade was still hung with the imperial coat of arms. As Lenin approached it on the night of October 24, it was afire with lights. Inside, within its hundred big rooms all white and bare, its long vaulted corridors lit by rare electric lights, "great Russia was in travail, bearing a new world." And Lenin was out front being denied entrance.

Only after ten minutes of arguing with the guards did he convince them he was somebody important. Trotsky, hearing of his presence, sent down for him. Out of his disguise at last, he was shown battle plans and maps and updated on operations. Together he and Trotsky waited as their revolution mounted toward a climax. By early morning, October 25, the Bolsheviks had occupied two of the main rail stations, the state bank, and the central telephone exchange. By ten o'clock the Military Revolutionary Committee declared the provisional government overthrown. Throughout the afternoon one building after another fell to the Bolsheviks. By nightfall only the area around the Winter Palace, where the beleaguered leaders of the provisional government huddled, remained outside Bolshevik control.

That afternoon Lenin appeared for the first time at a session of the Petrograd soviet. "Comrades," he began, "the workers' and peasants' revolution, which the Bolsheviki always said must come, has been achieved." He ended with, "Long live the world socialist revolution!" That night the assault on the Winter Palace began when two Bolsheviks on bicycles peddled up to the staff headquarters of the Petrograd Military District and demanded that the palace be surrendered within twenty minutes or be shelled. The ultimatum went unanswered, ten minutes were added to the deadline, and then the headquarters were rushed and seized. Only the palace itself now remained untaken. Armored cars were wheeled into the square and a blockade was raised. At nine in the evening an expropriated cruiser, the *Aurora,* began bombarding the tsar's former home.

In the early morning hours of October 26, only a thin line of guards stood between the besieged ministers and Bolshevik victory. Every government minister was in that chamber but Kerensky himself, who had left for the front the day before to try to rally armed help. The door to the ministers' chamber burst open. Vladimir Antonov-Ovseyenko, chairman of the Military Revolutionary Committee, rushed in on the crest of a wave of revolutionaries, "which poured in after him and, like water, at once spilled into every corner and filled the room."

Antonov was a rakish little man with long red hair, trimmed mustache, and small beard. His face was weary from lack of sleep, but his eyes glowed with victory. Staring about the room through eyeglasses perched delicately on his nose, he spoke. "Where are the members of the provisional government?" he demanded.

"The provisional government is here," said one of the ministers. "What do you wish?"

"I inform you, all of you, members of the provisional government, that you are under arrest."

At that moment, two-ten in the morning, October 26, 1917, a new Russia was born.

THAT NIGHT AT NINE O'CLOCK, the Second All-Russian Congress of Soviets met in the great hall at the Smolny Institute. Trotsky was there. Lenin was also there, rising to speak. Trotsky himself described the moment: "Now Lenin, gripping the edges of the reading-stand, let little winking eyes travel over the crowd as he stood there waiting, apparently oblivious to the long-rolling ovation, which lasted several minutes. When it finished, he said simply, 'We shall now proceed to construct the socialist order.' "

Trotsky could see epiphany dawning in the hall as Lenin spoke. "Even those nearest," he said, "those who knew well his place in the party, for the first time fully realized what he meant to the revolution, to the people, to the peoples. It was he who had taught them; it was he who had brought them up—the man with the short, sturdy figure, the extraordinary head, high cheekbones and simple features, with the small, slightly Mongol eyes which looked straight through everything."

This was the meeting when the Bolsheviks would begin to construct their social order, announce the first moves of the new government, and name its officers. That night the first Council of People's Commissars was confirmed, consisting entirely of Bolsheviks, with Lenin its president, Trotsky its commissar for foreign affairs, and the obscure Georgian, Stalin, its commissar for nationality affairs. Russia was pulled out of the war, all land was wrested from the landlords, and private property was abolished. The infant government then turned to deal with its first and most pressing problem: consolidating the revolution. Since they still stood on very shaky ground, they could expect a counterrevolution—and they would get one, a civil war that lasted for three years. The struggle for Moscow was still undecided. Kerensky was even at that moment leading a drive toward Petrograd. The reins of government were in anything but knowing hands. Of the new commissars, not one had any serious administrative experience.

But they went to work, seventeen, eighteen hours a day. "Lenin's office and mine in Smolny were in opposite ends of the building," Trotsky recalled. "The corridor that connected us, or rather separated us, was so long that Vladimir Ilyich laughingly suggested establishing a bicycle connection. We were connected by telephone, and sailors were constantly running in bringing important notices from Lenin. . . . Several times a day I went through the endless corridor . . . to Vladimir Ilyich's room."

The civil war began in December, centered on the Don River and in the Ukraine. At first it was a hit-and-miss affair with little organization, much panic, and few casualties. Survival for the new government was also hit and miss. "The early part of 1918 weighed heavily upon us," Trotsky wrote. "There were moments when one had the feeling that everything was slipping and snapping, that there was nothing to hold fast to, nothing to support oneself on. On the one side, it was quite clear that without the October revolution the country would long ago have rotted. But on the other hand, in the spring of 1918 one asked the question unconsciously whether the life forces of the exhausted, shattered, despairing land would last until the new regime was in the saddle. Provisions were not at hand. There was no army. The state apparatus was being put together. Conspiracies were festering everywhere."

Chaos attended the civil war, virtually prostrating the country. The Bolsheviks only intensified the suffering with an economic plan called War Communism, which called for the nationalization of everything, "down to the last inkwell." The state took over all means of production—not only factories, railroads, and banks, but private houses of any size, large libraries, and all privately owned objects of any value. All labor and means of distribution were nationalized. Everything was centralized to the extreme and money was abolished altogether. It was a deadly hammerlock on the economy that plunged the country into depths unknown even in the worst of the tsarist days.

Three years of this left the country hungry, disease-ridden, exhausted, and embittered. The mood of rank-and-file workers was sullen and menacing. The Bolsheviks' first program had become an even greater threat to the young government's existence than civil war itself. So they abandoned this maximum control in favor of a less suffocating arrangement called the New Economic Policy.

At no time in the three years of civil war and economic distress was there any sign of a rising up of proletariats in surrounding states. The Russian revolutionaries were forced to go it alone in the world. They survived only because they were not seriously attacked from without and there was no one charismatic leader, common idea, or popular movement unifying their enemies from within. They survived the hunger and fighting. They survived a brief war with Poland in 1920. They survived bullets. Lenin himself took two of them in an assassination attempt in August 1918—one in his neck and one in his shoulder. There were times, until the Bolsheviks organized their sixteen red armies, when the revolution hung by a thread. Had not Trotsky bent all his energy and administrative skill to organizing the army and taking charge of the young revolution's security, the thread clearly would have snapped.

At the Bolshevik party congress following the revolution, the slogan "All power to the Soviets" was discarded. In its place appeared a new maxim: "Dictatorship of the proletariat and the poorest peasantry." To the discerning eye it was a tip-off of what was to come. From the start Lenin believed the revolution was too important to be left to the soviets or to any other forum of the people. All power was to be vested instead in his little Bolshevik hierarchy. There was not to be a dictatorship of the proletariat envisioned by Marx, but a dictatorship over it and over everybody else, operated by Bolsheviks, wholly self-constituted and irremovable. The dictatorship quickly became the dictatorship of one man, Lenin himself. The proletariat and the rest of the country was politically expropriated.

This dictatorial machinery was fueled by terror and tolerated few freedoms. In the earliest days following the October Revolution, Lenin discovered that the control his shaky government sought was virtually impossible to attain without terror. So at first tentatively, then with increasing sure-handedness, he wielded it as the chief instrument of policy. He discovered that it was so formidable a tool that few others were necessary. Trotsky noted that Lenin at every opportunity was now preaching the gospel of terror. "There are, pardon the expression," Lenin said in one outburst, "revolutionaries who imagine we should complete the revolution in love and kindness. Yes? Where did they go to school? What do they understand by dictatorship? What will become of a dictatorship if one is a weakling?"

After the attempted assassination the crackdown quickened. Trotsky says Lenin's " 'good nature' gave way. The party steel received its last tempering. Firmness and, when necessary, ruthlessness grew out of it." Freedom of the press was abolished. "It cannot be denied," Lenin wrote, "that the bourgeoisie all over the world is still much stronger than we are. To hand it yet another weapon, such as political freedom, which includes freedom of the press . . . means to help the enemy of the working class. We do not intend to commit suicide. . . . We do not intend to lend the world bourgeoisie a helping hand."

Lenin's old friend Rosa Luxemburg, the German socialist, abhorred this dictatorship. She was in prison in Germany at the time, but she could see from there where the revolution was tending. She applauded the revolution itself but saw the rising dictatorship as no better than the autocracy it replaced. "The ultra-centralism asked by Lenin is full of the sterile spirit of the over-seer," she had written earlier. "It is not a positive and creative spirit. Lenin's concern is not so much to make the activity of the party more fruitful as to control the party—to narrow the move-ment rather than to develop it, to bind rather than to unify it . . . to surround it with a network of barbed wire. . . ."

Now she saw that same sterile spirit about to make a totalitar-ian state in Russia. "But the remedy which Trotsky and Lenin have found," she cried, "the elimination of democracy as such, is worse than the disease it is supposed to cure; for it stops up the very living source from which alone can come the correction of all the innate shortcomings of social institutions. That source is the active, untrammeled, energetic political life of the broadest masses of the people." She predicted what would come of it: "With the repression of political life in the land as a whole, life in the soviets must also become more and more crippled. Without general elections, without unrestricted freedom of press and assembly, without a free struggle of opinion, life dies out in every public institution, becomes a mere semblance of life, in which only the bureaucracy remains as the active element. Public life gradually falls asleep, a few dozen party leaders of inexhaustible energy and boundless experience direct and rule. Among them, in reality only a dozen outstanding heads do the leading and an elite of the working class is invited from time to time to meetings where they are to applaud the speeches of the leaders, and to approve proposed resolutions unanimously—at bottom, then a clique affair—a dictatorship, to be sure, not the dictatorship of the proletariat, however, but only the dictatorship of a handful of politicians. . . . Such conditions must inevitably cause a brutal-ization of public life. . . ."

Nobody has more accurately described what Communist rule in the Soviet Union came to be.

On March 10, 1918, Lenin moved his government under cover of night from Petrograd to Moscow and installed it in the Krem-lin. From there, in a bare room without draperies, with a potted plant in one corner, maps and bookcases in another, three telephones on his table, and a portrait of Karl Marx looking on, he ruled Russia absolutely.

But there was one thing Lenin could not control, and that was his own death. His health began to fail in March 1922. Two months later the first stroke hit, leaving his speech slurred and his right side partially paralyzed. In December a second stroke left him powerless. He would never again exercise effective control in Russia. In March 1923 he was struck by still a third stroke. Ten months later, on January 21, 1924, he died.

From Tiflis Station, Trotsky asked and answered his own questions: "How shall we continue? With the lamp of Leninism in our hands. Shall we find the way? With the collective mind, with the collective will of the party we shall find it."

They would find the way for more than half a century, eventually controlling a third of the world with their rigid doctrines, and keeping the rest of it in ceaseless turmoil. What took the place of the tsar's autocracy was another authoritarian regime, run by Bolshevik socialists operating more like an army of occupation than a political party. The party, which Lenin described as "a party of iron, tempered in struggle," in effect became the state, a new tsar, only more authoritarian. It was more brutal, untrusting, and intolerant of free speech and political opposition. It brought more hunger and distress than the worst of tsarist days. What Russia got out of the revolution was not the stateless socialism of Marx's dreams, but the authoritarian communism of Lenin's design.

What Lenin accomplished must rank him with the most important men in world history, and as its foremost revolutionary. This modest-living, iron-willed man, as one historian has said, "destroyed more, created more, affected the lives of a far greater number of people" than Peter the Great. Lenin "was the incarnate doctrine of militant Marxism, the revolutionary Word become flesh." He had had little to do with creating the revolution. His genius was in conquering it, mastering the anarchy it created, and turning Russia into the most authoritarian state in the world.

Chapter 3

THE BUSINESS OF

AMERICA IS

BUSINESS

KARL MARX SAW IN AMERICA the excesses of modern capitalism. A "bourgeois republic," he called it, "where swindle has reigned sovereign for so long." In America, a "capitalist economy and the corresponding enslavement of the working class have developed more rapidly and more shamelessly than in any other country."

"Upon us," wrote Clinton Rossiter in *Marxism: The View from America,* "Marx unleashed the brunt of his attack. . . . We have no social arrangement—our welfare capitalism, the ascendancy of our middle class, the variety of our groups and interests—for which he can say not one kind or even understanding word. We have no institution—church, family, property, school, corporation, trade union, and all the agencies of constitutional democracy—that he does not wish either to destroy or to transform beyond recognition. We have no ideals or ideas—from the Christian ethic through patriotism to individualism—that he does not condemn out of hand. The essence of Marx's message is a prediction of doom for the Western, liberal, democratic way of life. He announces that prediction not sadly but gladly, not timidly but furiously, not contingently but dogmatically."

Except for brief—and intense—interludes, Americans have

never much cared what Marx thought. Capitalism dawned in America at the beginning of the nineteenth century and was well on the ascendancy by the time Marx was born in 1818. The 1820s and beyond were decades of enormous expansion of trade and manufacture on both sides of the Atlantic. In America the expansion—buoyed by the continent's riches, westward expansion, the transcontinental railroad, and increasing urbanization—progressed steadily through the following decades. While there were as many class distinctions in young America as anywhere—upper and working classes, exploiters and the exploited—there was no inherited nobility in the European sense. The opportunity to move out of one class and into another was ever present. Indeed, most of our nineteenth-century millionaires started out poor. There was no sharp social-class conflict, the grist for a Marxist-style revolution, no fixed aristocracy to revolt against, no peasant class, no classic proletariat from which to build a revolutionary movement. What the country had in those early years were farmers who were incipient capitalists and workers who were incipient entrepreneurs. The American pie was big and growing, and the main problem was how to slice it and who was to get what part.

By the late nineteenth century a deep gap existed between the rich and the poor, but there was no fire to ignite revolution. Most of the poor accepted their lot. Some dreamed that they, too, would hit it big—if not on this earth, then in the hereafter; or if not them, then their children. Many believed emphatically in the dream of rags to riches.

As American capitalism continued to expand through the late 1800s and early 1900s, the working class expanded with it. But there was still no strong working-class consciousness to detonate a revolution. The Marx scenario didn't follow as he said it would, from economic misery to class consciousness to proletarian militancy. America's expanding middle class never sank into impoverishment as the Marxist model required; it was going in the other direction, toward rising wages and living standards.

As Rossiter states, our system, unlike the Marxist system, "has its bedrock beliefs in the dignity of man, the excellence of liberty, the limits of politics, and the presence of God; but on these beliefs, even in defiance of the last, men are free to build almost every conceivable type of intellectual and spiritual mansion." Marx hadn't counted on that. Given those beliefs, red-tinted radicalism has seemed to most Americans over the years not so much wrong-headed and dangerous as simply irrelevant.

By the 1900s, Americans thought nearly everything not American was irrelevant. We had been intensely isolationist before World War I, and we longed to be that way afterward. For three years, as Europe fought, America tried to keep out of it. The Democratic president, Woodrow Wilson, was reelected in 1916 in large part because he and his party promised to keep the country out of the war. "Over There" had no appeal for most Americans.

But then German U-boats began sinking ships with Americans aboard. To Americans, shielded for many decades behind isolationism, the submarine terror on the Atlantic seemed barbaric. It played havoc with Wilson's neutrality policy and finally became too much to endure. Wilson went to Congress on April 2, 1917—about the time Lenin was racing toward Petrograd's Finland Station—and declared that a state of war with Germany already existed.

To justify to the American people his going back on his campaign promise, Wilson characterized this "most terrible and disastrous of all wars" as the one that would end them all, the forerunner of eternal peace. "The world," he said, "must be made safe for democracy." Americans went reluctantly to war. But once into it, we did a complete flip-flop from hands off to hands on. Antiwar sentiment was replaced by war fever, which hardened into chauvinism, which solidified into hatred of anything German or different. Many Americans grew intolerant, and there were fierce crackdowns against immigrants, aliens, radicals, pacifists, socialists, German-Americans, and Industrial Workers of the World.

Nobody believed more avidly that this war would end all wars than President Wilson himself, the idealistic former professor of jurisprudence and political economy at Princeton University. In a sharp break not only with the American tradition of isolation, but with traditional protocol, an American president went personally to Europe to try to arbitrate an everlasting peace among nations. He returned with a treaty that included the basis for the League of Nations. But he also returned to a truculent and stubborn Congress, which refused to confirm it, and to a nation once again turning inward.

The fight for ratification of the League Covenant soon polarized into a struggle between isolationists and internationalists, which the isolationists won. Although the war had made the United States the preeminent power in the world, Americans wanted no part of such responsibility. Disenchanted with internationalism's bitter fruits, uneasy at the prospect of the spread of Bolshevism in Europe, yearning to be left alone, we retreated within ourselves.

By 1920 the country was rigidly isolationist and voting in droves for a Republican president, Warren G. Harding, because he promised the country a "return to normalcy." Normalcy meant the noninvolvement of prewar times. It meant no more revolution, agitation, experimentation, or internationalism—Harding was to pronounce the League of Nations issue "as dead as slavery." And it meant keeping America an Anglo-Saxon outpost, as free as possible from alien immigrants, alien ideas, and alien products. Immigration was restricted, and a quota system was imposed. In 1930, against the advice of virtually every important economist in the country and over the protests of thirty-four nations, Congress passed and the president signed the Smoot-Hawley Tariff Act, the most severe barrier to world trade in U.S. history.

Americans did not react positively to the Bolshevik revolution in Russia. Indeed, the threat of its crossing the ocean and contaminating us threw the country into a short fit of hysteria. The red scare that followed World War I started with the creation in Moscow of the Third International in March 1919. It was not the Russian Revolution itself that excited our alarm, but the idea that it might spread and engulf the Western world. Because it seemed so successful in Russia, Bolshevism was well liked by what few American radicals there were. It stirred them up and made them seem more numerous and more dangerous than they really were. Suddenly, Americans saw red everywhere. There were no more than 75,000 Americans who could in any way be called pro-Russian Communists, but every act of terrorism, every bombing, every shock to the body politic was blamed on a domestic Communist-led conspiracy to capture control of the government by violence. This led to crackdowns against labor unions, which went too far and soon brought the country to its senses. Within a year the scare ebbed, and by the end of 1920 it had died out in the reassuring glow of Harding's "normalcy." Moreover, it had also died out in Europe as well. The United States once more felt secure from external threats, and many realized the internal dangers had been wildly exaggerated.

As much as Americans embraced a new isolationism, reality was steadily pulling them in the opposite direction. The seeds of internationalism planted by Wilson never died out, but lived to blossom in another time. We were a world force whether we wanted to be or not; the war had made us so. Even more important, we were a growing economic power. By 1929 the U.S. national income exceeded that of Great Britain, Germany, France, Canada, Japan, and seventeen other nations combined. Soon after the war New York replaced London as the financial capital of the world. Even with our high tariff walls we continued to import on a massive scale. Our commerce became increasingly involved in a world economy that we did not fully understand. So when the stock market crash came in 1929 and we drastically reduced our direct investment abroad and scaled back our purchases of foreign goods, the world economy collapsed.

EARLY IN THE twentieth century many Americans didn't trust businessmen. The idea of the concentration of great economic power—power of any kind—in only a few hands was contrary to

the ideals of democracy. In the election of 1912 the major leading presidential candidates were "agin the trusts" in one way or
another. Monopoly had reared its head and people didn't like it.
Theodore Roosevelt had come to power and made his reputation
in part as a "trustbuster."

But World War I was an eye-opener. American industry and
its captains emerged from the conflict as heroes no less than the
soldiers who had carried the rifles. Their mobilization of the
nation to wage the war had been remarkable. By the twenties the
country was less and less inclined to question the virtues of American capitalism, its leaders, or its tenets. The virtues of competition, rugged individualism, and above all, laissez-faire, had been
elevated to the status of sacred creed.

American business operated in an atmosphere of virtual noninterference from government. Indeed, not only did government
not interfere, it bent every effort to grant business any favors it
needed to advance its interests. When Warren Harding succeeded
to the presidency in 1921, replacing Wilson, he said, "This is
essentially a business country." When Harding died in midterm,
his successor, Calvin Coolidge, carried that idea even further.
"The business of America is business," Coolidge said.

The decade of the twenties became a time of unity between the
Republican Party and corporate power. "It was something more
than a coincidence," wrote William Allen White, the eloquent editor of the *Emporia* (Kansas) *Gazette,* "that the United States Chamber of Commerce housed itself during the Coolidge administration in an imposing marble palace across Jackson Park from the
White House." The *Wall Street Journal* wrote: "Never before, here
or anywhere else, has a government been so completely fused
with business."

The president of the National Association of Manufacturers
thought that only proper. "It is unthinkable," he said, "that a government which thrives chiefly upon its industries will withhold
from them for a single unnecessary moment the protection which
they so sorely need and deserve." With Coolidge in the White
House the government didn't.

The nation's business leaders demanded the least possible federal interference with business—unless it was to help them—and a weak presidency. They got both. Coolidge believed that since all prosperity rested on business leadership, his duty was to give business its head and see that government got out of the way.

When Herbert Hoover succeeded him in 1929, it was clear he intended more of the same, saying that every "expansion of government in business poisons the very roots of liberalism—that is, political equality, free speech, free assembly, free press, and equality of opportunity." Tax policies were pushed that benefited the rich. The Supreme Court ruled repeatedly against the labor movement, sanctioning yellow-dog contracts (agreements by workers not to join a union), striking down an anti-injunction law, two child labor laws, and a minimum wage for women.

The twenties was a business-run, business-loving decade in which the federal executive, Congress, and the courts saw eye to eye with corporate power and ran the country that way. It was a decade in which federal intervention was seen as a sin, and capitalism went on an unfettered binge. It didn't seem an evil thing. Quite the reverse. The economy soared. The twenties became the "dollar decade." "Dancing," historian Page Smith said, "was more important than politics, and making money most important of all."

Industrial output nearly doubled. The number of cars tripled; to accommodate them, highway construction boomed. Stock prices went up, up, then up again. National income soared, millionaires multiplied, spending skyrocketed. For millions of Americans it was the best of times, with a home of their own, a car, and a garage to put it in. Many felt they had done or were doing well; or if they weren't, they hoped to be in the near future. Most who were not doing well believed it was their fault.

Riding the most productive wave in American history, the country in the twenties achieved the highest standard of living in the world. Annual income per capita jumped from $480 in 1900 to $681 in 1929. Workers were paid the highest wages ever. Their real earnings—what their dollars could buy at the store—shot up after having hovered essentially unchanged for the thirty years from 1890 to 1918. Many never had it so good. The number of hours worked was cut. U.S. Steel, the nation's biggest industrial employer, abandoned the twelve-hour workday and put its Gary, Indiana, plant on an eight-hour shift. Henry Ford instituted a five-day week. And International Harvester introduced the electrifying innovation of a two-week annual paid vacation.

The twin keys to this prosperity were innovation and its handmaiden, increased efficiency of production. The assembly line was invented in this decade, and on October 31, 1925, Ford took it to incredible heights, rolling a completed automobile off his assembly line every ten seconds. Machine power replaced human labor or made it easier. Electric power became commonplace, and the electric motor displaced steam, that flywheel of the industrial revolution. A cornucopia of new products poured into the market—cigarette lighters, oil furnaces, wristwatches, reinforced concrete, paint sprayers, book matches, dry ice, Pyrex glass, panchromatic motion picture film. It was the decade of the skyscraper, those towering wonders that the historian William E. Leuchtenburg has called "as certain an expression of the ebullient American spirit as the Gothic cathedral was of medieval Europe ... a radiant, defiant display of American energy and optimism."

American enterprise developed the automobile industry in a single generation, perhaps the greatest achievement of modern technology. This wonder industry became then what it remains today, the bellwether of the economy. And it was booming then. In 1900, 4,000 cars were produced annually; in 1929, 4.8 million rolled off the assembly lines, and Americans owned 26 million cars and trucks—1 for every 5 people, nearly 1 per family. In Great Britain it was 1 for every 43 people; in Italy, 1 for 325; and in Russia, 1 for 7,000.

It was a fabulous decade. Americans could buy things with their paychecks they had never been able to buy before and go places in their cars they could never go before. The merger movement mushroomed in American banking, and chain stores proliferated. The salesman and promoter entered our lives to stay.

It was a crudely materialistic decade in many ways, but it had its more altruistic side as well. The country in the twenties spent twice as much as it had before the war on libraries, and nearly three times as much on hospitals. We spent as much for education in 1928 as all the rest of the world combined. In 1900 an American child had 1 chance in 10 of going to school; by 1931 it was 1 in 2. In 1900 when a youngster reached college age, he had 1 chance in 33 of getting a higher education. By 1931 it was 1 chance in 7. The workers, by investing in the stock market, open to all, could own a share of industry itself. The taciturn Calvin Coolidge boasted, "We are reaching and maintaining the position where the propertied class and the employed class are not separate, but identical." That was Marxism turned on its head.

It was also inaccurate. For beneath the veneer of production and prosperity was a harsh underside. Millions of Americans did not participate in the prosperity at all. Amid the boom and the plenty, many still lived in poverty. The prosperity was raggedly uneven. While average worker income went up 11 percent from 1923 to 1929, corporate profits increased by 62 percent, dividends by 65 percent. By decade's end seven of every ten American families had incomes under $2,500, considered to be the minimum for a decent living. The 36,000 wealthiest families in the nation had as much income as the 12 million—42 percent of all families—who lived on $1,500 a year or less. Five percent of the population received a third of the country's income.

The twenties were golden, but only for a prosperous and privileged few. There was a disturbing undertow of high unemployment. For millions of workers the eight-hour day and five-day week with a two-week paid vacation was a myth. Most still worked ten- and eleven-hour days, and a twelve-hour shift was not uncommon. In the southern textile industry, conditions were dismal and poverty widespread. The textile workers sang the "Cotton Mill Colic":

> I'm a-going to starve,
> Everybody will,
> Cause you can't make a living
> In a cotton mill.

The labor movement was weak. In 1920 union membership had stood at 5 million. By decade's end it was down to 3.4 million. "America," an Australian visitor noted in 1928, "is an employer's paradise." In many cases the employer was not benign. Autocratic methods were widespread. "We govern like the Tsar of Russia," boasted the manager of a textile mill in South Carolina.

THE BEST YEAR of all in this decade was 1928. The *New York Times* on New Year's Day 1929 hailed it "a twelvemonth of unprecedented advance of wonderful prosperity," the end of a ten-year period of the greatest increase in national income the country had ever known. In that decade we had physically doubled our national production of goods and services. We had become more efficient industrially than any country in the world. Weekly cash wages and real wages on that first day of a promising new year were at the highest point in our economic history. Real wages had more than doubled since 1914.

Then the bottom fell out.

In the summer of 1929 speculative fever on the stock market turned into a frenzy. Every market indicator shot through the roof. Then abruptly, mysteriously, for no apparent reason—as in a moment of calm before some terrible storm—the upward surge halted. Prices hovered shakily for more than a month. Speculators grew uneasy, uncertain whether to cut and run for cover or wait it out, hoping for the boom to resume. The market began to edge ominously downward as one investor after another sold out. The market went into a slow freefall. It didn't happen all at once, but in a series of sickening collapses and cruelly delusive rallies.

Then came the most sickening jolt of all. On "Black Thursday," October 24, 1929, nearly 13 million shares—three times as much as on a normal day—passed over the counter at fractions of their previous prices. The forces that had been building up the market through the decade went into reverse, shattering stock values at a geometric rate as they rolled backward. Five days later, on October 29, the hurricane struck. John Kenneth Galbraith described it as "the most devastating day in the history of the New York stock market, and it may have been the most devastating day in the history of markets. It combined all the bad features of all the bad days before."

The three most calamitous years in American economic history followed.

Novelist Harvey Swados wrote: "The American people were as absolutely unprepared for the Great Depression as if it had been a volcanic eruption in Kansas or Nebraska, pouring red-hot lava from coast to coast and border to border."

By 1932, American industry was turning out less than half the volume of 1929. New investment plunged from $10 billion to $1 billion. Blue-chip stock prices tumbled. Gross farm income dove from nearly $12 billion to $5 billion, and farmers, in trouble even before the crash, were driven to bankruptcy and destitution. The bottom dropped out of consumer spending, closing shops and factories wholesale. The gross national product dwindled from over $103 billion in 1929 to $58 billion in 1932. National income shrank from $81 billion to $41 billion. Foreign trade fell from $10 billion to $3 billion. In those three terrible years 85,000 businesses folded, with liabilities of $4.5 billion.

Banks shut their doors by the hundreds and then thousands— 659 in 1929, 1,352 in 1930, another 2,294 in 1931. Nine million personal savings accounts were obliterated. Just before Christmas in 1930, the Bank of the United States, with 400,000 depositors, failed, wiping out the savings of a third of the people of New York City—the biggest single bank failure in U.S. history. Half of the automobile plants in Michigan shut down, and by 1932 the auto industry was operating at one-fifth of its 1929 capacity. Mines, foundries, textile looms, railroads—all lay idle. All the gains of the golden twenties were wiped out in a few months.

For workers the Depression was a long nightmare of joblessness. In the two months from the stock market crash in October 1929 to the first year of the new decade, unemployment soared from half a million to 4 million. In one two-week span it jumped from 700,000 to 3.1 million. The nation's big industrial centers, "the pride of American capitalism," were hard hit. By 1932 there were a million jobless in New York City and 660,000 in Chicago. In Cleveland, half of the workforce was out of a job. In Akron, six of every ten workers were unemployed; in Toledo, eight in ten. In the three years following the crash, 100,000 Americans lost their jobs every month. On New Year's Day 1932, 11 million were out of work. Between the fall of 1931 and the spring of 1933, workers were to endure economic and social hardships without equal in our history.

At the end of 1931 a Philadelphia relief authority announced: "We have unemployment in every third house. It is almost like the visitation of death to the households of the Egyptians at the time of the escape of the Jews from Egypt." Detroit's mayor, Frank Murphy, told a U.S. Senate subcommittee that his city's relief rolls embraced not just the poor and the middle class, but doctors, lawyers, ministers, and "two families after whom streets are named."

Those on the economy's bottom rung were the most vulnerable and suffered the most—the poor, women, blacks, tenant farmers, migratory workers. The Depression also devastated the middle class. Most of the 273,000 evicted from their foreclosed homes in 1932 were middle-class Americans. A huge class came into being consisting of the unemployed, the reliefers, the transients riding the rails looking for work, the homeless, the vagabonds, the hoboes.

The longer the Depression continued—and it appeared to have no end—the more it threatened to engulf everyone. America's industrial captains, who had seemed to know so much about making money, knew nothing of how to deal with this disaster. They were as paralyzed as the economy itself. Their answer—and therefore the answer of the Republican administration—was simply to continue as they were, making the business of America business, even though it was patently not working. "We should go back to the policies that have thus far made us great," said the president of the Chamber of Commerce. And for a while Americans believed that the wisdom of our bankers and industrialists would save us in the end, if we did as they said, and resisted any temptation to involve the government in the economy.

President Hoover addressed the situation with platitudes: faith in business leadership, trust in voluntary relief, emphasis on local action, and absolutely no intervention by federal power. The big cities were left to attack the problem without help and with varying means and uneven results. They were soon at the end of their resources. In New York, Chicago, Philadelphia, and Detroit, private and municipal relief systems simply broke down. Many smaller communities did nothing at all. By the fall of 1931 municipal relief was bankrupt in virtually every city.

Even when it became indisputable that the crisis cried for federal help for the millions of poor and jobless, Hoover did nothing. Finally, in 1932, he established the Reconstruction Finance Corporation. But it was designed and empowered to help business. There would be no direct federal relief for people; Hoover didn't believe in it. Because he didn't, the country continued to wallow in misery. Hoover's strategy failed because it assumed the impossible—that a national problem could be managed on a local scale with local means.

Not only did American capitalism appear to be going under, but it was taking the rest of the world with it. With the crash, American investments were recalled from abroad, and the whole international economic structure tumbled. One national economy after the other fell in the wake of the American disaster. By the early 1930s most major advanced economies were in deep trouble, beset by a drastic fall in production and widespread unemployment. And everywhere but here governments were intervening in their economies in ways unthinkable only a few years before.

Edmund Wilson, one of America's leading intellectuals, looked at the economy crashing around him and wrote that the Depression "may be nothing less than one of the turning-points in our history, our first real crisis since the Civil War." He believed capitalism had run its course. "May we not well fear," he asked in late 1929, "that what this year has broken down is not simply the machinery of representative government, but the capitalist system itself?—and that, even with the best will in the world, it may be impossible for capitalism to guarantee not merely social justice but even security and order."

He was not alone in thinking this. In September 1932, fifty-three American intellectuals, among them Wilson, Sherwood Anderson, John Dos Passos, Thornton Wilder, Theodore Dreiser, and Lionel Trilling, denounced the two major parties as hopelessly corrupt, repudiated the socialists as do-nothings, and soon threw their support to the Communist candidates for president and vice president. Other people were beginning to think along the same lines. As the Depression deepened, many began to question the capitalist system itself. The phenomenon of want in the midst of plenty, which Marx and Engels had predicted for capitalism, was there for everybody to see. Gradually, the seemingly endless distress resulted in disenchantment with business leadership. It was clear that the great tycoons were as bankrupt of solutions as the president and everybody else; they oscillated between foolish optimism and deep frustration and bewilderment. Going down in the chaos was the rule of the industrialists and financiers. As the presidential election of 1932 approached, talk of revolution was common. It was suggested that what the nation needed was a strong leader, a Moses to lead us out of this economic wilderness.

IN JANUARY 1932 the energetic and charismatic governor of New York, Franklin D. Roosevelt, announced his candidacy for the Democratic nomination for president. On July 1 he was nominated, and the next day he boarded a Ford trimotor plane for Chicago and a unique in-person acceptance. At the Chicago airport crowds pressed in on him, whisking off his hat and knocking his glasses askew. Dapper in a blue suit with a red rose in its lapel, he entered the Chicago stadium and pandemonium erupted. Crippled as he was by polio, Roosevelt made his way stiffly and painfully across the platform on one of his son's arms, and steadied himself at the podium.

He knew as he stood taking in the thunderous applause that if elected he must end the economic crisis, and even more important, he must do it in such a way as to preserve civil liberties and make the country more just and humane. The ends were clear, the means uncertain. He knew that the country must become more radical if it was to avoid a full-scale revolution. But he could not govern as either a Lenin or a Mussolini, even if he had wanted to. "I pledge you," he told the convention and the country, "I pledge myself, to a new deal for the American people."

The November election was a landslide. Roosevelt received 22,809,638 votes to Hoover's 15,758,901. He carried forty-two states with 472 electoral votes. Hoover won only six states and 59 electoral votes. Roosevelt carried into office on his long coattails solid Democratic majorities in both houses of Congress. Seldom in American politics has there been so dramatic a reversal in so short a time. Only four years earlier Hoover himself had won an enormous victory over Al Smith. That margin had been obliterated. The American workers had spoken. Indeed they had cried out, voting overwhelmingly against joblessness and Hoover's failure to deal with it.

In the four months between Roosevelt's election and his inaugural, another bleak winter set in, and the economy slid closer and closer to irredeemable disaster. Total collapse was in the air, palpable everywhere. In the three years since the crash more than five thousand banks had closed. On the morning of Roosevelt's inaugural most of those still open had also closed. The New York Stock Exchange announced it, too, was closing. The nation's financial system was disintegrating. Wall Street and the business community were throwing in the towel, surrendering all initiative to the president-elect as he began his ride down Pennsylvania Avenue to take the oath of office.

On that day one of every three wage and salary earners in the

United States was out of work. Towns and cities and industries everywhere were devastated, as though they had been visited by a natural disaster.

The only hope now lay with the big crippled man with the broad smile and the jaunty air. He seemed to be the only confident man in America.

Chapter 4

THE TWIN HAMMERS

OF CHANGE

LENIN TRIED TO WARN THEM. In early 1923, a year before he died, he dictated a postscript to a testament intended for the Soviet party congress.

"Stalin," Lenin's postscript said, "is too rude, and this fault . . . becomes unbearable in the office of General Secretary." He urged his fellow Bolsheviks to find a way to remove Joseph Stalin from this key post and appoint a man "more patient, more loyal, more polite and more attentive to comrades, less capricious."

Once again Lenin had seen the situation more clearly than most. He saw in Stalin unbridled raw ambition and personal vindictiveness of a dangerous order.

Stalin knew nothing of the postscript as he stood by Lenin's bier in the Kremlin a year later. Even at that moment he was being what Lenin would have considered rude. Even though Stalin had disregarded Lenin since the series of strokes had removed the old leader from power, he had now taken personal charge of the funeral arrangements. He had overseen the autopsy, the embalming, and the transporting of Lenin's remains to Moscow. He had ordered the pomp and ceremony and the public interment in the ornate red marble mausoleum in Red Square. And now he was standing conspicuously beside the bier, basking in the glare of Lenin's sun, as brilliant in death as it had been in life.

Joseph Stalin had long dreamed of succession and power. Now he would make his dreams come true.

When the postscript to the testament was read to the party's central committee four months later, those dreams hung precariously in the balance. Everybody knew that to cancel or override an edict of the now canonized dead leader was out of the question.

"Terrible embarrassment paralyzed all those present," Boris Bazhanov, a member of the Secretariat and an eyewitness, recalled. "Stalin sitting on the steps of the rostrum looked small and miserable. I studied him closely; in spite of his self-control and show of calm it was clear that his fate was at stake."

Grigori Zinoviev, Lenin's longtime lieutenant, who could not see the future as clearly as his leader could, intervened. "Comrades," he said, "every word of Ilyich [Lenin] is law to us . . . we have sworn to fulfill anything the dying Ilyich ordered us to do. You know perfectly well that we shall keep that vow."

Many in the room looked away from Stalin and shifted uncomfortably as Zinoviev continued: "But we are happy to say that in one point Lenin's fears have proved baseless. I have in mind the point about our General Secretary. You have all witnessed our harmonious cooperation in the last few months; and like myself, you will be happy to say that Lenin's fears have proved baseless."

Lev Kamenev, another Lenin stalwart from the old days, introduced an appeal that the damning postscript be kept from the party congress. Lenin's wife objected; that would violate her husband's wishes. Leon Trotsky, only a notch below Lenin in public stature and esteem, might have protested and ended it there. But he said nothing. Zinoviev made a motion that the postscript not be read to the party congress. The central committee voted for the motion 40 to 10.

Zinoviev and Kamenev were confident they had nothing to fear from Stalin. They believed that their real rival for power was Trotsky. In the first few years of Bolshevik rule Stalin had been modest and self-effacing—a bit hard to get along with and short-tempered at times, but a hard-working, effective party member. They did not see the driving, ruthless ambition within. They did not then know that in saving Stalin they had sealed their own death warrants and indeed set in motion the ultimate doom of virtually every person in that room. They had no idea that their act of mercy would vitiate everything the revolution stood for and condemn to death tens of millions of Russians.

Joseph Stalin, the son of a poor cobbler and his washerwoman wife, was born in a small town in the Caucasus in 1879. His father, often drunk on vodka, regularly beat him, making the boy "as grim and heartless as was his father." His mother, the daughter of a serf, wanted her only son to become a priest. However, expelled from the seminary for his antiauthoritarian reading matter and behavior, by the turn of the century Stalin had joined the political underground. Not a gifted orator, writer, or thinker, he became a doer. He was soon on the street, organizing strikes, demonstrations, and secret meetings, and courting exile and banishment. Nicknamed Koba, meaning "the indomitable," he sided with Lenin in the Bolshevik wing of the Russian socialist movement.

Koba's fighting, even though he carried it out on the dodge and behind numerous disguises and deceptions, soon landed him on the wrong side of tsarist authority. Between April 1902 and March 1913 he was arrested seven times and sent to prison or into exile. In 1913 he was banished to Siberia, not to surface again for four years, when he turned up in Petrograd after the revolution in the spring of 1917.

On the night following the revolution that October, Stalin, a Bolshevik stalwart throughout the long dark years of political banishment and exile, found himself the new government's commissar for nationalities, the equivalent of a cabinet-level post. Two years later, at Zinoviev's urging, he also took control of the workers' and peasants' inspectorate, with the power to appoint and remove party members to and from jobs. In 1922 he made one final acquisition—the most potent of all—the post of the Central Committee's general secretary.

Using these three positions, Stalin began building a power

base. Little by little, position by position, he placed people unswervingly loyal to him into posts of power. And nobody suspected. For Stalin was but a rough-hewn Georgian, a stolid, pockmarked, plodding man with none of the mental quickness of a Zinoviev or the forensic brilliance of a Trotsky. Some mistook his unintellectual exterior for a lack of intelligence—a fatal miscalculation.

"There were any number of men on the Bolshevik staff alone," Trotsky would one day write, "who excelled Stalin in all respects but one—his concentrated ambition."

With the office of general secretary came enormous power. The position had been created to coordinate the work of the many growing and overlapping branches of the new government. It was where the course of the party was shaped. In Stalin's hands it soon transcended even the Politburo, which was supposed to be the governing arm of the party.

When Lenin died, the peasant from Georgia was still little known in the country at large and totally unknown outside of it. Only years later did Trotsky realize—too late—that Stalin chose his men by their hostility or indifference to his opponents. He taught those closest to him to organize their local political machines on the pattern of his own. He taught them how to recruit collaborators, how to capitalize on their weaknesses, how to dissimulate, how to set comrades at odds with one another. On all occasions, under any pretext and with whatever result, he did everything possible to make trouble for his stronger rivals and strengthen his own hand. And from the first he never forgot or forgave an offense. In line with the Caucasian blood-feud tradition, he was leechlike in plotting revenge. He would one day say that his idea of a perfect day was "to plan an artistic revenge upon an enemy, carry it out to perfection, and then go home and go peacefully to bed."

After some seven years of laying a foundation, and after surviving the close call of Lenin's postscript, Stalin was ready to make his move. With Lenin gone, those Bolshevik leaders left at the top of the power pyramid had to feel their way. Chief among them were Politburo members Trotsky, Zinoviev, Kamenev, and

Nikolai Bukharin. The struggle for power was already under way, and nobody was better positioned than Joseph Stalin.

In the two years Lenin lay disabled by stroke, Stalin had conspired with Zinoviev and Kamenev against their common rival Trotsky, Lenin's most likely heir. In 1925, after they had separated Trotsky from effective power, Stalin turned on his two allies, ruthlessly wielding the considerable political leverage he had built over the years. By 1928, all of them—Trotsky, Zinoviev, Kamenev, Bukharin—had been drummed out of the Politburo and driven from the party. Trotsky was in exile, never to return.

Stalin's Georgian surname, Djugashvili, literally meant "son of iron." In the earlier days of Bolshevism he had changed it to Stalin, which meant "steel." And those two hard synonyms exemplified his political philosophy: to seize the machinery of power by the most handy, convenient, and underhanded means. There were no scruples evident, no regard for public opinion, and an utter contempt for the party's intellectual elite. Hidden all those years, these despotic traits now came coldly into full view.

BY THE END OF 1929, Stalin stood alone at the pinnacle of power. Huge portraits of him hung from walls in Moscow. Statues and busts of him filled the public squares, buildings, and shops. The public now knew him well—as "the Lenin of today." Now everybody saw the true Stalin. Trotsky, whose vision had cleared entirely by 1926, called him the "gravedigger of the revolution." Bukharin's vision was to become even clearer, indeed prophetic. "*He* is the new Genghis Kahn," Bukharin said. "*He* will slaughter us all . . . *he* is going to drown in blood the risings of the peasants."

Lenin's Marxist revolution was in the hands of the man he had least wanted to have it. The question now was how that man would keep it and how he would use it.

His office was on the third floor of the Central Committee Building at the edge of Red Square. It was a drab place, sparsely furnished with a long table and chairs, several telephones, a couple of bookcases, and portraits of Marx and Lenin. He would use the ideas and the words of these two mentors to disguise his own political ends; Marxism and Leninism would come to mean whatever he needed them to mean at any given time.

As he looked out from his office window overlooking Lubyanka Street, he could see an overwhelming number of domestic and international problems crowding in on him. But he was ready. He had surrounded himself within the Politburo with a coterie of faithful adherents. Also at hand hovered a sinister branch called the Special Section, which would swell in numbers to as many as several hundred. Its main job was to keep secret files on important party members, including their past histories and their sins and errors. This sinister section would play a central role in the years of terror to come. Stalin's work habits, shaped in his revolutionary days, did not change. He arose around noon and worked through the afternoon and the night, into the early hours of the morning. It was said that when he entered a room, at whatever hour, every Russian in it froze into an uncomfortable silence.

FOLLOWING THEIR REVOLUTION in 1917, the Bolsheviks had faced a serious international problem. They were a rickety ship cast upon a hostile sea. All about them were nations that wished them ill. The problem was how to maintain their fragile existence in that unfriendly world until more like-minded regimes emerged to shield them. Central to Lenin's thinking was the conviction that similar revolutions would sweep Europe following the Russian example. The world war had so severely damaged the capitalist systems that he was sure proletarian revolutions were inevitable. He believed the Russian overthrow could be readily transplanted elsewhere, particularly Germany. That belief sustained Lenin and Trotsky through the revolution and through the difficult early months of civil war and economic chaos. In 1919 they launched the Third International (also known as the First Comintern) to prepare the way. Zinoviev was named its president, and he confidently predicted, "Within a year we will already begin to forget that there was a struggle for communism in Europe, because within a year all Europe will be Communist."

The Comintern was to organize the worldwide revolution and plot its strategy. For a while the prospect looked promising. At the Second Comintern in 1920, Lenin laid down his twenty-one conditions to make the international movement in the image of Bolshevism. His main purpose was to keep out anybody not committed to creating Soviet-style regimes designed primarily to protect Russia. By 1921 there were Communist parties in Germany, France, Italy, Norway, Sweden, Poland, Britain, Chile, Uruguay, Argentina, and the United States—organizations shaped in the Bolshevik image and bent on infiltration and overthrow everywhere.

But then—nothing. The revolutions failed to materialize. If they had seemed but months away in the Second Comintern, by the Third they appeared to be years away. By the Fifth Comintern in 1924, Lenin was dead, and so, it seemed, were the proletarian revolutions he so desired.

Indeed, they were worse than dead. As early as October 1922, counterrevolutions, not revolutions, were beginning to take shape in Europe. Fascists had seized power in Italy. Within two years Mussolini had established an anti-Marxist dictatorship and the labor movement in Italy lay in ruins. A Nazi Party was rising in Germany, driven by a charismatic Communist-hater named Adolf Hitler. The economic depression would soon drive the unhappy masses in Germany not into the arms of communism, as Marx had predicted, but toward something he had never heard of. Fascism, not communism, was the specter now haunting Europe.

The American Marxist C. Wright Mills tells us that Stalinism was based on one fact and two decisions. To Stalin the fact was quite clear: the revolutions in other countries weren't going to happen. Decision number one, based on that fact, was that the Soviet Union must therefore go it alone. The second decision, forced from the first, was that the Bolsheviks must make an industrial revolution happen in their painfully backward country and make it happen immediately. It must be done, Stalin reasoned, by any means available—no matter how barbarous, murderous, or terrorizing.

He said: "We are fifty or a hundred years behind the advanced countries. We must make up this lag in ten years. Either we do it or they crush us." Stalin had just won the argument that had split the nation for a decade—not a difficult thing to do if you hold absolute power, as he now did. The traditional argument of Lenin and Trotsky was that socialism could not be built in a single country as backward as Russia without proletarian takeovers in other surrounding nations. The reason for revolution by their time had thus drifted far from Marx's original rationale—to free the exploited masses. Revolutions had become desirable not as ends in themselves, but as a way to strengthen the Soviet state against its enemies. Stalin's argument, forced by facts, was that there weren't going to be any other revolutions; therefore, it was going to have to be "socialism in one country"—his. That became his program, and therefore Russia's program. It would constitute the official canon and central dogma of the Soviet Union for the next three decades.

Stalin believed that "with the dictatorship of the proletariat we have . . . all the factors necessary to finish building an entirely socialist society." He began without delay to build it. It would not be a socialist society Marx would have recognized.

Isaac Deutscher, a leading authority on Soviet history, has written that Stalin became "completely possessed by the idea that he could achieve a miraculous transformation of the whole of Russia by a single *tour de force.* He seemed to live in a half-real and half-dream world of statistical figures and indices, of industrial orders and instructions, a world in which no target and no objective seemed to be beyond his party's grasp. He coined the phrase that there were no fortresses which could not be conquered by the Bolsheviks, a phrase that was in the course of many years repeated by every writer and orator and displayed on every banner and poster in every corner of the country."

Stalin knew he had to move quickly on two fronts—in agriculture and industry. Since the country was in the grip of extreme food shortages in the cities, he collectivized agriculture. This involved stripping the nation's peasants of everything that was their own, including their food, making it the state's, and forcing on them impossible, backbreaking production goals. Stalin collectivized everything, Trotsky was to write, "not only horses, cows, sheep, pigs, but even newborn chickens. They 'dekulakized' [dispossessed the *kulaks,* Russia's small-farm-holders], as one foreign observer wrote, 'down to the felt shoes, which they dragged from the feet of little children.' "

The process began in 1929, and in the first months of 1930 peasants were forced into collective farms by the millions. When disorder, death, and dislocation fouled the system, Stalin called a temporary halt, and the peasants fled the collectives in droves. Blaming not himself but his subordinates, Stalin reinstituted the collectives in 1931. The harvest that year was a disaster, so he seized all of the peasants' grain reserves. The 1932 harvest was another disaster, but the cities still needed grain, so he sent troops to collect it. In the Ukraine and in the North Caucasus millions of peasants starved to death. With a furious violence he forced millions of others to uproot and become industrial workers. Nearly 20 million peasants are believed to have been torn from rural Russia and sent to the cities and towns against their will in this mass uprooting.

Stalin turned with particular ferocity on the *kulaks.* The term soon came to mean any uncooperative peasant, anyone who stood in the way of Stalin's plans. He said: "We must smash the *kulaks,* eliminate them as a class. . . . We must strike at the *kulaks* so hard that they will never rise to their feet again." And he did. More than 5 million were dispossessed, arrested en masse, shot, exiled, or sent to the growing network of concentration camps and worked to death. As Stalin promised, they ceased to be a distinct class; they were obliterated.

Experts have put the death toll of the peasantry in these early years of collectivization at 10 million, more than the total dead of all the belligerents in World War I. They were thoroughly broken, forced into the grip of a centralized administrative hierarchy without precedent in any agrarian country. They could now be bent to any economic or political purpose the dictator wished.

There were two major parts—"twin hammers of change"—to his Socialism in One Country. Stalin intended to swing the second hammer—industrialization—with equal force and violence. If anything, the pace Stalin set for the industrialization and modernization of his backward nation was even more frantic and inhumane.

The economic aim of this crash industrialization was to increase national wealth, raise the standard of living, and employ the uprooted peasantry. Its military aim was to build up heavy industry, the basis of modern warfare, to be ready for the attack from the encircling capitalist world when it came. Its Marxist aims were to multiply the numbers of the working class who supported socialism and diminish the numbers of peasants who didn't—by whatever means necessary. But the first priority was to heighten the power of the state machine and to solidify Stalin's grip on it.

Since his country lacked the basic skills to industrialize at such a killing pace naturally, Stalin compensated with brute force. Workers were regimented, mobilized, and strictly directed. The first of a series of five-year plans was imposed on the country and impossible production targets were set. If they weren't met, then the managers were treated as saboteurs, and heads literally rolled. Managers, fearing not just for their jobs, but their lives, drove their workers without mercy.

The brutal pace of industrialization ended any possibility that the Soviet Union would become the worker's state of Marx's dreams. Forever lost were his reasons for revolution. The output of basic goods for human comfort was sacrificed to the overweening industrial goal. There was no rise in the standard of living. Clothing, food, and housing were scarce, and social problems were legion—and left unsolved. Stalin had replaced exploitation of the masses with outright repression.

By the time the war he had so long expected did come in 1939, he had built a state and an army equal to the times. But the price had been horrendous. Unity became the byword, work the standing order. No disagreement of any kind was tolerated. This "revolution from above" rapidly and permanently altered the face of Russia as not even the October Revolution had. It dislocated, ruined, or ended the lives of millions. Stalin was the "super-judge, super-architect . . . a modern super-Pharaoh."

Russia became in his image a totalitarian state remarkable in its control over social, economic, and political life, using all the techniques of repression and terror necessary for its continued existence.

The terror began in 1930 with the first so-called show trials. Stalin brought to "justice" the scapegoats of his brutal industrialization drive—engineers, scientists, and managers who hadn't lived up to his impossible expectations. He put on trial historians, former Mensheviks, and members of the Socialist Revolutionary Party. He purged the churches. He tightened his grip over literature and the arts, creating a cultural and intellectual organization with the power to bend all of art, literature, and the social and economic sciences to the emergency goal.

But that was only the beginning, the prelude to 1936–39, when he would unleash "a storm of homicidal fury." Stalin in the mid to late thirties began wholesale purges that swept from the face of the earth every enemy or perceived or potential opponent that his warped vision could see. And he saw them everywhere. It became a settling of old accounts in the Georgian blood-feud tradition. He executed or murdered the old Bolsheviks: Zinoviev, Kamenev, Bukharin, Trotsky, and hundreds of others. Any who opposed his policy, or those he simply wanted eliminated for any reason, were done away with. He massacred Lenin's closest collaborators, and even his own supporters.

Most of his millions of victims were never brought to trial; they simply disappeared. Half of the twelve Politburo members were purged. Three-quarters of the members of the Central Committee disappeared. Obliterated were thousands upon thousands of party secretaries, party officials of lower rank, party members in nonparty jobs, non–party members, army officers from the highest ranks to the lowest, foreign Communists who had the bad luck to be exiled in Russia, and Finns, Poles, Yugoslavs, Germans,

Estonians, Lithuanians, Latvians, Hungarians, Rumanians, Greeks, French, Bulgarians, Danes, and Italians.

Stalin exterminated more Communist leaders—friends and enemies, Russian and foreign—than Hitler, Mussolini, and all other dictators and semidictators of his time combined. No other killer, not even Hitler, approached the purges of Joseph Stalin. Doomed was any person, group, or nationality that fell under his suspicion. No fewer than 20 million people died at his hands.

Even Stalin's young wife was an indirect victim of his rage. He had married her in the midst of the civil war following the 1917 revolution. She was one of Lenin's secretaries, a striking beauty named Nadezhda Alliluyeva, twenty years younger than Stalin. A woman of tender feelings, she had grown more and more concerned about the famine and purges of the early thirties. At a social gathering in the Kremlin in 1932, she spoke openly of her feelings. Stalin burst into a violent rage and upbraided her publicly. That evening she shot herself through the head with a small pistol. Stalin stood at the side of her coffin for a moment, then gestured as if to push it away. "She left me as an enemy," he said. He did not attend her funeral, and he never visited her grave.

JOSEPH STALIN USED political power more mercilessly than any other figure in history. He extended the limits of tyranny in an appalling outpouring of inhumanity and immorality, becoming one of the most fearsome and feared rulers of all time. The Russian theologian and philosopher Nicolas Berdyaev, who had left the USSR in 1922, described his rule as "a peculiar sort of Russian fascism." Indeed, Stalin held his people in the same iron grip Hitler would hold his. Communism and fascism, polar opposites ideologically, and sworn enemies, nevertheless were the same in practice.

This said, Stalin did industrialize the Soviet Union, and he did it in a relatively short time. It was no small achievement. He created a mighty military-industrial complex by the time Adolf Hitler plunged the planet into a second world war. He transformed Russia from a backward nation into an industrialized military power, but the price was unendurably high—in the process he destroyed every shred of individual freedom in his country.

He also made himself the embodiment—and Russia the mecca—of world socialism. For thirty years Stalin and Stalinism would dominate the Marxist canon. From the time of the October Revolution to the rise of Communist power in China, Russia was the only successful socialist revolution in the world, and it dominated Marxist ideology worldwide. Yet—and what irony there was in this—Stalin and Stalinism were nakedly anti-Marxist in practice, "the incarnation of the totalitarian state that orthodox Marxism had visualized as the final stage of capitalist barbarism."

By 1939, another totalitarian state, Marxism's bitter enemy, was rising in Germany and threatening world peace. What was happening was the opposite of what Stalin had intended. Far from making Russia safe from its enemies, he had put it in mortal peril.

Chapter 5

THE COMMUNIST–HATERS

THE FACE WAS UNFORGETTABLE. It was mobile and expressive, set in a large head with a powerful outthrust jaw and a broad and eloquent mouth. The eyes were large, black, and piercing.

It was the face of Benito Mussolini–the face of anger, hatred, and violence–the face of fascism. The year was 1922, in the late autumn, and Mussolini was standing before 40,000 roaring followers who had come to Naples from every corner of Italy to hear him thunder against the government they wished to displace and the enemies they despised.

He did not disappoint them. Standing erect, swaying gently from the hips, his words were explosive and his gestures electric. Indignation, contempt, determination, and cunning marched across his ever changing face. Everything he uttered, in perhaps the most beguiling voice his listeners had ever heard, was direct and to the point.

"It is now a matter of days," he shouted, "perhaps hours. Either they shall give us the government or we shall capture it with a march on Rome. I tell you, I assure you, I swear to you that the orders if necessary, will come!"

His followers, whipped to a frenzy, took up the chant: "Roma! Roma! Roma!"

Born in 1883 in the Romagna district of central Italy, young Benito was quarrelsome, violent, and unmanageable from birth, a bully at school and moody and introspective at home. He also read voraciously and widely, and by 1910 was a twenty-seven-year-old agitator, journalist, and orator with a growing national reputation as one of the most gifted and dangerous of Italy's young socialists. But then he changed his course. At first he was violently against World War I and Italy's involvement in it. He wrote stingingly antimilitarist, antinationalist, and anti-imperialist articles. But abruptly he changed his mind, convinced that if France was lost, all liberty in Europe was lost. Italy must therefore intervene in the war against the Central Powers. Overnight he was as violently prowar as he had been antiwar, as rabidly nationalist as he had been antinationalist.

He went to war himself, was wounded, and returned home an unrelenting foe of socialism, with a growing sense of his own destiny. As early as 1918, he was calling for a dictator for Italy who would replace the men in power he believed had betrayed the country at the peace tables and would now betray it to the hated Bolsheviks. A dictator would restore Italy to glory and fulfill its destiny, and he did not hesitate to suggest that the dictator might be himself. By the next year he was head of a party prepared to support that idea. He called his following a *fascio di combattimento,* a group of fighters bound by ties as close as those that linked the *fascinae,* the bundles of sticks bound with an ax wielded by the magistrates of ancient Rome. Thus fascism was introduced to the world as a word and as a movement.

For the next two years Mussolini's black-shirted Fascist toughs roamed central Italy stirring up trouble, breaking up meetings, and cracking skulls. Communists, socialists, pacifists, democrats, liberals, and anybody else who wasn't as ultrapatriotic, militaristic, and hypernationalistic as themselves were targets. There was no fighting on a large scale, only small marauding, hit-and-run clashes. But they were widespread, constant, wearing on both victims and the general public. Soon the Fascists were in control of large parts of central Italy, often in connivance with Communist-hating local army authorities. When the old labor parties called a general strike in August 1922 to force the government to stand against this usurpation from the right, the Fascists broke it up and ravaged the country anew.

By October 24, when Mussolini was mounting the podium to speak to his 40,000 followers in Naples, the whole country was weary of the turmoil. The man in the street in Rome was by then for letting Mussolini try his hand at government.

Within days after the Naples speech King Victor Emmanuel III had also given up and called Mussolini to Rome to offer him the government. Mussolini arrived in the ancient city on the train from Milan, smiling from the window and waving an olive branch. A day behind him marched his black-shirted Fascist army. On October 31, 1922, at the age of thirty-nine, he became the youngest prime minister in Italy's history.

In the end, his Fascist coup had been less a military revolution than a holiday excursion. All the fighting and killing that had made it possible had been done in the weeks and months before in central Italy, where the Blackshirts had gradually beaten the reds in a long campaign. The Fascist entry into Rome—and to power in Italy—was instead a carnival-like procession of "smiling, cockawhoop lads, whom chieftains on bicycles, horseback, or in small cars, tried to marshal into order."

Thus, Mussolini "saved" Italy from both Bolshevism and democracy. His vision of a dictatorship of himself had been realized. The first fascist totalitarian state in history had been born.

MUSSOLINI'S SUCCESS IN Italy was not lost on an odd little man in Munich, Germany, named Adolf Hitler. He and the obscure political party he led were relatively new on the scene and little known. But in August 1922, only two months before Mussolini marched on Rome, Hitler was speaking at a mass protest demonstration in Munich to thousands of Germans who were as unhappy with their government as the Italians were with theirs. They felt they had been deceived, stabbed in the back, when the war they thought they were winning had ended in humiliating surrender. Now their country was suffering all the indignities and penalties of defeat–demeaning occupation, limited right of rearmament, and crushing reparation payments. Their lives were racked by inflation and grinding unemployment. Pressure was on from the left for a Communist revolution and dictatorship in the Bolshevik style. The government, the democratic Weimar Republic, was unable to cope.

Adolf Hitler and his National Socialist German Workers' Party followers, known as Nazis, goose-stepped into the Königsplatz under the bright summer sun in their brown shirts and swastika armbands. Their banners snapped in the breeze, marching songs swelled, and the thousands of Germans, in a flush of national pride, roared approval.

Hitler stood silent for a moment at the podium, then began to speak, quietly and ingratiatingly at first. Soon his voice had risen to a hoarse shriek. "His words were like a scourge," said Kurt Ludecke, who was seeing him for the first time and would soon become his follower. "When he spoke of the disgrace of Germany, I felt ready to spring on any enemy. His appeal to German manhood was like a call to arms, the gospel he preached a sacred truth. He seemed another Luther. I forgot everything but the man; then, glancing round, I saw that his magnetism was holding these thousands as one."

HITLER, BORN IN AUSTRIA in 1889, son of a civil servant, longed as a youngster to be an artist, but his father wouldn't hear of it and enrolled him instead in a technical and scientific school. He dropped out and drifted until 1913, when he moved to Munich. Politics interested him, but it took World War I to set him on the path to his destined calling. Turned down three years earlier when he tried to enlist, in February 1914, with war approaching, he was suddenly drafted. "I am not ashamed to say," he would later write in *Mein Kampf,* "that, overcome with rapturous enthusiasm, I fell to my knees and thanked Heaven from an overflowing heart for granting me the good fortune of being allowed to live at this time."

He lived in the trenches for the next four years, finding there a purpose in life. A messenger on the front lines, he was a crafty and courageous soldier. Wounded in 1916 and gassed two years later, he was twice decorated for gallantry under fire. He took the war seriously, identifying himself wholly with the German army and its cause. He became known to his fellow soldiers as "Mad Adolf" for his ravings on how the war ought to be fought.

In 1919, the war over, he was still in the army. He had no party, no following, no prospects. Then he was sent by the army—he was then in its political section—to investigate the German Workers' Party, an insignificant collection of malcontents also with little following and few prospects. It was a small knot of ex-soldiers bound together by their refusal to accept the "betrayal" of the army, committed to a program of nationalist and socialist principles, but uncertain of its aims and divided in its leadership. Of its twenty-eight members, only six were active. It wasn't much. But it was a means to an end. Hitler joined in July 1919 as its seventh active member. By August 1921 he was out of the army and running the party absolutely, his power undisputed—the way he liked it.

With his flair for organization, propaganda, oratory, and demagoguery, in his hands the party, with "National Socialist" added to the name, began to grow, drawing members mainly from the many private military organizations abounding in Germany after the war. The party was known for its militancy, its implacable hatred of the Versailles Treaty and anyone associated with it, its quasi-military approach, its conviction that Aryans were the "master race," and its burning passion to crush the enemies of "true

Germany," particularly Marxists, democrats, Communists, and Jews. Many Germans in those agonized and chaotic times liked what it stood for.

Hitler traveled tirelessly. Everywhere he promised a purged and regenerated Germany. He promised it in backroom beer cellars, in living rooms, in huge auditoriums, and in the big rally in the Königsplatz in August 1922. By then his party had added an enforcer wing of brown-shirted "storm troopers" called the SA, a private army not unlike Mussolini's Blackshirts. Their function was the same: to protect party meetings and to attack socialists, Communists, and unbelievers—employing violence wherever possible because it gave the impression of strength.

Intoxicated by the rapid growth of his party that followed in the next year and struck by Mussolini's successful march on Rome, Hitler tried a putsch of his own. Organized in a beer hall in Munich, his premature attempt to seize power in November 1923 landed him in prison and convinced him that the road to power had to be legal. Hitler served but nine months of a five-year sentence in the lax and comfortable confinement of the Landsberg prison—the authorities tended to go easy on right-wing insurrectionists; it was the left-wing revolutionaries they feared. Hitler served his time writing of his past, his perceptions, and his plans in what was to become the first volume of *Mein Kampf*—his road map to power.

While Hitler was doing his time, his party, rent by dissension with its leader absent, nearly foundered. After his release he began slowly and systematically rebuilding it to seize power in Germany by legal means. There would be no beer hall putsch this time. He would adhere strictly to the Weimar constitution and go for votes in the Reichstag. The real revolution would come afterward. Like Mussolini, he began to shape alliances with some of the more powerful and respectable elements of society. Spinning out his Marxist-hating, Jew-baiting mob oratory and his simplistic analyses of causes of and remedies for Germany's ills, he also began winning supporters among the thousands of the disaffected lower middle class.

With an unerring instinct for stirring every breeze into a political whirlwind, Hitler began to undermine the political structure. "No official scandal was so petty that he could not magnify it into high treason," Ludecke remembers. "He could ferret out the most deviously ramified corruption in high places and plaster the town with the bad news. He shone in print, and positively dazzled on the lecture platform." Even in these early formative years, the party grew steadily. From 1925 to 1929, its membership rose from 27,000 to 178,000.

In 1929 the Depression struck Germany like a hurricane, virtually destroying its economy. For Hitler and his party the misfortune was heaven-sent. With the bad years, his good years began, for his revolution, like all revolutions, could only prosper in hard times. He had long been preaching that only he could rescue Germany from its postwar difficulties. Now that the predicament included a wracking depression and almost unbearable rates of unemployment, his pitch became ever more alluring. Germans in droves, still mainly from the hard-hit lower middle class, began believing in him—and voting for his party. He began winning active allies in the powerful upper reaches of German society—key army officers, moneyed backers, businessmen, bankers, and industrial leaders.

In 1928 the party polled 800,000 votes in the Reichstag election. In 1930 it drew over 6 million and won 107 of the 608 seats. In 1932 it doubled that vote and captured 230 seats. Suddenly, it was the largest party in the Reichstag, replacing the Social Democrats. Hitler was nearing his goal. Opposing parties mounted frantic efforts to slow his march to power, but nothing worked.

With his stunning electoral success, with party membership over a million, and with a feared private army 400,000 strong, Hitler had become the most powerful political leader in Germany. By the end of 1932 he struck a deal with other leaders on the political right to form a coalition that would make him chancellor. Paul von Hindenburg, former field marshal of the German armies, now president of the Weimar Republic—and nearly senile—called Hitler to Berlin. On January 30, 1933, the Austrian drifter emerged from the presidential palace as the new head of the German Reich.

Then the revolution began.

THE REICHSTAG BUILDING caught fire on the night of February 27, less than a month after Hitler became chancellor. A young Dutch radical was arrested at the site and confessed. But most historians agree that the Nazis themselves set the fire as a trigger for all that quickly followed. The next day Hitler called the fire a Communist conspiracy and asked for and got a fire decree "for the Protection of the People and the State." It gave him carte blanche to crack down without mercy on Communists, socialists, and any other supposed enemies of the state, actual or suspected. It eliminated constitutional rights and replaced them with government by decree. It was Hitler's ticket to absolute power.

He told Franz von Papen, an ex-chancellor, that his mission was to destroy and exterminate Marxism, and he would permit nobody and nothing to interfere. He believed the Jews had established a brutal dictatorship over the Russian people in unholy league with the Bolsheviks and now sought to extend it to the rest of Europe and the world. He would link the Bolsheviks to the Jews and tar all who opposed his racial intolerance with the same brush. Any lie for his cause would be a good lie.

He struck immediately. Freedom of speech, press, and assembly were suspended. The police were given virtually unlimited power to deal violently with offenders against the public order and security. Less than a month later, the Reichstag fixed the fire decree in concrete with the Enabling Act—"A Law to Eliminate the Peril to Nation and Reich." It vested in the Nazi regime unlimited power for a period of four years.

Hitler moved quickly to wield this unprecedented authority. He purged from their jobs all government employees suspected of being politically undesirable, or simply of being of non-German blood. The press, radio, theater, and films were all put under the strict control of the twisted minister of public enlightenment and propaganda, Joseph Goebbels. The universities and schools were entirely subverted to the minister of education. The Reichstag was dissolved and new elections held, this time giving the Nazis a clear majority. Between March and July all other political parties in the Reich were abolished, disbanded, or ordered to liquidate themselves, and it became a criminal offense to establish a new one. The trade unions, once the pillars of the Social Democratic Party, were taken over by the Nazis, their leaders arrested, their newspapers and offices confiscated. The Reichstag was dissolved again and elections in November left the Nazis in total control. In early 1934, Hitler seized supreme executive and legislative power. When Hindenburg died on August 2, Hitler became president as well as chancellor, and the undisputed master of Germany. That same day all soldiers in the German army were required to take an oath of loyalty, not to their country, but to the führer personally.

Hitler boasted that this new government, the Third Reich, his government, would endure for a thousand years, and in Nazi parlance it became known as the Thousand-Year Reich. It would last twelve years and four months. But before it fell came the systematic purges to cleanse Germany of all racial impurity. The Holocaust, the systematic murder of European Jews, had already begun.

LIKE THE PRUSSIANISM of Marx's day, Hitler's Prussianism was "thoroughly militaristic, extravagantly Pan-German, bitterly anti-liberal and anti-democratic," wrote the journalist Harold Callender, with "a sublime faith in force and a mystical veneration of the State as the embodiment of force, a thirst for greater power and more territory, a rankling envy of other nations, a militant and aggrieved nationalism preoccupied with its own dreams and consequently given to grotesque misjudgment of foreign events and opinion." To this the Nazis added some twists of their own: a revolutionary and dictatorial technique borrowed from Mussolini; a vague, half-formulated socialism that represented a revolt against big business and industry; and a racial myth that held Germans up as a superior race.

Hitler's chief tool, like Lenin's and Stalin's, was terror, a tactic he himself said was based on precise calculation of human weaknesses, which when properly used results in success with almost mathematical certainty. That Adolf Hitler and Joseph Stalin should have lived and held power at the same time was perhaps the greatest single misfortune to befall the twentieth century.

EUROPE'S TWO MAJOR fascist dictatorships succeeded by default. For that, both Mussolini and Hitler could in part thank their fellow dictator and archenemy, Stalin.

Italy went Fascist because its workers, its socialists, and its middle-class Catholics couldn't unite to save the democratic system. The Italian socialists, wholly under Soviet sway, antagonized and frightened Italy's industrialists and irritated its middle class and its patriotic elements by talking loudly of a revolution they did not make or intend to make. Their strikes disrupted, inconvenienced, and alienated nearly everybody. Mussolini and his Blackshirts slid into the void, winning favor first with the nationalists and then the army. They cornered the superpatriotism issue, so important in postwar Italy, and it was all over for the socialists and Communists.

In Germany the Social Democratic Party was riding high after the war. In 1919 it won 45 percent of the vote for the Reichstag, and remained the largest political organization in the country until July 1932, when it was displaced by the Nazis. But despite this pole position in Germany's political life, it could never muster a governing majority. When in the early thirties a stalemated parliament failed to come to grips with the nation's crisis, the Social Democrats and the Communists, on their short Soviet leash, stood by paralyzed. By default the Republic was yielded up to the Nazis in a dizzying succession of decrees and Reichstag elections that ended in July 1933 with the outlawing of every political party in Germany but Hitler's.

The meaning of the Nazi triumph in Germany was at first lost on Moscow. Even as the German left was collapsing without a fight, the Russian Bolsheviks were preoccupied with their own socialism. Stalin saw German fascism as but an inevitable transitional stage. When the magnitude of what had happened finally dawned on the Comintern in 1935, its answer was a so-called Popular Front, a "united front from above." Its strategy was to combine with anybody anywhere, even capitalists, to oppose Fascists, Nazis, and a new threat rising in the east, Japan.

The Popular Front didn't work. The years 1935 to 1939 were years of steady expansion and conquest for Hitler and Mussolini, cheap military triumphs for Japan, and setbacks for Marxism. In Italy and Germany antifascist groups were helpless. France and Spain were both lost to the left after a short-lived success. Elsewhere the Popular Front never stood a chance. In part, it failed because Stalin's real aim was not to defeat the rising power of the right but to strengthen and protect his own position.

Isaac Deutscher wrote much later in *The Unfinished Revolution: Russia 1917–1967* that the surrender of the left to Hitler in Germany was "the most crushing defeat Marxism ever suffered, a defeat which was to be deepened by later events and later Stalinist policies, a defeat from which the German and the European labor movements have not yet recovered. If the German left, and above all the German Communist Party, had not allowed itself to be goaded into capitulation, if it had had the sense to fight for its life, there might never have been a Third Reich and a Second World War. The Soviet Union might not have lost 20 million dead on the battlefields. The smoke from the Auschwitz gas chambers might not have blackened the record of our civilization. And meanwhile, Germany might perhaps have become a workers' state."

It turned out the way it did in part because of Stalin's single-minded obsession with Russia's internal security. In effect, far from wanting socialist revolutions in other countries, he feared them, because they might have upset the social-political balance within his own, on which his autocracy rested.

So, as the thirties neared an end, Europe had three entrenched totalitarian dictatorships—one on the "left" and two on the "right." In some respects all three looked alike. As Leon Trotsky, long since banished, put it, "Stalinism and fascism, in spite of a deep difference in social foundations, are symmetrical phenomena. In many of their features they show a deadly similarity."

There was a sardonic joke making the rounds in Central and Eastern Europe in the thirties. Question: What is the difference between communism, socialism, and fascism? Answer: When a farmer has six cows, communism comes and takes them all. Socialism takes three and leaves him three. Fascism lets him keep them all, forces him to feed them and take good care of them—then takes all the milk.

Again, the similarity was not so much in the principles as in the methods. In practice, these systems were not just despotic, they were totalitarian. Their aims were to reshape society in their image and to obliterate all enemies for all time. This was managed by terror, torture, and murder, the favorite tools of Hitler, Mussolini, and Stalin alike. Historically, despots censored the news media; totalitarian governments take it over, as well as education and every other institution, and bend them to their own ends. Their aims are to remold and transform human beings to conform to their ideologies, to control everything and everybody—all thoughts, attitudes, and actions. All three of these dictatorships were forms of crisis government, all were twentieth-century phenomena, all were children of the First World War.

The two dictatorships of the right were by the end of the decade looking to blanket Europe, if not the world, with their versions of totalitarian terror. Hitler and Mussolini both knew that they must either resolve the social discontentments that brought them to power, divert attention from them through war, or perish. Both had initial success resolving the worst of the problems. Mussolini transformed and reinvigorated his demoralized and divided country for a time. He carried out promised social reform and public works and became the most popular leader in Italian history. Hitler launched a four-year plan, which relied heavily on the production of armaments, and virtually wiped out unemployment in Germany. To maintain that economic momentum and to satisfy the dictator's lust for conquest, war was the only answer.

Again, Mussolini led the way. He believed imperialism was not to be condemned, but embraced, encouraged, and pursued; war was desirable and necessary for Italy to find her place in the sun. He aspired to build a new Roman Empire. So he invaded Ethiopia in 1935. The League of Nations condemned his aggression and leveled sanctions, but they didn't work. By then France was desperately preoccupied by the military power rising from the ashes in Germany, the British were not up to risking a war with Mussolini, and the United States was battered by the Depression and embedded in isolationism. So Ethiopia came under the Italian boot.

Hitler always intended to make war on his neighbors. Less than a week into his chancellorship he told his cabinet, "The next five years have to be devoted to rendering the German people again capable of bearing arms." He told them that he intended to attain full political power within Germany and then "to conquer new living space in the East and Germanize it ruthlessly." He believed that Russia, that hated bastion of Bolshevism, must be destroyed. One of his generals quoted him as saying, "The Jewish-Bolshevik conspiracy must be crushed forever."

Conquest had great appeal to Hitler. It would reverse the Versailles Treaty, revive the German army, enrich business, end unemployment permanently, maintain the viability of Teutonic discipline and demonstrate Aryan superiority, satisfy workers and peasants, and destroy the Jews and the Bolshevists—all at the same time.

Hitler would not move too fast at first. He didn't want to stir up unnecessary trouble for himself. So he began to make deals with unsuspecting neighbors. His nonaggression pact with Poland in January 1934 was the first of a series of bilateral agreements with which he would neutralize for a time any attempt to organize a united front against him.

In March 1935 he announced a conscription law. With a combination of improvisation, bluff, and deceit—old and familiar tools for him—Hitler began to throw his weight around in Europe even before he had the military muscle to back it up. He counted on the fact that nobody would be willing or able to stop him. For a while he was right.

Hitler made his first bold move in March 1936, occupying the demilitarized Rhineland. There were protests, but nothing more. Later that year he struck an alliance with Mussolini and another with Japan shortly after. In 1938 he annexed Austria. Early the next year he eliminated what was left of Czechoslovakia and began menacing Poland, invading that supposed ally in defiance of their bilateral pact on September 1, 1939.

This was more than an alarmed Europe could stand. He had to be stopped. He had brought the world to the brink of another gigantic and bloody war.

Chapter 6

THE SMILING BUS DRIVER

MIDNIGHT, MARCH 3, 1933, was one of the darkest hours in American history. The Depression paralyzed the country. Twelve-to-fifteen million workers were unemployed. A seventh of the nation's 124 million people were on public or private relief. Shut down were half the auto plants in Michigan, the iron-rich seams of the Mesabi and Vermilion ranges, copper mines of the West, and textile factories of the South. Locomotives rusted on sidings. Crops couldn't be sold for what they cost to harvest. Cattle weren't worth driving to market.

Now, in that dreadful midnight hour, even greater panic seized the country. That afternoon virtually every bank in the nation had shuttered its windows and closed its doors. America was at the edge of disaster. The machinery of capitalism, in the world's showcase of capitalism, had broken down. Marx's bleak predictions seemed about to be proven true.

From the White House, President Hoover, weary and dispirited, looked out at his stricken country and said, "We are at the end of our string. There is nothing more we can do."

In a few hours the country was to inaugurate a new president.

Never in our history had there been a change of executives against a backdrop so hopeless.

Inauguration Day was a Saturday, appropriately cold, gray, and bleak. The colorless light, the cast-iron skies, the numb faces of the crowd, made a grim tableau of the spiritless day. People clustered in quiet groups on the forty acres facing the Capitol. Some stood, others sat on benches or watched from adjoining rooftops. Some climbed bare, sleet-draped trees for a better view. Of exactly what, nobody knew. Franklin Roosevelt was about to be inaugurated, but what did that mean? He was a man "in whose soul the amount of iron was still an unknown quantity."

On this dismal March morning, Franklin Roosevelt turned to God, calling an unscheduled prayer meeting for his little entourage. "If ever a man wanted to pray, that was the day," Frances Perkins, the woman who was about to become his secretary of labor, later wrote. "He wanted to pray, and he wanted everyone to pray for him." So they gathered—he, his family, his cabinet and their families—at St. John's Episcopal Church, across Lafayette Park from the White House. Endicott Peabody, the rector of Groton, Roosevelt's prep school, officiated, and they sang together two of the president-elect's favorite hymns, "Oh God Our Help in Ages Past" and "Faith of Our Fathers." "We were Catholics, Protestants, Jews," Frances Perkins said, "but I doubt anyone remembered the difference."

After the service, at a little before eleven in the morning, Roosevelt, in formal morning attire of striped trousers and a silk top hat, arrived at the north portico of the White House in an open car to pick up the man he was to succeed. Army trucks rumbled across the White House grounds, removing the Hoovers' belongings and replacing them with the trunks and furnishings of the Roosevelts. Hoover himself appeared, dour and unsmiling, and took a seat on Roosevelt's right. The cavalcade, escorted by cavalry riding at a trot, rolled toward the Capitol, with Roosevelt lifting his hat to the crowd lining Pennsylvania Avenue.

In the Military Affairs Committee room at the Capitol, Roosevelt sat patiently for a time, waiting for noon. He looked over his inaugural speech once more and wrote a new opening line: "This is a day of consecration." But he seemed hardly able to restrain himself. Ten minutes too early he started to get up to go seize his destiny. "All right," he laughed as they stopped him, "we'll go back and wait some more."

At noon the U.S. Marine Corps Band struck up "Hail to the Chief." Braced on the arm of James, his oldest son, Roosevelt moved slowly up the maroon-carpeted ramp to the outside platform. A few rays of sunshine broke for a moment through the leaden clouds, then the sky turned gray once more.

After taking the oath of office from Chief Justice Charles Evans Hughes, Roosevelt turned to the spectators standing before him and the millions waiting beside their radios at home, and gripped the lectern with both hands.

His voice firm and resonant, he said, "Let me assert my firm belief that the only thing we have to fear is fear itself—nameless, unreasoning, unjustified terror which paralyzes needed efforts to convert retreat into advance." He told the country, "This nation asks for action, and action now." He also warned, "It may be that an unprecedented demand and need for undelayed action may call for temporary departure from that normal balance of public procedure." His wife, Eleanor, noted with some distress that the 100,000 spectators cheered that statement more loudly than any other.

Donald Richberg, a Chicago lawyer, could have told her why that was. Only a few weeks before, he had testified before a Senate committee, saying, "There are many signs that if the lawfully constituted leadership does not soon substitute action for words, a new leadership, perhaps unlawfully constituted, will arise and act." The country not only wanted action, it wanted somebody who would resolutely seize the authority to act. Roosevelt was promising both, and in that hour of national woe it was what the country needed to hear.

John Simpson, head of the Farmers' Union, warned that "the biggest and finest crop of revolutions you ever saw is sprouting all over this country right now." Ed O'Neal, head of the conservative American Farm Bureau Federation, predicted, "We'll have revolution in the countryside in less than twelve months." And on March 3 the *Akron Beacon Journal* said of the bank closings: "A blight has fallen over all American industry. A foreign invader making easy conquest of our shores could do no worse."

At dusk that evening Roosevelt had his cabinet quietly sworn in at a private ceremony in the White House. He then ordered his new treasury secretary, William Woodin, to draft an emergency banking bill within five days.

The next morning Roosevelt, acting like a commander-in-chief in wartime, called for a special session of Congress to convene on March 9. That evening he proclaimed a four-day bank holiday, meaning that the banks of the country, already closed, were to stay that way for the next four days while he tried to put the system on a new footing. It was a delicate business; Roosevelt knew the banks had to be reopened as soon as possible, with new rules, but not so new and alien that they would traumatize the business community or drastically change the way the country did its banking.

The Oklahoma humorist Will Rogers said of the bank holiday: "This is the happiest day in three years. We have no jobs, we have no money, we have no banks; and if Roosevelt had burned down the Capitol, we would have said, 'Thank God, he started a fire under something.' "

Bill Woodin, alternating bill-drafting with a few riffs on his ever present guitar, emerged the morning Congress was to reconvene and started up to the Capitol carrying the emergency banking legislation. Was the bill finished? the press waiting outside the White House demanded. "Yes, it's finished," Woodin sighed. "My name is Bill, and I'm finished, too."

Bill, his bill, and the president's banking message arrived on Capitol Hill before most of the House members had found their seats. None of them had more than a sketchy idea what the bill contained. There was only one dog-eared copy for the entire House, and it had last-minute corrections scribbled in pencil in the margins. The Speaker read the legislation aloud from that one copy, and after thirty-eight minutes of debate the House passed it, sight unseen, with a unanimous shout. It took the Senate, a more deliberate body, three hours to consider its copy and pass it by a vote of 73 to 7. At eight thirty-six that evening, scarcely twelve hours after Roosevelt had sent the bill to the Hill, it was returned to him and he signed it.

The bill permitted banks with liquid assets to set up again in business, and reorganized the rest. It was not wrenching legislation. It left the financial institutions of the country essentially as they were. But it extended the sphere of presidential power over banking and attempted to reassure both the nation and the bankers. Three days later, on March 12, Roosevelt went on the radio for his first "fireside chat" with the American people. Their savings accounts were now safe, he reassured his 60 million listeners. The country believed him, for the next day when the banks reopened, deposits exceeded withdrawals by $10 million. The bank holiday had lasted four days, six including the weekend, and the crisis, if not the hard times, was over.

Raymond Moley, one of Roosevelt's key New Dealers, would look back later and say flatly, "Capitalism was saved in eight days." The nation was once again calm; the fear had abated. And the "Hundred Days," a cascade of legislation that has no equal in American history, had begun.

On the same night that Roosevelt signed the emergency banking bill, he handed party leaders his second offering. And for the next three months, until June 16 when Congress adjourned, one major bill after another—fifteen in all—rocketed up from the White House to the Capitol to attack the American malaise. All were passed:

March 9—the Bank Bill.
March 20—the Economy Act, which cut government spending and veterans compensation.
March 31—the Civilian Conservation Corps was created, giving work to thousands.

April 19–the gold standard was abandoned.

May 12–the Federal Emergency Relief Act, which appropriated $500 million to initiate work programs for the unem-
ployed.

May 12–the Agricultural Adjustment Act, giving hard-hit farmers the price supports they so desperately needed.

May 12–the Emergency Farm Mortgage Act, which pledged
millions to save farms from foreclosure.

May 18–the Tennessee Valley Authority was born, establishing far-reaching experimentation in regional planning.

May 27–truth-in-securities protection was passed.

June 5–the gold clause in public and private contracts was
abolished.

June 13–the Home Owners' Loan Act was passed, which would
ultimately save the mortgages of one of every five homes in
the country.

June 16–the National Industrial Recovery Act, which tied
industry into the recovery with agreements or "codes" of
benign conduct and mutual cooperation.

June 16–the Glass-Steagall Banking Act, creating the Federal
Bank Deposit Insurance Corporation for guaranteeing individual bank deposits under $5,000.

June 16–the Farm Credit Act, to refinance farm mortgages on
long terms at low interest.

June 16–the Railroad Coordination Act, to reorganize and
improve the nation's rail transportation systems.

In effect, there was a sort of constitutional dictatorship in operation, such as one might see in a country on a war footing. The
Congress was never stifled; no legislation was rammed down its
throat. Yet, as one Democratic congressman said: "I had as soon
start a mutiny in the face of a foreign foe as start a mutiny today
against the program of the President of the United States."

Within weeks after Roosevelt took office, the country seemed
a new place. Hope was reborn. The government–to the horror
of many, to be sure–was suddenly interceding massively into the

everyday life and business of the nation. It earmarked millions for relief. A remarkable public works program to ease the plight of the nation's destitute was launched. And a sea change had been triggered in the nation's financial life.

It was a revolution, although not the one Marx had in mind. Neither were these revolutionaries what Marx would have called the proletariat. These New Dealers were professors, lawyers, bright young men and women, idealists all. They surged into Washington and set up shop in small groups with vague mandates and obscure lines of authority. Their composition was more often than not accidental, their office space nonexistent or makeshift. They met in government buildings or Georgetown houses, drafting, tearing up, redrafting, arguing, and working through the night for weeks on end.

Among them were Henry Wallace, the New Deal's secretary of agriculture, who would become Roosevelt's third-term vice president; Harry Hopkins, who had run Roosevelt's emergency relief program in New York State and was brought in to run the Federal Emergency Relief Administration; Harold Ickes, an ex-Republican and Roosevelt's secretary of the interior; and Hugh Johnson, ex–army cavalry general, head of the National Recovery Administration (NRA). In a whirlwind three months Johnson, using his considerable arsenal of persuasion, charm, and bluster, signed on most major industries. In the end, the NRA law would not do what it was intended to do—bring capital, labor, and business into a happy concert under a "broker state" tent. Indeed, the Supreme Court would declare it unconstitutional. And it would only marginally spur recovery. But it would do some good things nonetheless, curbing child labor, sweatshops, and many unfair trade practices.

On June 16, after exactly one hundred days of lobbing major bill after major bill up the hill, Roosevelt went there himself to sign the last four emergency measures into law before Congress adjourned. As he signed the last of them, he said, "More history is being made than in [any] day of our national life."

"During all time," added Oklahoma Senator Thomas Gore.

In those hundred days the Congress had passed the most extraordinary series of reform measures in our history. America was not the same nation it had been on March 4.

Yet there had been no rupture of the way the economy operated, no overthrown capitalism, no revolution, no vendettas against business or anybody else, no purges or assassinations. Roosevelt had jump-started the country, got the wheels turning again, stabilized the business situation, won a measure of government guarantee for basic social rights, and showed that a little government regulation was not all bad. And most important, as Arthur Schlesinger, Jr., has said, in those one hundred days the American people "threw off a sick conviction of defeat and recovered an old faith in their capacity to manage their own destiny."

Franklin Roosevelt was behind it all. With his twinkling pince-nez, his cockily uptilted cigarette holder, his double-breasted suit stretched across his powerful torso, and his cheery, mobile features beaming out on the dispirited world, he sat in the oval study next to his bedroom and brokered the recovery. No matter what chaos each day brought, he radiated exuberant self-confidence and a self-esteem that beguiled the nation. His eyes—"a cool Wedgwood blue"—were friendly, curious, and impenetrable. His manner was serene and high-spirited, even in the worst trouble.

Contemporaries remarked not only on his serenity in the stormiest of times, but on his gift for acting quickly, shrewdly, and earnestly. He was sometimes petty, occasionally two-faced, often abandoning principle for political expediency, and sometimes vindictive. But he had a cheerful heart, and a concern for the poor, the friendless, and the unfortunate that historian Allan Nevins thought "Lincolnian." He believed the needy must be helped, and that government must step in when private institutions could not do the job. He had a gift for doing the right thing at the right time, and the power of matching a desperate need with an impressive act: "effective greatness," Nevins called it.

He was willing to try anything, and to keep the best of whatever was working—a perfect practitioner of American pragmatism. He tried it as long as it worked and abandoned it if it didn't, rarely explaining why in either case. He cracked jokes, stroked egos, calmed agitated congressmen, comforted frightened businessmen, soothed jealous bureaucrats, gaily mixed politicians with professors, and "came out with policy." He had neither a lawyer's way nor a scholar's mind, but he had what the aged jurist Oliver Wendell Holmes, Jr., called "a first-class temperament," and a gift for grasping the essentials of a problem, making a decision, and acting on it quickly and clearly.

His actions were often improvisational, seat-of-the-pants, adopted suddenly, often at cross purposes, and not always successful. But it was action. As he said: "The country needs, and unless I mistake its temper the country demands, bold, persistent experimentation. It is common sense to take a method and try it. If it fails, admit it frankly and try another. But above all, try something."

THIS COMPELLING AND complex man was an unlikely sympathizer with the destitute and downtrodden. He was born in 1882, the only child of a wealthy patrician, James Roosevelt, and his wife, Sara Delano. Young Franklin was raised with extreme indulgence in a mansion on a high bluff overlooking the Hudson River, dividing his boyhood between Hyde Park and the poshest resorts of Europe.

When he went away at age fourteen to an exclusive prep school, Groton, and then on to Harvard, it was hardly into the real world. At Harvard he entered into a schedule of undergraduate extracurricular activities heavy on sports and social life, and compiled an undistinguished academic record. Subsequently, he left Columbia University Law School without a degree, but with enough knowledge, indifferently learned, to pass the New York bar exam. His path to manhood was hardly an upbringing to ignite political ambition or a lust for public power, much less empathy with the common man.

In his final year at Harvard in 1902, Franklin met his distant cousin, Eleanor Roosevelt, at a party. President Theodore Roosevelt's niece, she, like Franklin, had been born to wealth. Franklin soon proposed and on St. Patrick's Day in 1905 they were married. The president gave the bride away.

Franklin's admiration for Theodore Roosevelt soon had him leaning toward a life in politics. An opportunity to enter public life came in 1910, when the Democratic leaders of Dutchess County, New York, persuaded him to embark on an apparently hopeless campaign for the state senate. He ran a hard, unorthodox campaign, visiting villages and towns in the county. Benefiting immeasurably from a Republican split and his famous surname, he won, the first Democrat to capture the seat in thirty-two years. He was not quite twenty-nine years old.

In the give-and-take of politics, Roosevelt was soon converted to progressive reform, becoming the foremost champion in Albany of the upstate farmers.

In 1912, Roosevelt ardently supported New Jersey Governor Woodrow Wilson for president, and when elected, Wilson rewarded him with the job of assistant secretary of the navy, which he held through World War I. By 1920 the young Roosevelt was seen as a comer in national politics and was nominated for vice president on the Democratic ticket with James M. Cox. But the Democratic ticket was thoroughly drubbed by Harding and Coolidge.

In 1921 he was struck by polio. His legs were entirely paralyzed. It was widely thought that this would end his career in politics. But in 1928, New York Governor Al Smith, the Democratic nominee for president, persuaded Roosevelt to run for the seat he was vacating, believing it would strengthen the state's Democratic ticket. Roosevelt campaigned with all his youthful flair and energy. Smith was buried under Hoover's Republican landslide and failed even to carry his own state, but Roosevelt won by 25,000 votes.

He won on a platform of social and labor reform, and he soon became a master at finding ways to squeeze his program through a hostile Republican legislature. Early in his first term, with the country plunging into the Depression, he at first took a stand not unlike Hoover's—that government intervention ought to be kept to a minimum. But he soon saw that if government didn't intervene people faced disaster. He came to believe the government had a responsibility to protect its citizens. He became a thoroughgoing liberal, and in 1930 was reelected in a landslide, becoming overnight the leading contender for the Democratic nomination for president in 1932. When he was nominated, then elected, the country was ready for a savior.

With the savior it also got Eleanor. When Eleanor Roosevelt became Franklin's wife, she was shy, quiet, and unversed in politics. By the time she entered the White House, she was teaching, writing, doing radio work, and contributing to a host of charitable causes. At times she acted as her husband's eyes, ears, and legs, attending meetings he couldn't attend and meeting people he couldn't meet. He soon found that her observations and opinions were pungent and accurate, and he came to rely on them.

She had a staff of her own, held her own press conferences, and became a powerful force in women's, family, and minority matters. She traveled the country tirelessly, invading the areas of greatest poverty and despair, from the coal-mining camps of West Virginia to the slums of Puerto Rico. She looked and questioned and listened, and returned to the White House to tell Roosevelt what she had seen, heard, and felt.

As 1935 BEGAN, recovery seemed to bog down. Two million jobs had been added, but 10 million Americans, a fifth of the labor force, were still jobless: Unemployment seemed permanent. Twenty million Americans were still on relief. Sharecroppers and tenant and migrant farmers continued to be ignored, cheated, and crushed. Unwanted, unrepresented, they were forced from their land by bad faith, bad times, and drought. Soon dust storms in the Midwest would drive many of them to California, where the welcome would be nonexistent and the times no better. National income had risen by a quarter, and the economic system had been saved, but the bad times were not over. The country had weathered the crisis but failed to install prosperity.

Much of big business was hostile to Roosevelt and his New Deal. So were most of the newspapers. Even in Congress, despite the big Democratic majority, there was unrest. Industrial labor, presumably Roosevelt's friend, began to organize and advocate strikes that threatened recovery. Adding to the trouble at this point was the behavior of Roosevelt himself. He seemed unaccountably irresolute, permitting his administration to drift and his opposition to take heart.

Many of his opponents accused Roosevelt's New Deal of high-handedly depriving Americans of their individual liberties. So Roosevelt put it to the people in a fireside chat in mid-1934: "Plausible self-seekers and theoretical diehards will tell you of the loss of individual liberty," he told them. "Answer this question . . . out of the facts of your life. Have you lost any of your rights or liberty or constitutional freedom of action and choice?" Turn to the Constitution, he urged them, read each provision of the Bill of Rights, "and ask yourself whether you personally have suffered the impairment of a single jot of these great assurances."

Most Americans hadn't, and they had become uncommonly fond of their president. He was overwhelmingly popular, with an affection that cut across all levels of society. Many believed he had worked a miracle. Many said he had saved their jobs, their homes, even their lives. In the midterm elections in 1934, an indirect test of his popularity, the country thanked him, resoundingly. Generally, an out party picks up seats in Congress in off-year elections, and the Republicans expected to pick up a few in the House. Instead, they lost thirteen more, their percentage falling to the lowest in party history. It was even worse for them in the Senate, where Democrats won a two-thirds majority, sixty-nine seats, the widest bulge either party had ever enjoyed in that chamber. Nine new Democrats were elected, including a judge from Missouri named Harry S. Truman. When the returns were in, the GOP was left with but a third of Congress, seven governorships, no popular leader, and no prospects.

Roosevelt's lassitude in the early months of 1935 turned out to be but the calm before a second legislative storm, a lull before another hundred days nearly as remarkable as the first. It started when Roosevelt refused to let Congress adjourn until it had passed five major measures he had ready. There was another banking bill, a further step toward centralizing the nation's banking system and bringing it under federal control; a Public Utility

Holding Company Act to break up the major electric power combines, which most agreed fleeced their customers, corrupted legislatures, and evaded state regulation; the National Labor Relations Act, forbidding employers from preventing unions from organizing and empowering a review board to enforce the law and oversee plant elections—one of the boldest legislative innovations of the New Deal; progressive tax legislation; and finally, the Social Security Act, perhaps the most far-reaching, people-helping legislation of our time. This last act was long overdue. Most other industrial societies had long since set up programs to shield their aged, their young, their destitute, crippled, and jobless. It was a landmark in American history, for it would alter our assumptions about the nature of social responsibility.

All of this important legislation—the so-called Big Five—went to the Hill that summer, and all was passed. With it was passed a hopper of other bills, some with consequences nearly as far-reaching—rural electrification, youth programs, natural resource protection, farm credit, work programs, and other spending measures for the needy.

The $5 billion that Congress voted that summer in work relief programs would begin to build public structures—hospitals, dams, schools, and airports—across the country. Tens of thousands of jobless would be put to work, not only laborers, but rootless young people, white-collar workers, and thousands of Americans with artistic talents—writers, artists, musicians, dancers, actors, and historians.

THE ELECTION YEAR OF 1936 brought the first direct electoral test of Roosevelt and his New Deal. On the last day of October, Roosevelt ended the campaign with a speech at Madison Square Garden. "For twelve years," Roosevelt began when the cheering that kept him from speaking for thirteen delirious minutes at last slackened, "this Nation was afflicted with hear-nothing, see-nothing, do-nothing Government. The Nation looked to the Government but the Government looked away. Nine mocking years with the golden calf and three long years of the scourge! Nine crazy years at the ticker and three long years in the breadlines! Nine mad years of mirage and three long years of despair! Power influences strive today to restore that kind of government with its doctrine that Government is best which is most indifferent."

He reminded the rallying Democrats that in the nearly four years since those dark days they had had, in contrast, an administration—his administration—which instead of twirling its thumbs had rolled up its sleeves. "I would like to have it said of my first Administration," he finished, "that in it the forces of selfishness and lust for power met their match." Madison Square Garden erupted in a storm of applause and stamping feet. "I should like to have it said of my second Administration that in it these forces met their master!" There was no longer any possibility in the Garden of hearing another word. Fresh waves of acclaim swept the crowd.

As it had for years, and as it would until 1956, Maine held its election in September. And since 1860 it had normally gone Republican. Surely it would do so again, and this time, unlike 1932, the nation would follow. It had so often happened that way that Mainers delighted in the slogan "As Maine goes, so goes the nation."

But the trend and the slogan went down a few weeks later under another Roosevelt landslide. The president buried Alf Landon of Kansas by 11 million votes and carried every state but Maine and Vermont, the biggest electoral margin of any candidate for president since James Monroe.

Jim Farley, Democratic national chairman, Roosevelt's friend, and soon-to-be postmaster general, laughingly coined a new slogan: "As Maine goes, so goes Vermont."

WATERVILLE, HOWEVER, DID its best for Roosevelt. In the election of 1932, he had carried the town by a landslide. The Chamber of Commerce led the effort to persuade local businesses to operate under the "codes" established by the National Recovery Act. Those who agreed to do so were hailed by the local press and citizenry. The C. F. Hathaway Company, then, as now, a manufacturer of shirts and a major employer, announced that it would accept a forty-hour week for its employees and would pay a minimum wage of $13 a week. This, according to the company, would enable it to increase employment by 50 percent.

But, as in the rest of the country, there were voices of dissent. A professor of economics at Colby College denounced the president's program as unsound. "How," the professor asked, "can any employer afford to pay workers a standard wage of $14 for a forty-hour week?" Besides, he said, it was unnecessary because "the recovery had already begun before Mr. Roosevelt became President."

My mother, a skilled weaver of woolen goods, was in demand—both before and after the Depression—in one or more of the many mills that operated in central Maine. If one slowed or temporarily shut down, another would be running around-the-clock. She moved from one to another, hardly ever missing a day's work.

But during the Depression, the shutdowns became more frequent, the long runs more rare. The gaps between jobs grew, income declined, and we all tightened our belts another notch.

Although for us there was difficulty, there was never despair. For the worst didn't happen. My father didn't lose his job. Because he kept working, he was able to keep his family together. Although he had never been interested in politics, during those years he developed a fierce loyalty to Franklin Roosevelt. That loyalty lasted through his life and was transmitted to his children. His way of dismissing a politician was to say of him, "He's no Roosevelt."

My father was a working man with a limited education. His whole life was lived on the edge of economic insecurity, plagued by anxiety and fear. Years later the fear was realized and he lost his job. The despair ate into his soul as lethally as flesh-eating bacteria eat the body, consuming his self-respect.

To him—and to millions like him—only one powerful person ever really cared, ever really did anything to protect him, ever fought for him, and that was a man as different from him as darkest night is from brightest day. That man was Franklin Delano Roosevelt.

Beginning in 1933, the local paper carried ever more upbeat stories about the great changes being wrought by Roosevelt's politics. Many of them hit home right in Waterville.

On August 1, 1933, the paper announced that the Maine office of the Federal Home Loan Board would be located in Waterville, rather than in Portland, Maine's biggest city, or in Augusta, the capital. Before the coming of the federal loan program, home ownership was an uphill and often unattainable goal. Mortgage loans were rarely available for terms of more than five years, and down payments of less than 25 percent were unusual. Loans were payable in quarterly sums and many had balloon payments which, if not made, would mean the loss of the home, plus all equity previously gained. The Home Loan Board was a significant support to the American dream of private home ownership.

For us the Depression would end in 1938, when my father and mother moved the family to a house just outside Head of Falls. For the almost unimaginable sum (to us) of $2,500, my parents bought a house on Front Street. Although there was only one bathroom for seven people, and we five children had to share bedrooms, it seemed to us spacious, even grand. Even though it was actually much closer to the railroad tracks, it was on the "right" side of those tracks, away from the river. It was, therefore, a huge step up. I was only five years old, and my memory of those days is dim, but I recall thinking, and hoping: maybe someday we'll be able to afford a car.

ROOSEVELT'S WORDS AT his second inaugural caused the nation to brace for yet another Hundred Days of nerve-jangling legislation. In the past five years the country had gone through two major traumas—the Depression itself and the New Deal's answer to it. Now Roosevelt said there was still more to do. "I see one-third of a nation ill-housed, ill-clad, ill-nourished," he said—words freighted with potential action if any ever were.

The action began two weeks later, but it was not the expected action to house, clothe, and feed the one-third of a nation; it was instead a bill to reform the Supreme Court, which lately had been overturning key sections of the Roosevelt program. On May 27, 1935, it had unanimously invalidated the NRA, Roosevelt's treasured centerpiece. And it might yet do more damage. To prevent this Roosevelt unwisely moved to expand the court's membership—with justices friendly to his New Deal. The court-packing legislation was a serious mistake, and it was defeated. But soon thereafter a justice retired and Roosevelt finally got a 5-to-4 court willing to approve his programs. The longer Roosevelt stayed in office and filled vacancies, the more friendly the court would become.

However, out of that turmoil emerged a far less friendly Congress. In the midterm election of 1938 the Republicans profited from a recession and made an impressive comeback, picking up eighty-one seats in the House, eight in the Senate, and recouping thirteen governorships.

By 1938 the New Deal had about spent itself. There were to be no more Hundred Days. All the efforts of the New Deal hadn't cured the cyclical ups and downs of the economy, and the hard times persisted, with 7.5 million still unemployed.

But the economy had been saved and democratic capitalism had survived. As huge an accomplishment as this was, the New Deal did even more: it changed the way Americans look at social problems and their solutions. Roosevelt had put it plainly: "Government has a final responsibility for the well-being of its citizenship. If private cooperative endeavor fails to provide work for willing hands and relief for the unfortunate, those suffering hardship from no fault of their own have a right to call upon the Government for aid; and a government worthy of its name must make fitting response."

Before the New Deal, before Roosevelt, most Americans did not conceive of the national government as an agency that acted directly for their benefit. By the end of his second term, the government was involved in the everyday life of the country.

Harry Hopkins had described what the New Deal was all about. "We are in a new fight . . . ," he said, "the war to insure economic and social security to every citizen of the country." In a speech in 1934 he said, "The end of government is that people, individuals, shall be allowed to live a more abundant life, and government has no other purpose than to take care of the people that live within our borders."

Frances Perkins described it as an attitude "that *the people mattered*." Roosevelt himself in 1936 said his objectives were "to do what any honest Government of any country would do; try to increase the security and happiness of a larger number of people in all occupations of life and in all parts of the country; to give them more of the good things of life, to give them a greater distribution not only of wealth in the narrow terms, but of wealth in the wider terms; to give them assurance that they are not going to starve in their old age; to give honest business a chance to go ahead and make a reasonable profit, and to give everyone a chance to earn a living."

Because government had acted on that belief, millions of Americans survived who might not have, and so did the economic system. Roosevelt made the adjustments that made Marx's revolution unnecessary and obsolete.

AT THE TURN OF the nineteenth century, economics in the Western world had for nearly two hundred years been dominated by a simple rule: that supply creates its own demand. Also called "the law of markets," it was unvarnished laissez-faire. Around 1800 a now virtually forgotten French economist named Jean Baptiste Say picked this rule up, dusted it off, articulated it, and gave it his name. Say's Law had been both the most fundamental—and controversial—law in economic theory ever since. Marx got all worked up and personal about it, calling Say inane, miserable, thoughtless, dull, comical, and a humbug, and his law preposterous, a paltry evasion, childish babble, and pitiful claptrap.

The twentieth-century British economist John Maynard Keynes was a far more deadly foe of Say's Law. He didn't just criticize it. He disproved it. When the Depression hit, with its breathtaking rates of unemployment, it became clear that supply was not creating its own demand.

The biggest adjustment Roosevelt made after his election was to slip the moorings of laissez-faire, which had governed the economy of the nation throughout its lifetime. It was a bold step, and it had its origins in World War I. In mobilizing to fight that war the national government intervened directly in the nation's economy, by allocating resources, regulating prices, supervising cartels, running railroads, and commandeering factories. It was a form of war socialism.

Elements of the approach persisted in a different form following the war. New government agencies sprang up—the Bureau of the Budget, the Federal Radio Commission. But in large part they existed by the will of business itself, which dominated the country, paying lip service to laissez-faire but insisting on government favors to advance their own interests.

Whether government or business acknowledged it or not, industrial growth was creating an economy that would one day require some degree of national regulation. The time was coming when pure competition could no longer be exclusively relied on to protect the interests of the people. The Depression would be the trip-hammer for that new order.

Keynes departed sharply from the classic concept of a free economy with his belief that state intervention was necessary to keep a modern economy going and joblessness under control. He advocated large quotients of public control over currency, credit, and investment, so that basic economic decisions would no longer be left entirely to private judgment. When the Depression struck he called for government public works programs, arguing persuasively for deficit spending as the way to maintain aggregate purchasing power. He was for bold action to stimulate business activity in hard times, bolder than anything even the New Deal dared propose.

Although he campaigned on traditional economic policies, Roosevelt came to power in 1933 at a time of crisis tantamount to war, and his administration embraced the lessons of World War I. Indeed, it knew of no other way to mobilize the country but by invoking the war experience. It had worked then. The New Dealers counted on its working again.

Keynes was as skeptical of socialism as he was of laissez-faire capitalism. To him the socialist program was "little better than a dusty survival of a plan to meet the problems of fifty years ago, based on a misunderstanding of what someone said a hundred years ago." He marveled at how a doctrine "so illogical and so dull" as Marxism could ever have influenced anyone. He saw the middle ground, managed capitalism, as the best bet.

Keynesian economics was to become the most influential economic theory of this century. It was to entirely displace Say's Law, surpass Marxism, and revolutionize economic practices worldwide. It would lead Raymond Moley, of the Roosevelt professoriat, to say flatly early in the New Deal that laissez-faire was dead, "the world which it once ruled is gone—forever."

Undiluted Keynesianism was more than Roosevelt could stomach, however. He was basically orthodox in his economics and had a hard time making heads or tails of Keynes. So even though Roosevelt was willing to try almost anything, Keynes never had the impact he might have had on the New Deal, although circumstances would eventually take Roosevelt a long way down that path. He would shun the massive deficit spending Keynes championed, but would also refuse to hold spending strictly to income if a situation required otherwise. He would care for the needy at whatever cost, convinced that in the end the economy, responding to the various New Deal enterprises, would take an upward sweep and lead to a balanced budget.

SOMETHING WAS CLEARLY necessary in the 1930s. Hugh Johnson, FDR's head of the National Recovery Administration, said, sometime after the crisis had passed, that no one will ever know "how close we were to collapse and revolution. We could have got a dictator a lot easier than Germany got Hitler." Many people believed this; some *desired* a dictator. Even as Roosevelt was being inaugurated in March of 1933, there were calls for him to assume dictatorial powers to meet the crisis. *Barron's,* the weekly business journal, called for "a mild species of dictatorship." The influential Walter Lippmann wrote: "The situation is critical, Franklin. You have no alternative but to assume dictatorial powers."

Others expected it. Edmund Wilson stood in the cold with 100,000 others that day and afterward wrote: "The thing that emerges most clearly is the warning of a dictatorship."

The makings for revolution and dictatorship were there. "The gunpowder," Arthur Schlesinger, Jr., wrote, "was loosely trailed across the land." All it needed was the spark. The precedent was also there: only two months before, Adolf Hitler had become chancellor of Germany; Stalin had seized total dictatorial power in Russia less than eight years earlier; and Mussolini was firmly installed in Italy. The political tide in the world was flowing to dictatorships of the left and right.

Roosevelt chose to work within the framework of democracy. He would one day say: "I have no inclination to be a dictator. I have none of the qualifications which would make me a successful dictator."

Novelist Wallace Stegner wrote that Roosevelt was "a leader with all the personal magnetism of the führers, but without their venality or their vanity or their incurable lust for a white horse."

But Roosevelt understood how close at hand revolution hovered. He believed that he could, if he wished, seize dictatorial power. Instead, in his own words, "we waged war against those conditions which make revolutions—against the inequalities and resentments which breed them." Many millions of Americans feared—or hoped—that capitalism was finished, disintegrating in the economic chaos of the times, a chaos with which the system seemed unable to deal. But Roosevelt's idea from the start was not to destroy or replace capitalism. His idea was to change it and by changing it, to save it. It would not be easy. He was to learn soon that to reform capitalism "you must fight the capitalists tooth and nail."

But *Fortune* magazine was able to write after the first three years of the New Deal that it was "fairly evident to most disinterested critics" that it "has had the preservation of capitalism at all times in view."

The dark predictions that the country was spinning toward either revolution or dictatorship or both went hand in hand with preordinations that capitalism was doomed. Edmund Wilson, yearning to see it gone, said: "So far as I can see, [Marx's] prophecy is now being fulfilled and he ought to be turning in his grave with glee."

Ever since the Bolshevik revolution, many intellectuals had turned to communism; the Depression accelerated their desire for a radical solution to America's problem. If not actually joining the party, they were at least drawn to it. Among them, besides Wilson, were some of the leading names in American arts, music, and letters: Malcolm Cowley, James T. Farrell, Heywood Broun, Theodore Dreiser, John Dos Passos, Sherwood Anderson, Langston Hughes, Waldo Frank, Granville Hicks, Nelson Algren, Erskine Caldwell, Josephine Herbst, Nathanael West, Richard Wright, Willa Cather, Lincoln Steffens, and Paul Robeson. Major novelists turned out proletarian novels, and the horizon was crowded with left-wing critics and journalists.

Although no one could have known it at the time, the issue was settled in the first weeks of the New Deal. It was not capitalism that was doomed in America, but Marxism. Capitalism was battered and reeling, but it survived, ultimately stronger than ever. Roosevelt had turned back revolution and turned his back on dictatorship. It was for that charged time no small accomplishment.

From that point on, the triumph of democracy over communism was inevitable. It would take another half century of dramatic events and daring leaders, but the die was cast. Roosevelt preserved and strengthened democratic capitalism and in the process doomed communism.

Most impressive was the way it was done.

Adolph A. Berle, Jr., a member of Roosevelt's "brain trust," said that what Roosevelt did was "not in the spirit of hatred manifested by the red revolutionary or the black Fascist abroad, but in the typical American spirit of great generosity and great recognition that individual life and individual homes are precious possessions."

Isaiah Berlin wrote that Roosevelt's greatest service to mankind was proving it possible "to be politically effective and yet benevolent and humane," that "the promotion of social justice and individual liberty" could be reconciled with "the indispensable minimum of organizing and authority." *Fortune* magazine said the first year of the New Deal proved it "possible for a democratic government retaining at least the democratic forms to act more rapidly and decisively than either Hitler or Lenin was able to act at the moment of assuming power."

Roosevelt wished not just to lift the nation out of the Depression but at the same time to build a more just and equitable America. Watching the rise of totalitarian regimes in Germany and Russia, Roosevelt concluded that the only counter to them was a stronger, more vital democracy in America. Not only did he see himself waging a war against want and destitution, but "a war for the survival of democracy. We are fighting to save a great and precious form of government for ourselves and for the world."

American journalist John Gunther witnessed and wrote of the striking difference between the two approaches. "For anybody who lived in the atmosphere of Mussolini and Pilsudski [the Polish dictator], Kemal Ataturk and the rising Hitler, all that I had witnessed [in America] was incredible—its openness, simplicity, lack of posture, lack of pressure. Nor could I avoid being impressed by the absence of fanfare in the White House itself— no trooping of the colors, no changing of the guard, no frock-coated underlings, no obsequious secretaries, no machine guns . . . no cordons of police blocking off the streets [as] near Wilhelmstrasse."

What Russia and Germany had for leaders were psychopathic thugs driving their nations deep into totalitarian nightmares. What America had in Roosevelt, wrote Allan Nevins, was this: "One remembers him as a kind of smiling bus driver, with that cigarette holder pointed upward, listening to the uproar from behind as he took the sharp turns. They used to tell him that he had not loaded his vehicle right for all eternity. But he knew he had stacked it well enough to round the next corner, and he knew when the yells were false, and when they were real, and he loved the passengers."

IN 1995, THE SPEAKER of the House of Representatives, Newt Gingrich, promised his supporters that the Republican majority in Congress would "renew American civilization [and] redirect the future of the human race." This was to be accomplished through a repudiation of what he said are the failed policies of the past thirty or forty years—ironically, a period that includes the zenith of middle-class prosperity in America.

Gingrich went on to say: "We're in a cycle where I believe the countercultural, redistributionist, bureaucratic welfare state model is just a disaster and people are very ready for a very profound transformation."

But the "profound transformation" took place sixty years ago. Franklin Roosevelt's New Deal was the profound transformation of American government in this century. And it is almost certain that, despite Gingrich's rhetoric, the Republican majority in Congress will not succeed in repealing the New Deal.

At most, the Republicans will trim a bit around the edges. But the fundamental accomplishments of the New Deal will remain largely intact for two reasons. The first is that the changes wrought by the New Deal have become firmly embedded in the fabric of American life. They cannot be removed without serious damage to that fabric, something the American people do not want and will not let happen. The second reason, arising from the first, is that all members of Congress, including Republicans, face continuing, sometimes contradictory pressures from their constituents. While they want restraint in government spending, they do not want the kind of wholesale uprooting that Speaker Gingrich seemed to suggest and came to symbolize. That was made clear in the election of 1996.

The most visible symbol of the New Deal, and the best evidence of its strength and endurance, is the Social Security system. It was bitterly opposed by Republicans (and some conservative Democrats) when proposed by Roosevelt. They claimed that passage would undermine the willingness of children to care for their parents. It was said that the 1 percent payroll tax would cause workers to abandon their jobs. After the law was enacted, and as the 1936 campaign heated up, some employers put slips in their workers' pay envelopes saying: "Effective January 1, 1937, we are compelled by a Roosevelt 'New Deal' law to make a 1 percent deduction from your wages and turn it over to the government. . . . You might get your money back, but only if Congress decides to make the appropriation. Decide before November 3 whether or not you wish to take these chances."

The turnabout was complete in 1972, when President Nixon had Social Security benefit envelopes carry the message that he had signed a 20 percent increase in benefits.

The strength of the program can be judged by those two appeals: one in which employers told workers to mistrust a Democratic president's Social Security plan; and a second, three and a half decades later, in which a Republican president took credit for an increase in Social Security benefits.

Radio spots in the election year of 1936 featured actors telling each other in shocked tones that the Social Security plan would require each worker to be assigned a number, and claimed it would also require fingerprinting—although fingerprinting was not part of the law. Some even went so far as to claim that people would be required to wear steel dog tags around their necks stamped with their Social Security number.

Those who paid attention to the midterm elections in 1994 might recall ads portraying a middle-American couple, actors known as "Harry and Louise," who were allegedly frightened by the idea of national health insurance. Some things have not changed in American life.

It was a massive and misleading assault on his programs that elicited from FDR his emotional outburst in that last speech of the 1936 campaign in New York's Madison Square Garden: "Never before in all our history have these forces been so united against one candidate as they stand today. They are unanimous in their hate for me—and I welcome their hatred."

Today, of course, Republicans vie with Democrats to portray themselves as protectors and defenders of Social Security.

In 1995, throughout the debate on a proposed constitutional amendment to require a balanced budget, Republican senators ranging from Majority Leader Bob Dole to Phil Gramm disavowed any intention of using the payroll tax dedicated to Social Security to help balance the federal budget. They even went so far as to say that in a resolution adopted by the Senate. The Republican whip, Trent Lott of Mississippi (now the majority leader), defended the resolution by saying, "There had to be some opportunity [for Senators] to express that they don't think Social Security should be used. That's the way you keep everyone together."

Lott was right, of course. His words verify the remarkable political transformation of Social Security from a Communist plot to the way you keep everyone together. The reason is simple: strong support by the American people for the program. The same is true of a host of programs created in the New Deal, including unemployment insurance, bank deposit insurance, and regulation of the stock market—programs we so take for granted it's hard to believe there ever was a time when we lacked their protections.

Republicans and Democrats continue to face a test in elections as their rhetoric collides with the interests of their constituencies. This often leads to humorous results. As one congressman replied when confronted with his prior inconsistent words, "That was theory, this is reality."

The Tennessee Valley Authority serves a nine-state area that was among the poorest in the nation in the 1930s. But thanks in large part to the TVA, and notwithstanding the rural pockets of poverty that remain, incomes in the region are now above the national average. The TVA provided not only low-priced electrical power, but the infrastructure to attract industry and jobs and give the region the boost it needed to enter the nation's economic mainstream. Republican ambivalence about the TVA is demonstrated by the fact that it appeared on one House list of federal properties that could be privatized and agencies that could be abolished, but at the same time the Senate Judiciary Committee expressly provided in its report on the balanced-budget amendment that no cuts be made in TVA funding.

Republicans are not alone in inconsistency. Many Democrats are inconsistent. Some, for example, loudly support—and voted for—an amendment to the Constitution to require a balanced budget, even as they consistently vote to increase spending on health, nutrition, and education programs.

However justified their impatience with the wastes and excesses of government, Americans recognize that the political stability and economic growth of the past half century and more has been in part due to the revolutionary changes made in their society by the New Deal. Clearly, there have been mistakes that must be corrected and excesses that must be curbed. But the American people want a modest course correction, not a reversal of direction.

If the smiling bus driver had saved capitalism, then what did that say about communism? It failed miserably in America, even when the country was at its most miserable.

Roosevelt's accomplishment involved far more than saving capitalism. In saving capitalism in this most capitalistic of the world's nations, he also set communism on the path to destruction. Rosa Luxemburg, that Marxist contemporary of Lenin, wrote: "If one admits . . . that capitalist development does not move in the direction of its own ruin, then socialism ceases to be objectively necessary."

If that was true, where did that leave things when the greatest of the capitalist societies failed to self-destruct, but changed and went on to become the most prosperous and benign society in world history? The answer, I believe, was to come nearly half a century after Roosevelt's death, in the self-destruction of communism in the greatest of the world's Communist societies—the Soviet Union itself.

But in the late 1930s, that time was still far away. A murderous world war and a chilling Cold War still lay between that day and this. In World War II, Roosevelt would at last find the key to full employment, the end of the Depression, and after it a prosperity unprecedented for the nation he had saved.

Chapter 7

ARMAGEDDON

AND HOLOCAUST

BY THE END OF THE SUMMER OF 1939, Europe had been through a year and a half of torment. It was nominally eighteen months of peace, but never outside of war had the Continent known such tension and fear.

Hitler had made himself clear. He was bent on carving out more "living space" for the German master race. "I have taken it upon myself," he bluntly said, "to solve the German space problem. Take good note . . . the moment I believe that I can make a killing, I'll always strike immediately and won't hesitate to go to the brink."

Like the common gangster he was, he struck without warning and without pity. He saw himself as a modern Genghis Khan bent on setting the course of history for the next millennium by his own relentless will. He had in mind a "new order" for Europe, a rule of a "pure and undefiled Aryan race" over subjugated peoples with "inferior" bloodlines. For him restraint would never be more than a temporary tactic. In those unsettling eighteen months he had already appropriated Austria and Czechoslovakia. All of Europe feared Poland would be next.

To the east lay the Soviet Union, led by Stalin, another thug without principles or restraint. From April to August of 1939, the French and the English pushed hard to head off the possibility that Hitler and Stalin might unite, by attempting to forge an agreement themselves with Stalin to oppose German aggression. But in May, Stalin demanded a political and military alliance with the British and French that went further than they were prepared to go. In the end, the effort failed.

So Stalin turned toward Germany. The Soviet dictator believed he could get something from Germany he could not get from the British and French. They were offering him a role in the defense of Eastern Europe's independence, while Hitler was offering him a piece of Eastern Europe. All he would have to do was stand aside and let Hitler have a free hand with Poland—then share the spoils. The price would simply be Stalin's agreement not to enter into any war against Germany. That was fine with Stalin; he was not ready for a war anyhow. Hitler for his part saw a pact with Russia as the way to isolate Poland and checkmate British and French interference.

It was an odd coupling. No two regimes hated one another more than the Bolsheviks and the Nazis. For two decades Hitler had hated only Jews more than he hated Bolsheviks. No agreement could change that. On August 11, 1939, only days before the unlikely agreement, Hitler said: "Everything I undertake is directed against the Russians. If the West is too stupid and blind to grasp this then I shall be compelled to come to an agreement with the Russians, beat the West, and then after their defeat turn against the Soviet Union with all my forces." A pact would just be another matter of temporary tactics toward a larger strategy.

But Stalin was Hitler's equal in employing temporary tactics for insincere ends. He was just as willing to deal with an enemy for the secret promise of half of Poland and freedom from the fear of being drawn prematurely into war.

So the agreement was made. The two dictators called it a nonaggression pact. But it was in fact an aggression pact against Poland and the Baltic states. It proposed to divide Poland into Soviet and German spheres of interest. Hitler would get more of the "space" he wanted. Stalin would get his fair share of Poland,

Estonia, Lithuania, and Latvia, which he quickly secured with his usual strong-arm tactics, rigged elections, trumped-up charges, arrests, and terror. It was a crude foreshadowing of the Stalinization of Eastern Europe that would follow the war.

The pact was signed on August 15, 1939. Hitler was now free to have his way with Poland.

He struck on September 1 with a blitzkrieg, a swift and sudden blow. His army stormed across the Polish border, crushing that unhappy nation within three weeks. Speed was critical, for time would work for Britain and France, who two days later declared war on Germany. But after Poland fell, time stood curiously still for the next six months, in what has come to be called the "phony war," when nothing of importance happened. The British did little. The French waited behind their Maginot Line, a barrier they believed unbreachable, and the Germans didn't attack. However, the pause was only that—a pause.

In the early spring of 1940, Hitler shattered the quiet. In April he hurled his army into Denmark, overwhelming that defenseless little nation in a single day. He swarmed from there into Norway. The "real war" had begun. Bypassing the Maginot fortifications, he struck Holland, then Belgium, and by the end of May they were his.

He then turned toward France. At the beginning of June the French and Germans faced one another along the Somme River, and it was over almost before it began. The Nazis overwhelmed the French and entered Paris on June 13. France simply collapsed, its army broken. On June 10, Mussolini, wanting to be in on this impressive kill, had declared war on Britain and France. It was becoming apparent he was being upstaged by Hitler's seemingly unstoppable German army. In fact, he would never be effectively in the war. He launched an offensive from Libya into Egypt in September, but was thrown back. He then plunged into an aborted invasion of Greece, from which Hitler was forced to extricate his broken army. A junior partner from the first, Mussolini was in the end to become Hitler's puppet.

In the summer of 1940, Hitler turned toward Britain. His original intention was simply to convince her to accede to his hegemony in Europe. But Britain stubbornly refused to follow his script and appeared ready to fight. So Hitler figuratively shrugged and made ready to invade and conquer her as well. He launched the Luftwaffe into the skies over England as a prelude, to crush the spirit of the British people. But for the first time he miscalculated. Britain's will to resist, under the inspired leadership of Winston Churchill, was a match for Hitler's will to conquer. In the epic battle in the British skies that followed, Hitler was thwarted. A combination of faulty German strategy and British technical skill began to turn the tide by September; the German momentum stalled. Hitler was not defeated, but neither had he won. He now faced a struggle of indefinite duration and doubtful outcome. So on September 17, he called the whole thing off and turned back to continental Europe to consolidate what he had won on his side of the channel.

Despite the check over British skies, Hitler was full of confidence. Following the stunningly successful military campaigns of 1939 and 1940, especially the easy conquest of France, he was convinced of his own infallibility in war as well as politics. He finished what Mussolini had clumsily begun in Greece, overrunning her and Yugoslavia and driving their governments into exile. Rumania, with no other recourse, threw in her lot with the Axis powers, and Hitler quickly forced the other Balkan states into line. He then pushed on from mainland Greece to overrun the island of Crete. By the early summer of 1941, he controlled in one form or another the greater part of the European continent. He had his "space."

But he was still not content. To the east was Russia, standing big and in his way. And he hated Russia.

Hitler originally believed he could not carry out his designs against Russia until he had secured all of western Europe. That was now completed, with the irritating exception of Britain. When he was unable to force Britain to admit she had lost, another thought occurred to him: Britain was depending on Russia; that is why she resisted him so stubbornly. Take Russia out and Britain would fold. The United States, Britain's other hope, would at that point drop any plans to interfere. "With Russia smashed," Hitler mused, "Britain's last hope will be shattered."

So in the early summer of 1941, in disregard of their mutual pact of nonaggression, Hitler massed his army on the Russian border. It was the largest force ever assembled for a single campaign–3.2 million men, virtually the entire German army. Hitler hurled this juggernaut into Russia in the early morning of June 22.

Stalin was stunned. He shouldn't have been. His navy commissar had tried to warn him: for days the Germans had been acting suspiciously, withdrawing their ships from Soviet ports. Told this, Stalin's chief lieutenant, Vyacheslav Molotov, said, "Only a fool would attack us." Stalin had had even earlier rumblings, disturbing reports about the deterioration of his pact with Germany, and he had tried to appease Hitler early in the spring.

It was too late. When the Germans struck across his border, Stalin for a time was paralyzed. The first strike had been terrifying and lightning fast, like all Hitler's blitzkriegs. The Wehrmacht rolled across Russia toward Moscow and appeared unstoppable. Up to the last moment Stalin did not believe it could actually happen. His daughter, Svetlana, was later to write, "He had not guessed or foreseen that the Pact of 1939, which he had considered the outcome of his own great cunning, would be broken by an enemy more cunning than himself."

For two weeks a demoralized Stalin remained in seclusion and said nothing. It was left to Molotov to tell the Russian people they were being invaded. Stalin knew he had built a respectable military force, reorganized and solidly armed. But its morale was uncertain. Behind the lines there appeared to be an alarming lack of fighting spirit. Rumors, confusion, and panic spread in the face of the German advance.

On July 3, Stalin emerged at last, to become the nation's commander in chief, seizing control of every detail of its defense.

By contrast, Hitler in those days was confidence personified. He did not doubt for a moment that the hated Russia, like the rest of Europe, would soon be under his heel. So confident was he that victory would not only be complete but swift that he had not bothered to issue his army winter clothing and equipment.

Hitler's armies advanced rapidly. By mid-October they had reached as far as the Crimean Peninsula and were approaching the gates of Moscow. Soviet resistance seemed about to crack. The government was evacuated six hundred miles to the east, and the city was put under martial law. But also in October the first rain mixed with sleet started to fall, turning the roads into bogs. An earlier German pause in its otherwise relentless advance now seemed to have been unwise. The Russian winter, not just the Russian army, was now Hitler's enemy, as it had been Napoleon Bonaparte's more than a century before. Stalin was meanwhile urgently preparing a counterblow of his own. He massed reserve armies and placed them to the east of Moscow, calling home three-quarters of a million experienced and well-equipped troops from the Far East.

On November 15 the final battle for Moscow began, on a snow-covered battlefield shrouded by freezing fog and assaulted by bitter winds. German machines froze and the attack ground to a halt on December 5. On that day, Stalin struck with his counteroffensive of 700,000 troops. The German army shuddered and fell back. For the first time Hitler's mighty army suffered a setback. It would shake him to his soul. He had expected a short, victorious campaign; instead, he was getting a bitter rebuke.

FRANKLIN ROOSEVELT WAS by upbringing, instinct, and experience an internationalist. And not just an internationalist, but an interventionist, as eager to redress problems abroad as at home.

But in the 1930s, America was more isolationist than ever in its history. A Gallup poll in the 1930s showed 94 percent of Americans strictly in favor of their government doing everything to stay out of another war in Europe, as opposed to doing anything to prevent it.

In that climate Roosevelt hid his internationalism. He had his hands full with the Depression at home anyhow. To protect his domestic policies, he more than muted his world instincts—he smothered them. He not only accommodated isolationist America; he joined it.

In 1935 and 1936, when the Congress passed a series of neutrality acts intended to keep the United States out of war and to set that policy in concrete, Roosevelt signed them. Called collectively the Isolationist, or Wishful Thinking, Laws by their few opponents, the neutrality acts outlawed government loans and the sale of arms and munitions to belligerents, and strictly prohibited American vessels from carrying supplies of any kind to any warring nation. American citizens were forbidden to travel on the ships of belligerent nations or to make loans to any nation at war.

Though Roosevelt talked isolationism with the best of them, in an address at Chautauqua, New York, on August 14 of 1936, he explained what our particular brand of isolationism *really* meant. "We are not isolationists," he said, "except in so far as we seek to isolate ourselves completely from war. Yet we must remember that so long as war exists on earth there will be some danger that even the Nation which most ardently desires peace may be drawn into war."

Even isolationist America could feel the tension gripping Europe. Events soon began to crowd American resolve. Roosevelt knew by 1939 that something must be done to halt fascist expansion. He began to extend limited help—as much as the prevailing sentiment and the neutrality laws would stand—to Britain and France. It wasn't much. Roosevelt fretted that the country did not yet have any deep perception of the world crisis, and that only a chain of events of compelling moment would give it that perception and free him to act.

In 1940, when Hitler overran Denmark, Norway, Holland, Belgium, and France, our isolationism was rocked to the core. The compelling events seemed to be happening. Suddenly, only Britain stood between Hitler and—what? Invasion of America itself? Americans for the first time felt vulnerable. Roosevelt not so subtly pointed out that German bombers could leave Europe or Africa and be over Omaha in a matter of hours. He requested money to mechanize and motorize the army and put planes in the air. By the end of May a sobered Congress had given him more than he asked. He would soon ask for still more.

Britain was putting pressure on the United States to intercede actively. As the European nations fell one after another to Hitler's Wehrmacht in the spring of 1940, Churchill cabled Roosevelt: THE SCENE HAS DARKENED SWIFTLY. THE SMALL COUNTRIES ARE SIMPLY SMASHED UP, ONE BY ONE, LIKE MATCHWOOD. . . . WE EXPECT TO BE ATTACKED HERE OURSELVES. He warned that France was about to go under as well, LIKE A DROWNING MAN, and predicted a NAZIFIED EUROPE if Hitler was not stopped.

But isolationism died hard in America. An America First Committee was formed in the Midwest to fight what it considered an ominous slide toward involvement abroad. It was clear, however, that with each German victory, isolationism as the driving force of America's foreign policy was waning—but not yet enough to permit the president to plunge the country into war.

Americans still pulled back from outright involvement. Even while asking Congress to repeal the arms embargo, Roosevelt promised the country he would continue to be guided by "one single hard-headed thought—keeping America out of this war." In November he was elected to an unprecedented third term in part on his pledge not to involve American boys in the foreign conflict.

Using his reelection—another 5-million-vote landslide—as a wedge, he pressed in late 1940 for massive aid to Britain to resist Hitler. To that end he proposed a lend-lease program of military assistance. The country was drifting ever closer to direct involvement, giving all assistance short of war, stretching its neutrality to the breaking point. Only one large provoking event now lay between the United States and direct participation.

December 7, 1941, was an uncommonly warm winter day in Washington. It was Sunday and the city basked placidly under a deep cerulean sky. At the White House, Franklin Roosevelt was enjoying a quiet Sabbath. The terrible showdown taking place just outside Moscow seemed distant, as if on another planet, in another lifetime.

It was also a warm Sunday in Honolulu, and the soldiers in the barracks onshore and the sailors on the battleships anchored in the harbor were sleeping in. Then planes bearing the insignia of the rising sun came roaring in from the southwest, undetected and unannounced over Diamond Head.

At about 1:50 P.M. Eastern time, E. E. Harris, radioman first class, who was manning the Washington-to-Honolulu circuit of the Navy Department Radio Central in D.C., was snapped out of his reverie. An alert had come over the wire to stand by for an urgent message from the Honolulu operator. The message read AIR RAID ON PEARL HARBOR. THIS IS NOT DRILL.

The Japanese, like the Germans, had been building a powerful military machine since the twenties, and they were longing to use it as Hitler was, to seize more territory. In 1931 the Japanese army had marched into Manchuria to begin a long, systematic drive to make China a client state. When the League of Nations protested, Japan simply resigned from the organization, ignored the protests, and went on with her conquests. As the third member of the Rome-Berlin-Tokyo Axis, Japan had been following developments in Europe with an eye to the opportunities. When Hitler overwhelmed France in mid-1940, Japan moved into Indochina. Britain and Holland were in no position to resist Japanese advances southward, and Russia was neutralized by the nonaggression pact. The only nation left that could offer any possible resistance to Japan's dreams of unresisted aggression in the Far East was the United States. In September 1940, the first-ever peacetime draft was passed, calling for service for one year. In August of 1941 a second measure extending service to eighteen months narrowly passed in the House, 203 to 202. By December 7, 1941, the United States had become enough of a frustration to bring the bombers of the Imperial Japanese Air Force roaring over Diamond Head to rain fire and death on Honolulu's harbor.

That did it. It was the provoking event that took the United

States into the war—and the world. American isolationism died forever in the flames in Honolulu. America would never be the same country again.

EVEN AT THAT moment the United States was already a greatly changed nation from the one that had emerged from the First World War little more than two decades before. It was a more industrialized America, more urbanized, more cosmopolitan, less deferential to business leadership, more kindly disposed to an activist federal government, more responsive to labor and ethnic groups, more willing to assume a role in world affairs—now that it had been forced into it—commensurate with its potential power.

It was that potential power that Roosevelt now had to harness to fight the greatest war the world had ever seen—the war America had vowed never to fight. The United States came streaking out of her isolationism to declare war on Japan, then on Germany and Italy. However, it took a while to mobilize, and 1942 was not good for the Allies: the Germans reached the Caucasus; the Japanese overran much of the western Pacific and reached the gates of India; Axis forces in Africa approached Alexandria—that they might engulf all of the Near East seemed a numbing possibility.

Since Britain and Russia were both on the edge of ruin, the United States gave early priority to the European and Mediterranean theaters, settling for a holding operation against Japan in the Pacific. But within a year of Pearl Harbor several events occurred that turned the tide.

Joseph Stalin was at his best in matters involving active violence. Immured at his desk behind the Kremlin walls—he would never visit any of his armies—he watched and directed the campaigns in the field. From his desk he oversaw the evacuation of over a thousand plants and factories from western Russia east to the Ural Mountains. Day after day he pored over military reports, made operational decisions, issued economic orders, and saw to diplomatic negotiations and arrangements. He appeared to grasp the technical aspects of war down to the most minute detail. He knew when to call up reserves and to put manpower and personnel where they belonged the moment they were most needed. The way he traveled from the Kremlin to his villa was a metaphor for the way he ran Russia: a motorcade of three Packards driven through Moscow's streets at breakneck speed, the position of each being frequently changed for security, the dictator himself sitting firmly beside the driver supervising every turn of the wheel.

That other dictator, amateur general, and practitioner of violence, Adolf Hitler, brought up short by his first inconclusive offensive in Russia, was in the summer of 1942 preparing his second. His target was Stalingrad (now Volgograd), on the Volga River. He hurled his army at that target with blitzkrieg force. But once again the terrible Russian winter was his undoing. The struggle dragged on through the fall and into the winter. Stalin, with his gift for timing, launched a counteroffensive before the city that took the Germans by surprise. Stalingrad would never be Hitler's. His devastated army, surrounded, its offensive power shattered, suffered a galling defeat.

Holding Stalingrad was the critical turning point in the war, arguably the most important victory in Russia's thousand-year history of being invaded from east and west. It not only destroyed an entire German army, it destroyed the myth of German invincibility. Not only had the Germans been outfought; they had been outgeneraled. It was a staggering blow to German self-esteem, the greatest single shock of the war. For Stalin it was his greatest hour. What did it matter that it was paid at horrendous cost in lives, a cost as unparalleled as the victory itself?

The tide of the war began to turn everywhere at about the same time. An Anglo-American force landed in Morocco and Algeria, and a British offensive in Egypt was launched at El Alamein. Both were successful. German Field Marshal Erwin Rommel's vaunted Afrika Korps was pushed back and finally smashed in Tunisia in May 1943. In July the Allies overran Sicily, and Mussolini's Fascist regime collapsed. When Italy sued for peace, Hitler occupied the country. It would be June 4, 1944, before Rome would be finally liberated, but by the summer before, its liberation had become inevitable. In a final humiliation, Mussolini and his mistress were captured by partisans, shot, and hanged, upside down, in a public square.

Only two days after Rome fell, the Allied armies landed on Normandy's beaches to begin the reconquest of France. The landing at Normandy—D-Day—was the beginning of the end for Hitler. In the closing months of 1944 overpowering Allied armies were approaching Berlin from both the east and the west. The noose was rapidly tightening. On May 7, 1945, at Reims, Germany surrendered, Hitler committed suicide in his bunker, and the European phase of the war ended.

Meanwhile, the war against Japan in the Pacific gathered force. Desperate air-sea battles in the Coral Sea and at Midway in the middle of 1942 proved to be the turning points. Over the next two years the Japanese were evicted island by island from their Pacific conquests, and by 1945 were in retreat from Southeast Asia as well. When American planes dropped atomic bombs on Hiroshima and Nagasaki in early August, the war with Japan ended as it had begun, with fire pouring from the skies.

THE DEADLIEST CONFLICT IN history had cost a staggering 50 million lives—20 million of them Russian. One of every ten Russians alive in 1941 had died at the hands of the Germans and their allies. Millions more—civilians, refugees, and prisoners—had been destroyed in this Armageddon, many millions of them as a result of Hitler's merciless policies. Towns, cities, and the countryside alike were devastated. Twenty-five million homeless lived in caves, trenches, and huts.

Even more monstrous was what Hitler had done in his own nation. The Nazis had shot, gassed, or buried alive some 6 million Jews in the most savage genocidal murder in history. Three to four million other passive or potential opponents of the Reich were slaughtered. As many as 2 million prisoners of war were shot or starved to death. Entire populations of hundreds of villages in Eastern Europe were destroyed by fire or bullet, often down to the last woman and child. Hundreds of thousands of ordinary citizens were enslaved, tortured, and otherwise abused to further the economic and military aims of the Third Reich.

Although 300,000 American lives were lost, the United States, alone among the great powers, had emerged from the war physically untouched except for the bombing at Pearl Harbor.

THERE WAS A final casualty. As the war neared its end, Franklin Roosevelt was also nearing his. He had been growing increasingly weak. The old joy and vigor were gone, sunk into dark eye sockets. In his last speech at a joint session of Congress, he could no longer stand and had to sit at a table before the podium. On April 12, 1945, he died of a massive cerebral hemorrhage.

I saw my father cry only a few times—this was one of them. Although I was not quite twelve years old, and did not fully comprehend what had happened, I shared my father's grief. The great man who had led America through two of the three greatest trials in its history—the Depression and the Second World War—was gone.

At the end of his life Roosevelt finally glimpsed the goal he had set for himself a dozen years before and that, until the war, had eluded him. The America of 1945 was a healed America, wholly different from five years previous. The Depression was over; the massive outlay of federal resources that had been required to wage the war had done what John Maynard Keynes predicted: it had produced astounding economic growth. Wartime demand had all but ended unemployment and restored full prosperity.

The country was firmly committed to the basic principles of the New Deal and to a lightly regulated free market economy rather than a laissez-faire economy. Roosevelt's reforms had been vindicated. Even the Republicans no longer wanted them repealed.

Gone was the fear. Ahead lay good times, rapid economic expansion, a sharp rise in the general standard of living, and an outpouring of goods and services of a quantity and variety unmatched in any society in history.

The whole world appeared opened to us. By 1945 technology

had, figuratively speaking, caused the protecting oceans to shrink. There was an urgency to immediately dismember our armies and bring the boys home, and a residual longing for the old protective ways. But there was no going back to the isolationism that until so recently had shielded us. Our military and industrial might, plus our monopoly of the bomb, had made us into a colossus. We were suddenly a nation with enormous international power and responsibilities.

Two of the world's three major totalitarian dictatorships had been obliterated. Fascism was dead in Germany, Italy, and the world. But there was still one great totalitarian regime left, in Communist Russia. In the war, that despotism had been our ally. Now it was about to become our enemy.

Chapter 8

THE COLD WAR

RUSSIA IS A LAND without natural geographic barriers to shield her from invading powers. There is no guarding ocean, no protecting mountains, no swamps, jungles, or deserts behind which she can hide. Nor did she have a protective cordon of friendly states to shield her. She has ever been at the mercy of her enemies: Mongols and Tatars from the east; Vikings, Poles, French, and Germans from the west. That was the history of Russia for a millennium. Centuries-old fear of invasion dominated the way she thought, the way she looked at the world, and the way she acted.

Stalin believed that must change. If he could not have natural shields, then he would create nation-shields, a buffer composed of satellite states, if not friendly, then at least servile.

Stalin did not delude himself that Poland, Rumania, Hungary, or any other nation that he occupied in the wake of the German retreat would become willing cogs in his defense machinery. "A freely elected government in any of these countries," he said, "would be anti-Soviet, and that we cannot allow." So he imposed his system as far as his army could reach. He pushed his frontiers westward, to shut the gate that had been forced open again and

142

again, and if possible lock it forever. This was not what his major allies in the war—the United States and Britain—had in mind. They wanted freedom for the nations of Eastern Europe.

The temporary reoccupation of the newly freed nations of Eastern Europe—Poland, Rumania, Bulgaria, Hungary, Czechoslovakia—was to be expected. The problem was that Joseph Stalin had no intention of ever leaving. This issue had begun to cloud Allied relations even before the war's end. It became a problem following the summit conference at Yalta between Roosevelt, Churchill, and Stalin.

The problem began with Poland. Was Poland to recover the eastern territories it had lost under the Nazi-Soviet Pact? Were the Poles to be free to shape their own domestic political and social order? The Western powers thought so; Stalin thought not. Allied relations worsened.

The Red Army moved into Rumania. There the issue became clear-cut and the breach bare and raw for all to see. Russia forcibly installed a Communist-dominated government in Rumania, which the United States and Britain refused to recognize. An undemocratic government controlled by force was clearly not in accord with the agreement at Yalta. The three powers had signed a Declaration on Liberated Areas, which called for representative interim governments and unobstructed elections in every freed nation.

However, there had been an earlier Churchill-Stalin agreement that had assigned spheres of influence in southeastern Europe. That agreement gave Greece to Britain and Rumania to the Soviet Union, but only for a period of military occupation following the expulsion of the German army. Stalin chose to embrace the bilateral agreement with Churchill, ignore Yalta, and make the occupation of Rumania permanent. It was the beginning of the contest that would reshape Europe and dominate world affairs for nearly half a century.

When the war in Europe ended in the summer of 1945, the Russian army occupied Eastern Europe all the way to a line one hundred miles west of Berlin. Stalin had simply replaced Hitler in the entire eastern half of Europe. With the rapid withdrawal of the eager-to-go-home American army from Western Europe, there was theoretically no military obstacle to the Red Army advancing to the English channel. A power vacuum was developing that Stalin found enormously inviting. The Western powers, having put down the terrifying specter of Hitler, were now confronted with the no-less-terrifying specter of a Soviet dictatorship. It was a sobering prospect. Equally sobering was the truth that Russia had not only pushed to a hundred miles beyond Berlin, but into Manchuria, into Korea to the 38th Parallel, into the Kurile Islands, and into the southern half of Sakhalin—all wrested from Japan as the war in that theater ended.

It had all come down, then, to what it had come down to repeatedly over the centuries—a seriously skewed balance of power. Russia's occupation of Eastern Europe at war's end once again pushed that balance, always delicate and tenuous, out of whack. In the twentieth century the principal European counterweight to Russia had been Germany. But Germany lay in ruins. Now the only power capable of maintaining the balance in Europe, and by definition in the world, was the United States. But we were intent on disarming and coming home.

Winston Churchill saw clearly what was happening. In March 1946, at President Truman's invitation, he came to America and delivered a speech in Fulton, Missouri. The speech was a warning. "A shadow has fallen upon the scenes so lately lighted by the Allied victory . . . ," Churchill said. "From Stettin in the Baltic to Trieste in the Adriatic, an iron curtain has descended across the continent. Behind that line lie all the capitals of the ancient states of Central and Eastern Europe. Warsaw, Berlin, Prague, Vienna, Budapest, Belgrade, Bucharest and Sofia. . . . Whatever conclusions may be drawn from these facts—and facts they are—this is certainly not the liberated Europe we fought to build up. Nor is it one which contains the essentials of permanent peace."

So it was to be yet more war, but a war unlike any other in history. It came to be known as the Cold War, a term first used by Bernard Baruch in a speech in 1947.

About the time Churchill was delivering his "Iron Curtain" speech in Missouri, a young U.S. diplomat in Moscow named

George Kennan was writing a memorandum describing life in the postwar world.

The facts of that life, he wrote, were alarming. The crippled world was at the mercy of two giants. As one scholar put it, "never since the breakup of the Roman Empire had power been so concentrated as it was in 1945." The moment the war ended, the traditional instincts of one of these giants, the United States, surfaced; the urge to pull back, bring the boys home, and disarm was overwhelming. But Russia, which we had never liked because of her communism, was not disarming. In fact, she was doing successfully what Hitler had failed to do: subjugating all of Eastern Europe and threatening the rest of the Continent. She was more dangerous to the world than the dragon we had just slain. A hundred million Europeans were under the Soviet boot, or soon would be. All of Eastern Europe to the western edge of a partitioned Germany was becoming "sovietized." There was to be no democracy anywhere from Moscow to Berlin. It was a situation filled with danger. For this was the same Soviet Union with the avowed aim of spreading communism worldwide and destroying capitalism—our way of life—forever. This was a new and very real threat of monstrous proportions.

That is what George Kennan in effect told his superiors in Washington in his sixteen-page memorandum from Moscow in the spring of 1946. He further said that this threat must somehow be contained. A new approach was called for, a new orientation toward the rest of the world. Thus a new policy, called "containment," was born. If Russia was to be contained, only the United States could do it. It was the only other power in the shattered world capable of making and enforcing global policy, the only superpower, with its resources, know-how, and its atomic monopoly, capable of making the now mighty Soviet Union back down. No other West European state, or all of them together, could stop what was happening. If there was to be containment, if the democratic way of life was to be restored and protected, the United States had to do it.

And so the last remnants of American isolationism scattered to the winds forever.

Kennan and the authors of the U.S. containment policy saw three dangers in this new Cold War world. One was that if and when the Russians developed an atomic weapon—and they were working at it full-time—it would throw the balance of power in the world even further out of line. A second danger was that any trouble between these two world giants could escalate into a disastrous nuclear war. Third, chaos anywhere in the free world could upset the balance of power in unpredictable ways. It all added up to an enormous responsibility for the United States. The containment strategy meant that in this new and strange kind of war we must always be ahead in the arms race. We must draw the lines of containment and prop up any free government in the world threatened by Communist takeover. These dangers and duties were soon to make many Americans paranoid, a paranoia that would be exceeded by Russia's.

ON WASHINGTON'S BIRTHDAY in 1947, Secretary of State George C. Marshall went to Princeton to deliver a speech. Marshall had been in office only a month, and he wanted to talk about America's new obligations in the world. "The development of a sense of responsibility for world order and security," he told the students, "the development of a sense of overwhelming importance of this country's acts and failures to act, in relation to world order and security—these, in my opinion, are great 'musts' for your generation."

Even as he spoke, the need to act was about to become a must in his own life. The afternoon before, after he had left Washington for Princeton, the first secretary of the British embassy came to the State Department with an important message from London. It said that Britain was no longer able economically or militarily to protect Greece and Turkey, its particular charges in postwar Europe. This was shocking news. For if Greece and Turkey fell under Soviet sway, the probable outcome of a British withdrawal, Europe would become sovietized to the very shores of the Mediterranean. The United States must act.

Marshall hurried back to Washington, and President Truman

went before Congress with a new doctrine. "I believe," the president said, "that it must be the policy of the United States to support free peoples who are resisting attempted subjugation by armed minorities or by outside pressures." He requested funding from Congress to replace British support in Greece and Turkey.

Marshall followed up the Truman Doctrine with the legislation that would bear his name and reach much farther into the world than just Greece and Turkey. The Marshall Plan, enacted into law in 1948 as the Foreign Assistance Act, had two basic aims—to halt the Communist advance into Western Europe and to stabilize an international economic environment favorable to capitalism. This far-sweeping policy signaled unmistakably the U.S. intent. American military power was to remain in Europe to check Soviet expansion and defend free nations from attack. A program of economic recovery was to be launched in Europe, erected on the structure of a North American Treaty Organization. By the middle of the 1950s, U.S. economic aid would rebuild Europe to new levels of prosperity, U.S. military might would underwrite Europe's security, and there would be a mutual defense network in place involving every free nation in Europe.

There would also be an inevitable Soviet response. When the United States halted and reversed its disarmament and remained in Europe, the Soviet Union was as alarmed for its security as we were for ours. In Russian eyes the United States was perhaps the most deadly enemy it had faced in its thousand-year history. For America had something the Soviet Union, or any other nation, had never had—the atomic bomb. Soviet leaders were concerned that Americans might drop it on Russian cities as they had on Hiroshima and Nagasaki. Just as the United States began to build a shield of containment in Europe, the Soviets fearfully gathered more tightly within their own protective armor.

Despite the fact that they initially intended to participate, the Russians came to see the newly adopted Marshall Plan as a declaration of war by the United States for control of Europe. In Stalin's view America intended to use its great economic might, if not its atomic power, to isolate the Soviet Union. His foreign policy hardened. There was no more hope for a Great Power consortium. The Russians established the Cominform, the Communist Information Bureau, as their answer to perceived American aggression. The Cominform, the coordinating body for national Communist parties in the Soviet Union and Eastern Europe, was, of course, dominated totally by the Soviets, and would tighten their hold on all of Eastern Europe. Where any political diversity still existed, it came to a sudden end.

The Cold War became firmly fixed. It would become a way of life for both powers, and for the rest of the world. Arthur Schlesinger, Jr., has written that it all began as the product not of a decision, but of a dilemma. "Each side felt compelled to adopt policies which the other could not but regard as a threat to the principles of the peace," Schlesinger wrote. "Each then felt compelled to undertake defensive measures. Thus the Russians saw no choice but to consolidate their security in Eastern Europe. The Americans, regarding Eastern Europe as the first step toward Western Europe, responded by asserting their interest in the zone the Russians deemed vital to their security. The Russians concluded that the West was resuming its old course of capitalist encirclement; that it was purposefully laying the foundation for anti-Soviet regimes in the area defined by the blood of centuries as crucial to Russian survival. Each side believed with passion that future international stability depended on the success of its own conception of world order. Each side, in pursuing its own clearly indicated and deeply cherished principles, was only confirming the fear of the other that it was bent on aggression."

Both sides would come to insist, and to believe, that the other intended to make itself master of the entire world. Both would conclude that the struggle could only be resolved by the total defeat of the other. Louis J. Halle, in *The Cold War as History*, wrote: "Western politicians, paraphrasing Lincoln, would announce that the world could not exist half slave and half free (although it always had). Communist leaders, citing Marx, would proclaim the inevitable doom of the capitalist world, its total defeat and destruction (which Marx had expected to take place not later than the end of the nineteenth century)."

The Soviet Union began a massive, bitter, coordinated verbal assault on the United States and its allies, in which the kindest word seemed to be "warmonger." "The ruling clique of American imperialists," one of Stalin's Politburo members, Georgi Malenkov, said at the founding of the Cominform, ". . . has taken the path of outright expansion, of enthralling the weakened capitalist states of Europe and the colonial and dependent countries. It has chosen the path of hatching new war plans against the Soviet Union and the new democracies. . . . The clearest and most specific expression of the policy . . . is provided by the Truman-Marshall plans. . . . Imitating the Hitlerites, the new aggressors are using blackmail and extortion. . . ."

A sphere of influence—a very large and well-padded one—was what the Soviet Union wanted, for only that would translate into their long-sought permanent national security. American leaders, believing the Soviet policy to be aggressive and expansionist, concluded that any communism in any country was too much communism. The very fact of Soviet totalitarianism aggravated everything, making any kind of postwar collaboration between the two giants impossible. One or the other would have to give up its modus operandi—we our democracy or Russia its communism.

There were two ways the United States could have gone at the end of the war. We could have opted for containment, which we finally did, or we could have gone along with the Soviet Union and carved up the world into spheres of influence and left each other to manage its sphere as it saw fit. While there was still a choice, some influential voices in the United States argued for the latter approach.

Secretary of War Henry L. Stimson told President Truman that he thought the Russians were more realistic than we were about their own security. He likened it to our own preferred position in Latin America and spoke of "our respective orbits." He was skeptical of the prevailing U.S. tendency "to hang on to exaggerated views of the Monroe Doctrine and at the same time butt into every question that comes up in Central Europe." Accepting spheres of influence seemed to him the way to avoid a head-on collision between the world's two superpowers.

In 1946, Henry Wallace, by then secretary of commerce, said: "On our part, we should recognize that we have no more business in the *political* affairs of Eastern Europe than Russia has in the *political* affairs of Latin America, Western Europe, and the United States. . . . Whether we like it or not, the Russians will try to socialize their sphere of influence just as we try to democratize our sphere of influence. . . . The Russians have no more business stirring up native communists to political activity in Western Europe, Latin America, and the United States than we have in interfering with the politics of Eastern Europe and Russia."

President Truman fired Wallace for saying that, for Truman believed in containment. Despite these dissenting voices, and despite a note in the briefing papers Truman carried to the Potsdam summit that said "Eastern Europe is, in fact, a Soviet sphere of influence," containment it was going to be. As Hans Morgenthau, one of America's foremost scholars of international relations, said in the early 1970s, America refused to reconcile itself to the fact of spheres of influence that would be Communist-controlled. "As the Soviet Union has reproached us for refusing to recognize its sphere of influence," Morgenthau wrote, "so we have reproached the Soviet Union for having acquired it."

There were several persuasive arguments for the United States to reject the spheres-of-influence approach: it could fatally destabilize the balance of power and lead to yet a third world war; it would militate against the newly formed United Nations, which the United States saw as the correct alternative to a balance-of-power world; it would prove a haven for American isolationists, who would attempt to turn us inward again, to our peril; it would betray the principles for which World War II was fought; it would alienate the more than 6 million Polish-Americans at home as well as others of East European origin. If the Russians were allowed to overrun Eastern Europe without an argument, would that satisfy them? Who would be their next victims?

The United States wanted the world to work through the United Nations and to be free, democratic, and capitalistic. The Kremlin, in concentrating on spheres of interest, tightly controlled and Communist, would consider it a betrayal of the principles for which they had fought and suffered so heavily in the war if they permitted Eastern Europe to revert to capitalism. There was no reconciling the two points of view.

There was also no altering the fact that the world was, in effect, carved up into spheres of influence anyhow, whether we wanted it that way or not, whether we called them that or not. The Soviet Union in the early years following the war had fashioned what one U.S. ambassador to Russia described as "a belt of pro-Soviet states to protect it from the influences of the West." Once the Cold War began, the issue was no longer whether spheres of influence should or should not exist. They already did. The question became how far either side's sphere of influence should extend.

But there was also containment. Just as the Soviet Union had erected its defenses, the United States had built its elaborate network of regional security alliances that ultimately linked it with forty-four nations in Europe, Latin America, Asia, and Oceania. It also had its equally elaborate and apparently permanent program of economic, technical, and developmental assistance to the friendly free world. The Soviet Union, so we hoped, was boxed in.

THE FIRST "BATTLE" of the Cold War was in Berlin in 1948, when Stalin threw up a blockade around the Western-held sectors of the city. President Truman answered with a massive airlift over the blockade. The air lanes over Berlin became supply highways, and Stalin was forced to back down and lift the blockade. The United States won this test of wills. But it was also a victory for the status quo: neither side dared make the cold war hot.

Just after the Berlin blockade and airlift came an event that would unsettle America: China went Communist.

Though we didn't see it then, it was nowhere near the victory for Russian communism we believed it to be at the time. There were many similarities at first between Chinese and Russian communism. China was no more the perfect setting for a classic Marxist revolution than Russia had been—it was even more peasant-based. The Bolshevik ideology began to seep into China in 1920 with the Second Comintern. Russia, the sole case in the world of a successful Communist revolution, was the only role model the small knot of Chinese Communists had. It was from Russia, therefore, that Mao Tse-tung and his followers got their Marxism. It wasn't until 1921 that the *Communist Manifesto* was translated into Chinese for the first time, seventy-three years after Marx and Engels published it.

The Chinese Communists tried a revolution in 1925–27 and couldn't pull it off—just as the Bolsheviks had tried and failed in 1905. It would take over twenty more years, a Japanese invasion and occupation, world war, and Japanese defeat to bring Mao's partisans to a point where they could again challenge the Kuomintang government of Chiang Kai-shek. By then Mao's time had come.

Throughout Chinese history, ruling dynasties had bloomed and then gradually decayed, becoming ineffective, feeble, and corrupt. In their decadence they would lose their legitimacy—what they called their "Mandate of Heaven"—and in the eyes of the Chinese people, their authority to rule. At some point in this inevitable downslide, a commanding figure had always risen up to lead a new dynasty that did have the Mandate of Heaven.

The surrender of Japan in 1945 unleashed a struggle for power in China between Chiang, now without the Mandate of Heaven, and Mao, the rising commanding figure. The Kuomintang had attempted too much with too few resources. Following the war they couldn't cement their hold over such a vast region as China. As poverty and discontent grew, police repression also grew, and against that the hatred of the people grew as well. Mao's Communists were better strategists. Unlike the Kuomintang, they carried out sweeping land reforms in the territories where they seized power. As the civil war dragged on, they won over the peasant masses and the intelligentsia of the North, especially the university students and professors—even the intelligentsia of the Kuomintang itself. In Chinese history peasants and scholars had always made potent partners. All the great dynasties of the past had had their support, and now Mao did, too. He also had three other things the revolution needed—his strong leadership, efficient party discipline, and trained cadres capable of taking over the administration of regions as they were conquered. In his two decades of guerrilla experience in the mountains of China, Mao had created a military and civil state machine that was more than a match for Chiang's.

What he needed least was the Russians. Up to 1927 the Chinese Communists had operated under Moscow's tutelage and followed its strategic direction. But after the failure of the first revolution, that was no longer the case.

When Peking and Tientsin fell to the Communists in January 1949, all over China the Kuomintang began to disintegrate. Within months it was finished. Mao's victory owed little to the Russians—little to communism for that matter. Louis Halle reminds us that the revolution in China was peasant-driven, Communist only in name—it could just as well have been called something else. The pity is it wasn't, since, as Halle says, "the nominal is always more real to us than the real." China had merely played out a pattern as old as its history. Its communism was merely its modern face. But to Americans the word was everything.

Since we saw it that way, that is what it became—China was seen as one of the true disasters of the Cold War. But Communist China had very little in common with Communist Russia. The main similarity was their shared totalitarianism. Mao's China quickly became what one scholar has called "a totalitarian hothouse," with a stranglehold over every aspect of life. Stalin quite rightly never trusted Mao and his cohorts, any more than they trusted him. Considerations of security, more than a shared socialism, drove the Chinese Communists toward the Soviet Union in the Cold War. The Kuomintang armies had been advised and equipped by the United States. With the world dividing into two blocs, China's new government had to choose sides. It turned to the Soviets for security and economic aid.

But it would never be an easy fit. Relations between the two Communist giants were strained from the start. Stalin's egoism and his ideological isolationism got in the way. It would continue to get in the way even after he was gone.

What the Chinese revolution did was to make ominously clear that a third of the world was now Communist. It also swung world attention to the Asian rim, where yet more trouble was brewing.

In June 1950 the armed forces of Communist North Korea swept across the 38th Parallel into South Korea. The second major battle of the Cold War was launched. The Communists swept to the tip of the Korean peninsula, to be rolled back by U.N.–mostly U.S.–forces led by General Douglas MacArthur. When MacArthur pushed on beyond the parallel to the very borders of China, the Chinese Communists entered the fight. There was another rollback in the other direction, and the fighting stopped at the 38th Parallel, where it had all begun. A demilitarized zone was created and the border slipped again into an unquiet peace. Communism had been contained, but the Cold War simmered on.

China may have been lost to the West, but at least Stalin's hegemony in Eastern Europe was showing signs of slippage. His postwar empire had reached high tide by February 1949. After that it began to ebb. Communist Yugoslavia successfully broke off. Stalin was finding that it was not a simple matter to hold unwilling states in line.

Something was happening in Europe that Marxism had not counted on. People in the Communist regimes continued in misery and economic stagnation while those in Western Europe enjoyed a rising prosperity. The contrast was striking. It would continue to be so, and in the end would undermine the entire Communist world.

The free world at the time, however, could not see that. The Cold War crowded out other considerations and skewed perceptions. Positions were fixed in cement. In the face of a hostile West, the Russians dared not release their hold on their East European satellites, whom they had by now profoundly antagonized. But neither could the West liberate them without terrible consequences—perhaps nuclear war. So by the early 1950s there was deadlock. Neither side could advance, neither would retreat, and no disengagement was possible.

There seemed only one out—that communism, boxed in and contained, would ultimately decay from within. George Kennan had suggested such an outcome in 1947 when he wrote, "The possibility remains that Soviet power . . . bears within it the seeds of its own decay. . . ." But in the early postwar decades, that seemed highly unlikely.

BY THE EARLY 1950s Joseph Stalin had grown more paranoid than ever. One day in 1951 he was walking on the grounds of his vacation dacha with Nikita Khrushchev and Anastas Mikoyan, two Politburo members. "I'm finished," he said. "I trust no one, not even myself." He was again seeing enemies everywhere, not a new symptom with Stalin, only more aggravated. Such feelings usually meant death for somebody.

His health was rapidly declining, but his capacity for destruction of human life remained intact. It is widely believed that by late in 1952 he was making arrangements for another purge of the magnitude of the 1930s, including the liquidation of most of his Politburo. But sometime between five and six in the morning on March 1 and three in the morning on March 2, 1953, his brain began to hemorrhage and he became paralyzed. For three and a half days he lingered on, in intense pain, dying at last on March 5.

On the morning of Stalin's funeral on March 9, pallbearing members of the Politburo, who might themselves have been dead if he still lived, carried his coffin to the Lenin Mausoleum, where he was laid to rest.

After Stalin was purged posthumously in the 1960s, all of his acts denounced by the new leaders in the Kremlin, his daughter Svetlana, who had defected to the United States, wrote a sad epitaph to his bloody career: "He gave his name to this bloodbath of absolute dictatorship. He knew what he was doing. He was neither insane nor misled. With cold calculation he had cemented his own power, afraid of losing it more than anything else in the world. And so his first concentrated drive had been the liquidation of his enemies and rivals. The rest followed later." No more violent and brutal figure has ever walked across history's stage.

THE WORLD CAUGHT its collective breath. Now what? What would Stalin's passing mean?

What it meant was a long power struggle. By the late 1950s, Khrushchev had won, and for a time the attitude of the Kremlin toward the world seemed to soften. But Stalin's passing did not end the Cold War. The same tensions, the same divisions and differences, the same desire to spread communism to the world—or at least lip service to that desire—persisted. The arms and space races and the containment policy continued, and the Cold War vocabulary persisted. We still talked of "the international Communist conspiracy," "missile gaps," "nuclear stalemate," "Iron Curtain," and "the domino theory."

By now the Cold War had become a blanket description to cover most postwar antagonisms throughout the world. And it continued to heat and cool. For a time after Dwight Eisenhower became president in the 1950s, his secretary of state, John Foster Dulles, talked boldly of not just containing the Soviet Union but of rolling back the Iron Curtain. But that was no more realistic than the Soviets' professed aim of making the whole world Communist. In November 1956 the Soviet Union brutally crushed a revolt in Hungary, and the United States did nothing. Khrushchev about the same time triggered a crisis in the Suez. In the summer of 1961 he tried again what Stalin had tried more than a decade before—to pry the Western powers out of Berlin. He finally settled for a wall through the middle of the city, which became a symbol of the persistent division of the world into two antagonistic camps. In 1962 he precipitated the Cuban Missile Crisis, a reckless attempt to intrude into what the United States regarded as its own sphere of influence. At about the same time, Russia and China split decisively. The quarrel between them had become acute over the years, and there was little Moscow could do to keep China in line.

It was a signal that the nature of the Cold War was changing. Through nearly two decades, through a huge buildup of nuclear arms on both sides, it was becoming apparent that neither open war nor clear-cut military victory of one side over the other was a realistic expectation. A debilitating war in Vietnam drove this fact home to the American people. And while there was still tension, the Cold War entered a new phase with the Nixon-Brezhnev détente of the early 1970s.

Other concerns became ever more pressing: Third World problems intruded; new centers of economic and political power emerged—a resurgent West Germany, Japan, China, India, Latin America, and Southeast Asia; important new institutions emerged—the European Community, the World Bank, and various U.N. organizations; revolutions in technology transformed lives everywhere.

One of the casualties of the Cold War was Marx's dream of turning all the world Communist. By the early 1960s the governments of a third of the planet held Marxism as their official doctrine and guide. But by the late twentieth century, it had been honored in the word and ignored in the deed.

Chapter 9

THE YEARS

OF HYSTERIA

RED SCARES IN AMERICA WERE NOTHING NEW.

The first flared in the twenties following the Russian Revolution, swept the country, then sputtered and died in that decade's roaring prosperity. Another picked up in the 1930s as a response to Stalin's Popular Front. The U.S. Congress passed the Hatch Act in that troubled decade in part to address the fear of Communist infiltration of the government. That legislation made membership in the Communist Party grounds for refusing federal employment. That was followed in 1940 by the Smith Act, which made it a federal offense to advocate the violent overthrow of the government. By 1941 federal agencies had begun investigating the loyalty of their employees, with the goal of rooting out Communists. That ended when Hitler invaded the flagship of communism, the Soviet Union, and that country was suddenly transformed into our wartime ally.

These early scares, however, were mild tremors compared with the earthquake-sized hysteria spawned by the Cold War.

In 1947, when Soviet-American tension began in earnest, a general loyalty program was established by executive order throughout the federal establishment—the first in our history. It was Congress's idea, not the Truman administration's, and originated as much from conservative loathing of New Dealers as from fear of Communists. Some conservatives, still embittered by the Roosevelt years, tended to lump all liberals with reds.

Partisan tensions rose in 1948 with testimony before Congress that two independent espionage rings had been operating in Washington for years, for the benefit of the Soviet Union. There were gasps of disbelief when Whittaker Chambers, an editor at *Time* magazine and a former Communist, named Alger Hiss, a former high official in the State Department, as one of his partners in espionage. Hiss sued Chambers for libel and Chambers produced papers, allegedly sequestered in a pumpkin, that supported his claim. Hiss, having denied any connection with Chambers, was prosecuted for perjury and convicted. During the case a young congressman from California attracted national attention with his aggressive anticommunism. For the next quarter century Richard Nixon was a dominant figure in American politics, and for most of that time anticommunism was his ticket to ever higher office.

Soon after the Hiss conviction, Truman unexpectedly won a second term in the presidential election upset of 1948, beating Thomas Dewey. Some conservatives turned up the heat on independent investigations of alleged Communists in government and elsewhere. It was an effort, at least in part, to tar the administration. As the Cold War tightened, the threat of Communist infiltration in high levels of government suddenly seemed a grim possibility, making the country receptive to virtually any public charge of subversion—against anybody. And come the charges did.

Hearings and investigations erupted around the country. Everything and anything that smacked of communism became intensely suspect. To have once been a member of the Communist Party was to become a pariah at best, a traitor at worst.

The fear of communism in the winter of 1948 was palpable. "Cold fear is gripping people hereabouts," reporter Eric Goldman wrote in Chicago after the violent Soviet putdown of Czechoslovakia in February. "They don't talk much about it. But it's just as real and chilling as the current 11-degree weather. Fear of what? Most people don't know exactly. It's not fear of Russia alone. For most think we could rub Joe's nose in the dirt. It's not fear of communism in this country. Few think there are enough Commies here to put it over. It's not fear of the atom bomb. For most think we still possess a monopoly. But it does seem to be a reluctant conviction that these three relentless forces are prowling the earth and that somehow they are bound to mean trouble for us."

Then came 1949. China fell to the Communists. The Russians had the bomb. Our own country seemed to seethe with traitors. Goldman called it "a year of shocks," which "loosed within American life a vast impatience, a turbulent bitterness, a rancor akin to revolt . . . quite without parallel in the history of the United States."

Containment was not a comfortable policy for a people who believed in immediate problem-solving. It was too slow and indefinite, especially since it didn't seem to be working. China was lost. That was hard enough to take. The Alger Hiss case suggested an appalling pattern of Communist infiltration in the government itself. Was there indeed a conspiracy right here at home, under our noses, in our own government? Many American leaders came to think so. Some even came to believe that the internal threat of communism was greater than the external threat. They believed there was something so appealing about communism that it had to be combatted by any means, fair or foul, peaceful or warlike.

On the other hand, many ordinary Americans believed that if Russians could only see and understand what a free system could do for its people, they would never choose to be Communists.

With the benefit of hindsight we can see that the confidence of ordinary Americans in their own system was right and the fears of many leaders were exaggerated and misplaced. There is, in fact, little attraction for a system in which a few unelected persons tell all others how to live, while there is a great deal of attraction for a system in which the vast majority of people tells its freely elected leaders how to govern.

During the red scare, people in many walks of life suddenly found themselves blacklisted for past connections, or for suspected or even mistaken connections, to Communist front organizations of any kind. The Truman administration, spooked by the general mood, created the Attorney General's List of organizations with known Communist, fascist, totalitarian, or subversive views. This gave the House Committee on Un-American Activities, the main anti-Communist investigator, a ready-made weapon. Americans who had been in any way associated or had sympathized with any of the listed organizations were presumed disloyal by the committee until proved otherwise. Part of the proof of innocence became a willingness to name other people's names. The penalty for belonging to a listed organization was to be blacklisted and denied work. The lists also made it necessary for people to be circumspect about who they associated with and where they went, even who they met. *Everybody* was suspect. The arts community, particularly Hollywood, became a special target.

Many cooperated with the committee and named names to save their own livelihoods. The historian Garry Wills wrote, "It was a humiliating little crawl men were learning, that early after World War II." Not everybody crawled. The playwright Lillian Hellman had been a longtime consort to the writer Dashiell Hammett, who was a known former Communist. Subpoenaed, Hellman wrote the committee that she would willingly testify about herself, but she would not implicate others. "I cannot and will not," she wrote, "cut my conscience to fit this year's fashions." But she was an exception.

The journalist Fred J. Cook described it as "a time of national paranoia in which the greatest power on earth expended its energies hunting for communists under every bed; in which millions of average Americans looked fearfully over their shoulders, wondering whether they would be tapped next to explain themselves before the grand inquisitors. . . .

"The entire nation ran cowed. A whisper out of the night could ruin a life, a career. Just to have a name similar to someone else's could be fatal. If one had ever in all innocence signed petitions or joined groups working for what had seemed at the time estimable causes, one became extremely vulnerable in the changed political climate a decade later when the Attorney General's office belatedly labeled many such groups as communist fronts. To have been connected with any of them, however tentatively or remotely, automatically stigmatized one as 'a communist fronter.'

"Such 'communist fronters' had no recourse. It was not necessary to show they had known that the groups with which they had been connected had communists in them. Such persons were not accused of any crime. They were not brought to trial in any court of law. They were simply branded—and often, professionally ruined." Several thousand federal employees—alleged security risks—lost their jobs in the tides of hysteria coursing through the country.

SOME MEN SEEM to be produced for their moment in time. Abraham Lincoln, an improbable candidate for the presidency in 1860, seems in hindsight to have been specially made and shipped to earth specifically to save the Union. When that was accomplished, he just as abruptly left the scene.

Though I hesitate to write of the two men in the same context, it seems that Joseph McCarthy was especially produced for the hysteria of his times. Elected to the U.S. Senate as a Republican from Wisconsin in 1946 following an undistinguished career as a judge and on a dubious record in the war as self-proclaimed "Tail-gunner Joe," his arrival on the national scene coincided with the beginning of the Cold War. For a while McCarthy hovered on the outer edge of national life, unnoticed and little known, but brash and ambitious. In his first four years in office his shopping about for a cause was notorious in the Senate. Then, one February night in 1950, in a speech to Republican women in Wheeling, West Virginia, he found it.

Waving a sheet of paper before the entranced audience, he told them that the U.S. State Department was full of Communists and that the secretary of state *knew their names*. They are there with the secretary's knowledge and approval, he charged, making policy for the United States of America. He, Joe McCarthy, had their names right here on this piece of paper. These were startling assertions. He was to repeat them in two follow-up speeches in Denver and Salt Lake City. The numbers of known Communists in the State Department changed with each speech, and he waved the piece of paper without reading any names. But the shock value was tremendous. He and his lists were to dominate American political life for the next four years. The whole postwar era of hysteria, charge and countercharge, investigation and innuendo, destroyed lives and careers, would soon bear his name. He had inaugurated in Wheeling a national search-and-destroy operation that would come to be known as McCarthyism.

The *New York Times* caught on right away to what he was about. In its February 22, 1950, issue it wrote that "Senator McCarthy has been giving a good imitation of a hit-and-run driver in his attacks on the State Department." But that hardly mattered to McCarthy. As Richard Rovere, his highly critical biographer, was to write some years later, if there were Communists in the State Department, McCarthy really didn't know who they were. The important thing, as Rovere wrote, was that "he had cued himself in. The lights played over him. Eyes were upon him. The show was his." A few weeks after the Wheeling speech he was in full stride, recklessly accusing the Truman administration itself of conniving with and being supported by Communists—all unnamed. He spoke of the Democratic years, which he hoped to see ended in 1952, as "twenty years of treason."

McCarthy's style soon became familiar to the country: brazen and reckless accusations, verbal abuse of all who opposed him, careless statements, and outright lies. The columnists Joseph and Stewart Alsop wrote that "McCarthy is the only major politician in the country who can be labeled 'liar' without fear of libel." Rovere wrote that "he lied with wild abandon; he lied without evident fear; he lied in his teeth and in the teeth of the truth; he lied vividly and with a bold imagination; he lied, often, with very little pretense to be telling the truth." Another critic, Thomas Griffith, wrote, "Over his grave should be written the simple epitaph THE TRUTH WASN'T IN HIM."

McCarthy doctored documents if necessary, waving them in the air whether doctored or not, as he drove home another undocumented statement. Rovere says there was "a bedlam quality" to McCarthy's speeches. What filtered through, as reported in the papers, was that a U.S. senator had delivered a long and angry speech giving what he claimed were details on persons he insisted were Communist in the State Department. It was all vague and chaotic and preposterous, bamboozlement of an extraordinary character.

It was also one of the most incredible performances in the history of American politics. But the fear of communism was so pervasive and his tactics so intimidating that McCarthy's performance won him reelection in 1952. He became chairman of the Senate's Governmental Affairs Committee, from which he launched high-profile hearings into alleged Communist infiltration not only of the State Department, but the Pentagon, the Voice of America, and other agencies. No American, no matter how lofty, was immune from assault. He was to tar even George C. Marshall, perhaps the most widely respected American of his time, charging that his conduct of affairs as Truman's secretary of state, particularly in the loss of China to communism, bordered on treason.

There had indeed been some Communist activity over the years, particularly in the 1930s. Communists never achieved any important electoral success, but for a time their influence was felt in many organizations. Writers, actors, and intellectuals widely sympathized for a time with Communist aims, especially during the Depression, and many of them became members or "fellow travelers." McCarthy might have been able to make a valid, though limited, case if he had tried to do so.

Early in his anti-Communist career, a special Senate committee looked into his charges that the State Department was riddled with Communists, and found them groundless, "a fraud and a hoax." That failed to derail McCarthy, however. Not even the election of Dwight Eisenhower and a Republican administration in 1952 made a difference. He turned the Communists-in-government issue against the administration of his own party just as he had turned it against the Democrats. He accused the new administration of coddling unnamed Communists, as well as practicing a "weak, immoral, and cowardly" foreign policy of "appeasement, retreat, and surrender" before communism. He was soon stretching the "twenty years of treason" to twenty-one.

McCarthy reached his apogee in 1953, the first year of the Eisenhower administration. The next year, after the fall midterm elections, he was finally brought down—by the Senate itself. His fellow senators had had enough and moved to censure him. Televised Army-McCarthy hearings that riveted the nation for weeks had revealed McCarthy for what he was. In the end, a Senate committee found that he had wrongfully defied the authority of the Senate and certain of its committees and had abused his colleagues. He soon lapsed back into political oblivion, and only three years later was dead, at the age of forty-seven. In the end, he was never to unearth a single certifiable Communist in the government.

He was surely one of the strangest objects ever to soar across the American political sky. The reason he happened—or at least had so much effect—is that he fit the nation's mood at that moment. That mood was ugly, and he knew how to capitalize on it.

McCarthyism was not simply a Republican phenomenon. Anti-Communist fear was bipartisan, infecting both parties alike and metastasizing throughout the body politic.

These were melancholy times, a dark chapter in our history. But times even more dark and melancholy lay ahead in a faraway field of battle called Vietnam.

IN 1930 THE INDOCHINESE Communist Party led by Ho Chi Minh was formed to resist French colonial rule, which dated to the 1860s. In 1940 the Japanese occupied Indochina, but they permitted French administrators to continue to govern. The Communists stepped up their opposition in 1941, creating the Viet Minh front and the People's Liberation Armed Forces. In 1944 a Communist general named Vo Nguyen Giap organized a Vietnam Propaganda and Liberation Army, which in turn became the People's Army of Vietnam, an underground guerrilla force that would come to be known as the Vietcong.

In March 1945 the Japanese ended French rule in Vietnam. In September Ho Chi Minh proclaimed Vietnam a democratic republic and appealed to the United States for support. He got no reply. Japan meanwhile had surrendered and the French army had returned to reclaim Vietnam. Ho Chi Minh announced he was prepared to fight for ten years if necessary to free it from the French grip. By the early 1950s, France was finding Vietnam a major headache. French occupation forces had mushroomed to 391,000 by 1951, and the clamor against the war had grown at home proportionately. In May 1950, France asked the United States for help to put down the Communists, and we answered this summons, for the Cold War was then in full cry. Our policy of containment was not selective. It was applied wherever the threat of Communist expansion appeared. It was also based upon our fear that one country falling to communism would inevitably cause others to fall, like a toppling row of dominoes.

So we sent in direct economic help and with it an economic mission and a military assistance advisory group of thirty-five men. The French suffered serious setbacks in September and October, and in December the United States signed a mutual defense assistance pact with France and the Associated States of Indochina for indirect military aid to fight the Viet Minh.

That was as far in as we intended to go. But the Viet Minh continued to hold large parts of North Vietnam, and in December 1953 launched an offensive that cut the country in half near its geographic center. The following April the Big Four nations—the United States, France, Britain, and the USSR—met in Geneva to try to resolve the Indochina war. But the Viet Minh, refusing to put anything on hold, took Dien Bien Phu even as the diplomats talked, crippling French military power in the country and thoroughly demoralizing its government back home. In June the French began evacuating the Red River Delta. The United States sent in Air Force Colonel Edward G. Lansdale to head a team of agents to engage in paramilitary operations and wage political-psychological warfare against North Vietnam. In July the negotiators in Geneva agreed to divide Vietnam into a North and a South along the 17th Parallel. Ho Chi Minh's Communists would rule the North; Ngo Dinh Diem, the anti-Communist head of government in Saigon, who had been set up in office by the United States, would control the South. Each Vietnamese would be free to pick whatever zone he or she wished to live in. All foreign forces were to pull out except French troops in the South. The United States didn't sign the agreement but agreed to abide by it. We thought the chances for a regime in the South strong enough to stand up to the Communists in the North were slim to none. Our National Security Council called the accords a "disaster," a "major forward stride of communism."

President Eisenhower approved a council recommendation for direct economic and military aid to South Vietnam through the French government. In October 1954, Colonel Lansdale's team sabotaged the Hanoi railroad, contaminated the oil supply for the city's bus system, and recruited and trained two teams of Vietnamese agents. By early 1955 we were simply bypassing the French, who opposed the Diem government, and aiding South Vietnam directly. By October the French were out of Vietnam altogether, and South Vietnam was an independent republic with Diem as president. The United States sent in 350 more military advisors.

In 1961, John F. Kennedy, who had succeeded Eisenhower that year, offered Diem $42 million in aid in exchange for much-needed military and civil reforms in the country. In October of that year the U.S. Joint Chiefs of Staff were talking about cleaning up the Vietcong threat once and for all. They estimated it would take 40,000 U.S. troops to do the job. While Kennedy wasn't ready for that, he did raise the U.S. military presence in Vietnam to 3,200 men, and sent in a U.S. army helicopter unit, the first operational troops to be committed.

Between January 1962 and October 1963 the number of U.S. troops in Vietnam grew from 4,000 to 16,732. The next month a military coup, with the tacit backing of the United States, overthrew the Diem regime. Diem was assassinated and a military junta took over. In January 1964 the junta itself was overthrown, and the new South Vietnamese premier called on Lyndon Johnson to attack North Vietnam. Johnson didn't do that, but he ratcheted up the level of U.S. military aid yet another notch.

In August 1964, Johnson and Secretary of Defense Robert McNamara reported that two U.S. destroyers in the Gulf of Tonkin had been attacked by the North Vietnamese. Johnson used this as a pretext to get from Congress the Tonkin Gulf Resolution, which basically allowed Johnson to take any military action he pleased in Vietnam. The vote was nearly unanimous, 416 to 0 in the House, 88 to 2 in the Senate. Only Ernest Gruening of Alaska and Wayne Morse of Oregon voted against it.

From that point on, U.S. military forces in South Vietnam mushroomed. By the fall of 1965, 148,300 American troops were committed. Almost as quickly, mass demonstrations against the war began in this country. By the following April, as protestors marched on Washington, the United States was raiding North Vietnam with B-52 bombers. In March 1968, his popularity plummeting because of the war, Johnson announced that he would not seek reelection. In March 1969 the level of U.S. troop involvement in the war peaked at 541,000.

By then Richard Nixon had become president, pledging to "end the war and win the peace." He didn't do either until 1973, in his second term. Long before that, the war had become a nightmare. By 1971 it had clearly become—even to government officials—a war we could not win. Assistant Secretary of Defense John T. McNaughton was privately saying it had become an effort "to avoid humiliation." Finally, on January 23, 1973, accords were signed, the fighting stopped, and the United States began evacuating, glad as France had been to be pulling out of the Vietnam quagmire. Nixon hailed it as "peace with honor to Vietnam and Southeast Asia." But by May 1975, South Vietnam was under Communist control.

It was a terrible time. I sadly quote Laurence Stern, who described the Vietnam experience and its toll on the American psyche. "It started imperceptibly," he wrote, "like a mild toothache. Then it ran like a pestilence through American society, impeaching 'the system' and its leadership in the eyes of a generation, bloating the economy with war inflation, disrupting universities, blighting political careers, spreading the plague of heroin, generally shattering the conventional faith in the decency of American purposes."

It had been the miserable war that wouldn't end, the longest and most unpopular in American history, and it had accomplished nothing. Lansdale himself, later a major general, called it a "strain on our social fabric" that "left at least a generation of Americans emotionally maimed."

Aside from the deep emotional scars it left on the American psyche, the war had cost the United States $135 billion. Far worse, 2.5 million young Americans went away to it, and some 57,000 of them returned dead. Another 300,000 came back crippled or wounded. It was America's paramount disaster of the Cold War era—or of any era.

Not since the 1930s had the American way been tested so severely. But despite the turmoil and fury, democracy once again proved well able to survive. The right of citizens to publicly disagree with their government was validated.

THE VIETNAM WAR was not the only long-lasting strain on our social fabric. There was also a nuclear arms race that lasted even longer and took its own emotional and economic toll on us—and an even more disastrous toll on the Soviet Union.

As soon as Stalin heard of the atom bomb—Truman told him of it at Potsdam only days before the first one was dropped on

Hiroshima—he wanted one. He *needed* one. Without the bomb, he saw no lasting security for his country, no matter how wide and deep his cordon sanitaire in Eastern Europe. For the next four years he turned every sinew of his nation's resources to getting it. In 1949 the Soviet Union tested its first device, and the Cold War reached a whole new level of terror.

Both the world's great military powers now had the ultimate weapon. If either nation used it against the other, it would assure retaliation and mutual destruction, and the possible destruction of the rest of the world. The first atomic weapon, when only the United States had one, was a "war-fighting" instrument. When the Soviet Union got one, it became primarily an instrument of "deterrence," its function not so much to win wars as to prevent them from ever happening. In a perverse way these terrible weapons became peacekeepers, for both attack and reprisal would be so devastating that neither the attacker nor the attacked could survive.

Once again, it was left to Winston Churchill to say succinctly what it all meant. "Safety," he said, "will be the sturdy child of terror and survival the twin brother of annihilation."

Through much of the 1950s the United States maintained a marked nuclear superiority to the Soviets. In that decade some military leaders advocated a first-strike strategy. Hit the Soviets now, they argued, hit them first while it can still be done with impunity, and have done with it. Eisenhower, of course, rejected such an idea, and gradually the doctrine of deterrence evolved. We would not attack first, but if attacked we would mount a second strike so devastating that no enemy could possibly consider using nuclear weapons. It meant always keeping ahead, way ahead, preferably, of the Soviet Union in numbers, megatonnage, and the accuracy of our arsenal. With the Soviets entertaining basically the same idea, we got the arms race. Over the following three decades the crude but effective atomic bombs of the 1940s were superseded by a fearsome proliferation of sophisticated weapons and delivery systems.

The 1960s were the heyday of the strategic arms buildup, tense years of proliferation on both sides. The United States developed what came to be known as the triad approach. We built a capability to launch missiles from land (from underground silos), sea (from nuclear submarines), and air (from constantly airborne bombers). If one of the triad was obliterated, the other two could still deliver the counterdevastation. It would be impossible for the Soviet Union to knock out all three before retaliation would wipe out at least two hundred major Soviet cities.

The Soviet goal was to maintain an arsenal so large that, whatever happened in an attack and a counterattack, they would win in the end. The Soviets were banking on the notion that no state would attack the USSR if it knew in advance that it would lose.

By the end of the 1960s both nations had met their respective launcher goals. So in the 1970s we got a warheads race—a struggle to increase the number of warheads carried by each launcher. This was the decade of the MIRV—the multiple independently targeted reentry vehicle. As the Soviet arsenal became more and more heavily MIRVed, U.S. military planners believed we had fallen behind, and there developed what American nuclear thinkers called a "window of vulnerability" that had to be closed, and closed quickly.

In the face of mounting Soviet megatonnage, greater mobility of our nuclear arsenal became the priority of the 1970s. During the years of the Carter administration, 1977–81, the concept of multiple protective shelters to shield us from multiple warhead attack came into vogue. Our retaliatory land-based missiles would become mobile, capable of being shuttled randomly from hiding place to hiding place. It was called the "racetrack" concept, and it lasted until Carter's defeat in 1980 by Ronald Reagan.

By the 1980s the arms race had spilled into space. Our space technology was way ahead, and Reagan began to push the idea of "Star Wars," the Strategic Defense Initiative. Nuclear war in outer space came to be viewed as a possibility, perhaps even a probability. In 1980, *Aviation Week and Space Technology* predicted that "space-based systems will constitute within 5–10 years the first line of defense against a Soviet strategic nuclear weapons attack." It was based on a concept as old as war itself. As one of our generals, Richard Henry, put it, "Space is the high ground in today's world." Aside from its virtues as a battlefield high ground, space was prized as a worldwide communications station and a perfect place from which to carry on espionage and surveillance.

The idea of mutual self-destruction could not go on long without both sides realizing that there had to be some kind of control—a form of disarmament, if possible. Woody Allen put it this way: "The world today is at a crossroads. One road leads to utter hopelessness and despair; the other road leads to utter destruction and extinction. God grant us the wisdom to choose the right road."

Over the years the two superpowers had tried taking several roads to disarmament and arms control. Disarmament implies weapons reduction of some kind, which leads to the second road the powers have tried to take together—arms control. If you can't disarm, then perhaps you can control how the arms are to be used or not used, managing the arms race rather than ending it. Either way, disarmament or arms control, or both, it all went back to maintaining a balance of power in a very dangerous world.

There had not been a lot of success in arms control as the world neared forty years of Cold War tension. Some believed that three decades of U.S.–Soviet negotiations to limit the arms race had only systematized it. But overall, by the 1980s, there was a general perception of decreasing danger. The superpowers had demonstrated over those four decades that, as the writer Michael Sheehan put it, "they were *not* about to exterminate each other and everyone else in a mindless Armageddon." But neither, as Sheehan also said, were all the world's swords about to be beaten into plowshares.

So over the last half of the twentieth century the arms race had created a nuclear stalemate. The paradox is that the presence of nuclear weapons was what kept the peace between the superpowers. Churchill was right: world safety *has* been the sturdy child of terror and survival the twin brother of annihilation.

The decades-long nuclear stalemate was clear to see, up-front and obvious. But something had been happening in the Soviet Union over the Cold War years that was not so clear and obvious. And a chain of events was now about to erupt within that country that would astonish the world.

Chapter 10

THE GREAT

UNRAVELING

IN EARLY MARCH 1931, about the time Franklin Roosevelt was considering a run for president, a baby boy called Misha was born in the gently rolling steppe country of southern Russia.

Roosevelt and Misha would one day be linked in history— Roosevelt because he would save a great system, Misha because he would end one.

Misha's father, Sergei, was a peasant farmer of Cossack stock living in Privolnoye, a village in Stavropol, the grain province of Russia. The 1930s were a bad time in the Soviet Union. Stalin was relentlessly driving farmers like Sergei off their land and into collectives. Famine prostrated the country. More than 50,000 people would die of hunger in Stavropol by 1933.

Misha—Mikhail Gorbachev—the second of Sergei's three sons, was but an infant when his paternal grandfather, Andrei, was shuffled off to the gulag in Siberia for resisting Stalin's reforms. "I knew that my grandfather had been arrested, another grandfather had been persecuted," Gorbachev told me in a long meeting we had in September of 1995. "But neither of those two men had a negative attitude to Soviet power. They were both born into very poor families. For them the Soviet power meant that it was their power and they could work their land under Soviet power. By the way, those two men were very different. One of those grandfathers was the creator of the collective farm in our area. The other refused to become a member of the collective farm (the kolkhoz) for a long time. This is how my family was. Within my own family, within that family nucleus, there were the tensions and the contradictions of that time."

Andrei was a "middle peasant," one who owned the land he farmed but was not a big enough landholder to hire help. But he was a kulak nonetheless, and he was sentenced to nine years in the gulag, not to return to Privolnoye until just before Hitler launched his blitzkrieg into Russia in 1941. Both Misha's father and his older brother were drafted into the Russian army and sent to the front, where his brother died. Young Misha, then about ten, fell under the care of his refugee grandfather from the gulag.

Three family members belonged to the Communist Party: Misha's maternal grandfather and both of his parents. "I am a man whose origin *is* in that world and in that system," he took pains to point out to me. "I'm not some kind of an exception. I'm not some kind of Messiah. When I was graduating from school, my essay for my diploma was entitled—you will be surprised— 'Stalin Is Our Combat Glory; Stalin Is the Flight of Our Youth.' That is from a poem by a famous Soviet poet."

From the time Misha was in college, attending Moscow State University and studying law, he was inclined to politics. He became active in the Young Communist League, and was a party member by the time he was twenty-one. "It was much later that I really began to give thought to those problems [of communism], to the country, and to the world," he told me. "Certainly, my studies at Moscow University gave an impetus to my thinking about the system, even in Stalin's time. The university still generated some democratic traditions. There was always a certain opposition within Moscow University. In Stalin's time, of course, it was not open opposition. But a certain attitude of criticism was always present there. In addition to that, and what's very important, I was studying world history, the history of state and law, of political doctrines, and diplomacy, international public and private law, political economy. All of these subjects gave me a certain view of the world that was much broader than before."

After graduation in June 1955, and by now married to Raisa Maksimovna Titorenko, Gorbachev returned to Stavropol, where he took a job as a party organizer and began his climb up the Communist ladder. As a rising young apparatchik he knew how to work within the stern forms and rituals of the party. But he also had something special: charm, and an extroverted personality. Equally at home swapping stories with farmers in a field or operating in the realm of ideas, he could hold his own in any company and was brilliantly persuasive when he needed to be. He was widely read, articulate, and well-spoken, with a slight southern accent, but he was also at home with the *ruski mat* (Russian mother), the rich compendium of native obscenities. He was not a bureaucrat by nature, but a politician, always preferring to be out talking to people.

For twenty-three years he was a party official in Stavropol, shaping his political vision. At thirty-nine, he was the top-ranking official in the province, prematurely bald, with a distinctive red birthmark on his forehead. It was 1970 and he was one of a hundred first secretaries in the Soviet party system, exercising, as they all did, immense local power and autonomy. He also had a very well-placed mentor in Moscow, Yuri Andropov, chairman of the powerful KGB, who vacationed in Stavropol and had taken a fancy to the personable and intelligent Gorbachev. Andropov saw in the younger man a comer who combined an acute and ironical awareness of the flaws and absurdities in the Soviet system with a devoted attachment to it. The two men found themselves agreeing on many key policy issues. Both were concerned with the worrisome signs of economic and social decay that were visible in the system in the late 1970s. They both feared that their party and their country, ensnared in bureaucracy and too rigid to deal with their problems, was headed for disaster.

Andropov began pulling Gorbachev upward in the party. By 1978, Gorbachev had moved to Moscow and become a secretary of the Central Committee in charge of agriculture. He was in the highest ranks of the country's leadership—among the top twenty or so in the party—and at forty-seven the youngest Politburo member by far, twenty years younger than the average.

In 1982, Andropov reached the summit of the hierarchy. As party general secretary, he began initiating some of the economic and social changes he and Gorbachev had discussed in Stavropol. But Andropov fell ill only months later, and died in February 1984. However, before he died, he broadened Gorbachev's domestic responsibilities far beyond agriculture and drew him into foreign affairs, a field then little known to the younger man.

At this point Gorbachev was well positioned, but not well enough to succeed to total power just yet. The mantle of leadership went instead to an old-liner named Konstantin Chernenko who had been the long-time right hand of Andropov's predecessor, Leonid Brezhnev. Chernenko had no program of his own, except to oppose Andropov's. He couldn't reverse the forward momentum of the dead leader's reformist policies, however; he could only slow them. One senior official later said, "It was like having the driver take his foot off the accelerator."

As Chernenko was taking his foot off the accelerator, Gorbachev was positioning himself as the leader of the coalition put together by the dying Andropov, as well as clarifying and refining his views of the country's problems and the kind of leader he meant to be when he took power. He clearly intended to take power. He shored up his alliances and got ready.

Chernenko died only a year after Andropov, on March 10, 1985. As funeral dirges played on national radio and TV, Gorbachev and his supporters made their bid. His most potent ally in the charged meeting of the Central Committee that convened to pick a successor was Andrei Gromyko, the senior Politburo member, a man well known to Americans as an obdurate cold warrior.

"Comrades," Gromyko is reported to have told the three-hundred-member Central Committee, "this man has a nice smile but he's got iron teeth." Gromyko spoke of the "brilliant" analytical skill behind the teeth, the younger man's political gifts, and his people skills, "not given to everyone." The veteran of the Cold War assured his fellow party old-liners that the young Gorbachev had an excellent grasp of foreign affairs. "I was the youngest member of the Politburo," Gorbachev said. "But the old men could no longer appoint one of themselves, and they understood that the times required a new man."

The vote was close. Gorbachev had fewer ties to the main branches of the party and state administrations than any other top leader in Soviet history. But it was enough. Four hours after Chernenko's death was announced to the nation, it was followed by the news of Mikhail Gorbachev's election as general secretary, the seventh supreme leader of the Soviet Union.

He now turned to face the problems. This descendent of Cossack horsemen was about to take his country on the most astonishing ride of its existence.

WHAT GORBACHEV SAW was a gigantic failure. For a decade, during Andropov's summer vacations in Stavropol, the two men had commiserated over their country's economic and political decline. Communist ideology had collapsed and they knew it. As Robert G. Kaiser, a close and astute observer of the Soviets, put it, "There were no more true believers."

Unfortunately, ideology was still all-important. It was Communist ideology—Lenin's legacy—that drove everything. It was ideology that justified the organization of Soviet society, the lack of freedoms, the disastrous system of collective agriculture and trade, the captivity of Eastern Europe, the educational system—everything. But nobody any longer really believed in it.

And nobody any longer was intent on exporting it. Their ideological mission had simply collapsed. Russians, particularly those who had traveled in the West, no longer believed that history was on the side of Soviet communism, that capitalist nations must collapse and become Communist. What Russians who traveled had seen in the West in no way squared with that scenario.

In free economies the visiting Russians saw standards of living risen to unprecedented heights. Industrial production was vigorous. Farm output was soaring.

By contrast, the Soviet Union Gorbachev saw as he took power in 1985 was in deep trouble. "The amazing thing is that the words 'We cannot go on living like this' were said by me on the night I came back home on the day when Chernenko died and we had the Politburo meeting," he told me. "After I returned from that Politburo meeting, at four A.M., Mrs. Gorbachev and I took a walk on the grounds of the dacha, and I said to her, 'We can no longer live as before. We need reforms. We need very far-reaching changes.' By the way, today in Russia many people are saying, 'We can no longer live like this.' Once again, they're saying the same phrase." The economy was worse than stagnant. American farmers, who accounted for but 2.5 percent of the U.S. population, not only fed their country but sold huge amounts of their surplus output abroad. Nearly twenty times more Soviet farmers were unable to produce enough food to feed their own country, let alone export a surplus. The USSR's economic growth had been smothered by the military demands of the Cold War. The country was not competitive in world markets.

The Soviet Union was a military superpower and an underdeveloped country at the same time. The standard of living of its people was lower even than most of its East European vassals, no match at all for developed Western countries. Central planning and the tight hold of the totalitarian state simply couldn't cope with the complexities of a modern economy. Nor could it compete technologically. The only reason the Soviet Union was a superpower was because of its army and its nuclear arsenal.

What the Soviets did produce—space research, steel, oil, ICBMs, MIRVs—took two to three times the energy per unit of output of its leading Western rivals. The USSR could match U.S. military power only by spending 15 to 20 percent of its gross national product on defense, compared to about 6 percent for the United States. In computer development and associated advanced technologies the USSR was more than a decade behind the United States and the gap was widening. The country could send cosmonauts into space and probes to distant planets. It could find Halley's comet in deepest space and reach Venus. But the quality of Soviet refrigerators left a lot to be desired. The country that could probe the galaxy couldn't produce enough basic consumer goods and food to meet the needs of its people. Soviet housewives spent endless hours waiting in long lines for everyday necessities. As Gorbachev picked up the reins of power, the economic system, a product of the 1930s, had reached its limits and had begun literally to bankrupt the country.

The political situation was no better. In the last dozen years of Leonid Brezhnev's long rule, corruption had replaced ideology in the party; dachas and automobiles and the perks of power had superseded ideological fervor. David Remnick, another sensitive observer of the Soviet malaise, wrote: "The Communist Party apparatus was the most gigantic mafia the world has ever known. It guarded its monopoly on power with a sham consensus and constitution and backed it up with the force of the KGB and the Interior Ministry Police. . . . It was as if the entire Soviet Union were ruled by a gigantic mob family." One Russian admitted to Remnick, "The mafia is the state itself."

Gorbachev knew these things. He suggested to me that he sensed the rotting nature of the system as early as the 1960s. He knew that a continued downslide would eventually turn the Soviet Union into a second-rate power. Someone, someday, would have to bite the bullet and change the system. He understood that if there was to be change, he would have to bring it, for time was running out. He understood the kind of leader he would therefore have to be: audacious, resolute, and strong of nerve.

Gorbachev knew that Russia's economy must be modernized. He knew that he must somehow overcome the enormous technological and consumer gap with the Western world, and that to do this the system must be radically changed. He knew that to radically change the system, the party itself would have to change. He knew there would be tremendous resistance to change in both the party and the country. It would be a high and dangerous road. But he also knew that somebody would have to begin telling the Soviet people the truth. The reform Gorbachev was talking about soon had a name; it was called *perestroika*—reconstruction.

GORBACHEV SET OUT on that road cautiously at first. It would not do to hit the party and the country with change too hard and too fast. As he told me in 1995, "If I had said, in the first period of perestroika, that perestroika would be done outside the CPSU [Communist Party of the Soviet Union], it would have taken five days for them to get rid of me, five days for the members of the Central Committee to gather at another Plenum and to dismiss me." He first had to consolidate his power. After all, he had barely been elected general secretary and his opposition was still powerful. Nonetheless, strange and unfamiliar words—for a Communist—began coming out of his mouth as early as April 1985, one month into his job, when he addressed the Central Committee: words like retooling, streamlining, cost-accounting, flexibility, supply and demand, modernization, decentralization, worker participation, and, heresy of heresies, market economy.

He was also beginning to say things about politics the hardliners wanted to hear even less, explosive things like election reform, sacrifice, and an end to tenure. "Everyone must change," he said, "from the worker to the minister to the secretary of the Central Committee. . . ." These were words of radical reform. And the fact that they were coming out of the mouth of this young, unpredictable general secretary meant it might actually happen.

"Brezhnev's regime, by that time, had come into real conflict with the cultural potential of our society," Gorbachev told me. "The society already consisted by that time of people who were capable of showing initiative, of really acting, and that system was really shackling that initiative, shackling the people. Perestroika was really an attempt to somehow resolve that contradiction. Initially, we did think that the system could be improved by discarding the distortions. But then we saw something that had happened in history before. Any old system wants to protect itself, wants to preserve itself. This particular system was unique. It was tough as nails, it did not accept any kind of deviation. And there-fore we understood that we needed to replace the system. We wanted to do it in a democratic way. We wanted an evolution. That's why we conducted free elections, that's why we intro-duced glasnost, freedom of information, a multiparty system, var-ious forms of property. Those were the prerequisites of freedom that began to work, and people have begun to show their real potential."

He went on: "An interesting fact: 90 percent of the people, by the time perestroika began, had been born under the Soviet power, in the Soviet period. And that's why we felt that our path of change should be evolutionary. We should have a kind of five-year horizon and move step-by-step."

Nobody had quite expected the zeal with which Gorbachev would push perestroika. Gorbachev had always been a good and faithful party man, a little different in style than the rest, but not one to favor radical reform.

The Communist Party at that time was 19 million strong. Its rank and file represented 7 percent of the Soviet Union's total population. The *nomenklatura,* the leadership cadre, the back-bone of the party, was much smaller—about 450,000. And many of them could be expected to dig in their heels against anything approaching radical reform. For many of them the party was less an instrument of action than a way of life they did not wish to see changed. They stonewalled from the start. They did not resist openly at first; they went along rhetorically but privately waged a battle of resistance and foot-dragging—what hostile bureaucra-cies do everywhere.

This, of course, would be nothing new, not even for the Soviet Union. Bureaucratic drift, "the powerful force of inertia," thwarted even Stalin. Even during his reign of terror, "people did not go where asked, found ways of doing things their own way, exploited any loophole to play or outplay the system, and helped themselves through networks of friends, acquaintances, briberies, and adventurous risks," points out Moshe Lewin in *The Gorbachev Phenomenon.* Stalin's attempted remedy, of course, was his stan-dard remedy for everything—terror and murder. But even that didn't always work. Every state measure, control system, interdiction, or exhortation triggered some resistance.

If Stalin couldn't always quickly move the powerful force of inertia, how could Gorbachev with his "revolution without shots"? Gorbachev believed that if the Soviet Union was to be changed his way, the party was the instrument he must use. That meant that the party must be opened up and made more democratic, a concept totally foreign to Soviet politics. He began saying that true socialism was impossible without democracy. "We need democracy like air," he said. Without it, "our policy will get choked, and perestroika will fail."

Gorbachev in his first year moved cautiously but steadily forward with his reform program, getting the blueprint for perestroika ready. It was tough going. His second in command, the chairman of the Secretariat, an old-line Communist named Yegor Ligachev, resisted, becoming a leader of the conservative opposition.

After a year in office, Gorbachev found that perestroika was barely making headway. Even small decisions were dying in the morass of bureaucracy. He came to understand that if perestroika were to succeed, he must go over the heads of his party opposition to the people themselves—a tactic not within the Soviet experience. So a second great term was added to the vocabulary—in truth, resurrected, for the concept was as old as the tsars. But it had a new meaning and was to become a stirring buzzword along with perestroika. This was *glasnost,* which, roughly translated, meant "openness." Gorbachev did nothing less than turn Soviet society loose to say and think what it wished, and the media, so long enchained and controlled, to write what it pleased, investigate what it pleased, expose what it pleased.

He introduced yet another unthinkable policy by releasing many of the critics of past regimes from prison, starting with Andrei Sakharov, the nuclear physicist and Nobel Peace Prize laureate whom past Soviet leaders had considered too dangerous to leave free. These dissidents were now not only free, but able to go where they wished and say and write what they pleased.

Further, Gorbachev went directly to the media, revealing the shortcomings, outlining the problems, taking a match to the immobile bureaucracy and prodding it with a glasnost hotfoot. It was a jarring tactic for a society that had been closed for so long.

A joke about it all was circulating by the summer of 1986. The Soviet Union was likened to a train that had been stopped because there were no more tracks up ahead. Each Soviet leader, the joke went, would deal with the crisis in his own way. Stalin would have had the conductor and engineer shot. Khrushchev would have rehabilitated them. Brezhnev would have closed the curtains and ordered the train shaken from side to side to create the illusion of movement. Gorbachev had simply opened the curtains, leaned out the window and shouted, "We're out of rails! We're out of rails!"

Glasnost alarmed the party's old guard, who came to hate it at least as much as they hated perestroika. The floodgates Gorbachev opened, exposing in detail the sordid Stalinist past, could get out of hand and wash away the party's credibility, and with it them and their positions and power.

Gorbachev's moves in foreign policy soon became as breathtaking as his moves at home. Though inexperienced, he moved boldly, pursuing a healing relationship with the United States almost from the moment he assumed power. Détente abroad, he believed, was a necessary condition of restructuring at home. He knew the Soviet Union couldn't afford to remain belligerent and armed to the teeth and still resurrect its economy. In a rapid series of moves he called for an end to the "ice age" that had blanketed U.S.–Soviet relations for decades.

He frankly and publicly acknowledged the permanence of the non-Communist, capitalist world, the first Soviet leader ever to do so. Officially dropped from the canon was the old Bolshevik expectation of the downfall of imperialism and the worldwide triumph of communism and socialism. It was not a great sacrifice; the idea had been dead in practice for a long time. Gorbachev began to downplay the struggle between capitalism and communism, between the Soviet bloc and the West, replacing it with a concept he called "historic competition." He was going to save his system, in effect, by competing peacefully with what had for so long been the mortal enemy. Any other course seemed suicidal to him. He said Moscow was no longer in the business of "stimulating revolutions" in other countries, nor would it insist that the Soviet mode of socialism was the only true one.

Gorbachev not only put the brakes on the long rivalry and arms race, he dramatically threw them into reverse. It began with a summit meeting in Geneva in 1986 with President Reagan. From that meeting there followed a seeming transformation in Soviet–American relations. The world watched in amazement, disbelief, and gratification as tensions eased and the knottiest issues that had separated the two superpowers dissolved in the glow of a new friendship. Gorbachev also began making moves to pull the Soviet army out of Afghanistan, a sore point in U.S.–Russian relations since Jimmy Carter's administration. Afghanistan wasn't Gorbachev's war; it was Russia's Vietnam, a "bleeding wound," he called it.

The four summits that followed Geneva over the next two years brought about a revolution in world affairs. The first, at Reykjavik, Iceland, was relatively barren of results. Reagan was still pushing the Star Wars program, the one element of U.S. nuclear policy that worried Gorbachev more than any other. The Strategic Defense Initiative was something the Soviet Union could not hope to match, and trying to do so would make economic reform at home impossible. But the next three summits were productive, in Washington in December 1987, in Moscow in May and June 1988, and in New York in December that same year. Together they took the United States and the Soviet Union farther down the road to nuclear accommodation than anybody dreamed. The supreme leader of the Soviet Union had refused to accept the prospect of an indefinite nuclear arms race, and as a result, the world suddenly found itself in a whole new era.

BY THE END OF 1986, nearly two years after Gorbachev assumed power, the Soviet Union was in a new and uncertain era. Perestroika, its blueprint for radical change, was about to be put for approval to the Central Committee. Gorbachev had done what he could to grease the tracks. He had gradually planted his own people in the party's top echelon, in the Politburo and the Secretariat. But the Central Committee—that uncertain middle ground of the party hierarchy—hulked in his path. He had no guarantee his program would be approved. And even if approved, could it be implemented?

For better or worse, perestroika was on the table as 1986 ended. It seemed to me to be, as Bill Keller of the *New York Times* called it, a "jerry-built economic machine . . . faltering from early design flaws and an unexpectedly rough road." Gorbachev himself knew it was still rough around the edges. Nonetheless, the goal was to have it approved, whatever it turned out to be, by the Central Committee in its meeting in the summer of 1987, and up and running by January 1, 1988. It was a very tall order. The centerpiece of the perestroika blueprint was the Law on Socialist Enterprise, which stopped short of full market reform. It recognized profit as a mechanism for reaching higher economic efficiency and producing things people wanted to buy. Price reform, bank reform, industrial reorganization, were all implicit and certain to follow. The Law on Socialist Enterprise was major surgery, cutting deep into the entire economy and through virtually the entire society. It theoretically decentralized the economy, dispersing economic power. By 1991 the country's industry and agriculture would be out of the hands of the central planners, whose job then would be merely to map long-range strategy. No longer would they dominate from top to bottom. The state itself would become but another customer.

The whole thing was breathtaking, a major turning point in Russian history. Gorbachev himself had become a historic figure in a little over two years. He had already moved his nation and had changed the world because of it. He was asking the Soviet people to radically change their mindset and their ways. And he was telling them it was for their own good.

Gorbachev knew the program would face a wall of opposition when the showdown finally came. But he also probably believed that his hammer blows would soon demolish that opposition. What he would encounter instead, even worse, was not so much a wall as "a spongelike resistance," indifferent to the mightiest hammer blows.

Working the party, pulling every lever, Gorbachev got perestroika through the Central Committee and enacted into law by the Supreme Soviet in June 1987. It was the year of the seventieth anniversary of the Bolshevik revolution. Even as that milestone was being celebrated, he was pushing a program that fundamentally repudiated it.

Putting together perestroika had taken two years of hard work. And the trouble was just beginning. As one of Gorbachev's key economic advisors said, "We are going into the unknown, and people are trying to stop us." What one observer called "a glasnost free-for-all" raged throughout the summer of 1987.

To try to make perestroika more stable and irreversible, Gorbachev began to change the party itself. "Stalin's system was in crisis," he explained to me in 1995. "This was the system we inherited, and it was in crisis. Therefore, during that Party Conference, I spoke about the need to build a new system, a system that would have political and economic freedom. I said this would be socialism with a democratic face, this would bring together socialism and democracy." Gorbachev introduced legislation calling for political and civil rights, freedoms foreign to the Soviet experience. He insisted these changes remain within socialist boundaries. It was to be a *socialist* democracy, a *socialist* political pluralism. "What I think we can say today is not that socialism, broadly speaking, has been defeated, because if you look at socialism—what does the word 'socialism' mean to the ordinary person, to the man in the street? It has to mean the recognition of democracy, the recognition of freedom and social justice. People don't want wealth to be polarized between the very rich and the very poor. People want solidarity. That is something that goes back to Jesus Christ. Whether or not people call themselves socialists, those are the values that will continue to exist. So the defeat was not of the socialist idea as a whole, but of the blueprint of a scheme that was imposed on our society through repression, by violating the historic process."

Despite these conciliatory words, to the old-liners and the con-

servatives it sounded very much like Western bourgeois heresy—
very much, indeed, like treason. The Soviet Union was no longer
to be a totalitarian system, but a pluralistic hybrid, over which
they no longer had control.

By late 1987 both perestroika and political reform were stalled
in the face of conservative intransigence. Nobody, not even Gorbachev himself, was more disturbed by this than Boris Yeltsin,
the Communist boss of Moscow. Yeltsin, a beefy man with a
surge of white hair, was a charismatic populist, who, unlike every
other prominent Soviet politician, loved to press the flesh. He
rode the streetcars like other Muscovites, drank with them in
bars, stood in line with their wives at the meat market. They
loved him for it. For Yeltsin perestroika and glasnost were virtually religions. Some said he was exactly the symbol of what perestroika and glasnost stood for. He was also a man who was making his way across a no-man's-land between orthodoxy and
heresy.

YELTSIN WAS BORN IN Sverdlovsk province in the Urals in February 1931, a month before Gorbachev. Sverdlovsk had been the
home of his forebears for as long as there had been Yeltsins.
Nearly drowned in the baptismal tub by a drunken Orthodox
priest, he was raised in poverty. His first years, hard years of
famine in the Urals, were passed in a small house with a gentle
mother, a quick-tempered father who beat him with a strap, his
two siblings, and a cow. When the cow died, the family left their
native village to live for the next ten years in Berezniki in neighboring Perm province in a single room in a drafty wooden barracks housing twenty families. The Yeltsins slept together on the
floor with the family goat, huddled up for warmth.

Boris from the beginning was a contradiction. He invariably
glittered academically, easily passing every subject and just as
invariably flunking conduct. "I've always been a bit of a hooli-
gan," he was later to confess. Forty years later he was high up in
the Communist Party echelon, a member of the Politburo, one
of the Soviet Union's elite. He was building a reputation with the

old guard as an unregenerate, theatrical populist. He was forever in their hair, undermining the Soviet party monolith with his maverick ways.

The conservative foot-dragging over perestroika angered Yeltsin, as did Ligachev, the Kremlin's second-in-command and the leader of the old-line opposition. Perestroika and glasnost were going too far for Ligachev. When he signed on for pere-stroika, he had very much favored it. But he was not prepared for private property, open criticism of Soviet history, and politi-cal pluralism. While never openly splitting with Gorbachev or being disloyal, by 1987 he nonetheless had become the leader of the foot-draggers.

If perestroika and glasnost were going too fast for Ligachev, they were going too slow for Yeltsin. Not one to suffer foot-dragging lightly, Yeltsin had already had several near-collisions with Ligachev. Finally, by October 21, 1987, he had had enough. Without any advance warning, he took to the dais and slammed into Ligachev personally and all the conservatives by association. Yeltsin had always had a sharp tongue, a disrespect of rank, position, and name—and all those things came thundering out. He accused Ligachev of obstructionism amounting to conspir-acy against perestroika. He painted him as an intriguer and a "false man who adheres to the old and condemned style of lead-ership."

A dead silence followed Yeltsin's tirade—then immediately after, a fierce counterattack from the right. The upshot was that Gorbachev had to sack Yeltsin to stay on the good side of the con-servative opposition. Yeltsin was kicked out of the Politburo, out of his Moscow job, and demoted to a position as a first deputy chairman of the State Construction Committee. His fate, how-ever, showed how much Soviet politics had changed. Stalin would have had him shot. The old-liners of the perestroika age would no doubt soon wish they had done the same, because Yeltsin would be back to make their lives—and Gorbachev's—miserable.

The Yeltsin affair signaled a breakdown in party discipline that would open a Pandora's box of trouble. By the summer of 1989 an earthquake of reform was sweeping through the Soviet cordon sanitaire. The East European satellites were slipping their moorings one by one and defecting unchallenged from the Communist orbit.

Poland got a non-Communist government. Hungary's Communist Party changed its name. Communist governments fell in Bulgaria and Czechoslovakia. The last Stalinist dictator, Nicolae Ceauşescu, was ousted and executed, Stalin-style, in Rumania. Finally, the Berlin Wall itself, that symbol of a world divided into East and West, crumbled.

The seeds of revolution that Gorbachev allowed to germinate in Eastern Europe soon began to flower within the republics of the Soviet Union itself. The sweet smell of reclaimed national identity wafted across the eleven time zones of the Soviet Union. Lithuania was the first to separate, in March 1990. Then the "virus of independence" became an epidemic. Estonia and Latvia followed, then the larger republics along the southern Soviet border, then Russia itself, the largest of the republics, then the Ukraine. The Baltic states marked off 1990 with an open revolt against Moscow. By the end of 1991 the fifteen Soviet republics had proclaimed their sovereignty and reclaimed their nationalities. What had begun as a restructuring had become a demolition.

It was astounding, one of the most spectacular collapses in history. Mikhail Gorbachev became in Western eyes the man of the hour, the year, the decade, and was hailed as a political magician. They awarded him the Nobel Peace Prize and *Time* magazine called him "the Copernicus, Darwin and Freud of communism all wrapped up in one."

WHILE HAILED ABROAD, Gorbachev by 1991 was on his last legs at home. The hard-liners of the Kremlin were also amazed—that their country, their party, their lives had come to this. They pounded him openly now, their fury mounting daily. They demanded that he turn out his most reform-minded advisors—and he did. They blamed him for the "loss" of Eastern Europe, for the "triumphs" of the West, the "ruin" of the country and the party, the "degradation" of the armed forces. They condemned perestroika as the road map to the destruction of the Soviet Union.

One of them wrote: "For the West, Gorbachev is the destroyer of the communist monster, but in so doing he's destroyed everything that we believed in, everything that kept us together. Gorbachev hasn't built anything new, he hasn't thrown us a life ring. The people, myself included, are on a sinking ship, on a plane that's crashing, and that's what terrifies us."

The conservative Yuri Bondarev also obliquely likened Gorbachev to an airplane pilot "who has taken off, but does not know where he is going to land."

Indeed everything at home seemed out of control. Perestroika was dead in the water. The economy seemed as desperate as when Gorbachev assumed power six years before, if not worse. A joke had been going around Moscow since early 1990: "There are two ways—one realistic, the other fantastic—for resolving the crisis of the Soviet economy. The realistic way is to have people from outer space come and straighten out the mess. The fantastic way is for the Soviet people to sort it out on their own."

The conservatives had mounted an open attack against perestroika in 1988, issuing what Gorbachev's supporters later called an "antiperestroika manifesto," calling for a decisive turn away from Gorbachev's policy. In the showdown this triggered, Gorbachev won. But the fight had just begun, and more and more he found himself forced to compromise with his enemies simply to keep perestroika alive.

This in turn raised the hackles of that critic of an entirely different stripe. The unsinkable Boris Yeltsin had made a comeback. In 1988 he ran for a seat in the Congress of People's Deputies—the Supreme Soviet—and was elected in a landslide. Nobody in Russia could match either his charismatic style or his popularity. In June 1991 he was elected president of the split-away Russian republic, the first elected president in Russia's thousand-year history. He was also the first purged politician who had ever made a successful comeback in the Soviet Union. Having "garnered daredevil fame" for being cast from the Politburo for criticizing the party establishment in 1987, he was now, in 1991, openly attacking Gorbachev himself.

In contrast with the conservatives who were demanding a life preserver, Yeltsin was demanding that the ship be abandoned altogether, left to sink—and good riddance. He had become what Francis X. Clines of the *New York Times* described as "the virtuoso in the evolving communist art of campaigning against communism." He wanted an end to the party itself, and a sharp turn to democracy. "Those who still believe in communism," he said in late 1989, "are moving in the sphere of fantasy. I regard myself as a social democrat." Gorbachev, however, still regarded himself as a Communist, "a convinced Communist. For some that may be fantasy. But for me it is my main goal."

Many, however, now believed as Yeltsin did, that the "culture of Marx and Lenin" was disintegrating before their eyes. A few of the more radical were saying, in effect, why not give it up? Why not admit that the past seven decades of sacrifice and effort had been based on a flawed doctrine that had inflicted endless agony, suffering, and death, and all for nothing? This was the ultimate heresy, a final condemnation of the Marxist-Leninist dream.

Gorbachev at last had to retreat even on the matter of communism and the party. In February 1990 he asked the Central Committee to give up the party's constitutionally guaranteed monopoly on power. This was grudgingly granted. The implication of this act was profound. It meant that he was abandoning the central tenet of Lenin and Stalin—dictatorship of the proletariat—and reversing Russia's centuries-old heritage of autocratic rule. Russia seemed headed for what Lenin had once defamed as "bourgeois democracy," with its competing political parties and meaningful elections.

WARNINGS OF A COUP were everywhere in Moscow in the summer of 1991. In early August, despite them, Gorbachev and Raisa flew to their vacation dacha in the Crimea.

The first sign that something was amiss was on August 18 when

Gorbachev picked up his telephone to make a call. The line was dead. A delegation arrived at the dacha soon thereafter and told Gorbachev he either had to go along with a planned conservative-proclaimed state of emergency in Moscow or resign. He defied them, saying he would neither go along nor cooperate with a return to dictatorial rule, and they left. At four the next morning two tractor-trailers manned by the KGB blocked the runway at the airfield near the dacha. The coup had begun.

Boris Yeltsin was eating breakfast that morning at his own dacha in the village of Usovo near Moscow, when the calls started coming in. The military had launched the coup and gone on the air at six that morning. Tanks were in the streets in Moscow. One Muscovite, confessing he had no idea what it all meant, said, "All I know is nothing good can come from tanks."

Yeltsin had seen the signs as had everybody in the upper ech-elons. Now it was happening. With Gorbachev in the Crimea, somebody had to act or risk a return to dictatorship. Yeltsin strapped on a bulletproof vest, pulled on a shirt and suit over it, and headed full speed for the White House on the Moscow River, the hulking building that housed the parliament of the Russian republic.

By nine-thirty in the morning tanks had surrounded Moscow's city hall. Soldiers had taken down the Russian red, white, and blue tricolor and replaced it with the red Soviet hammer and sickle. The tanks by then had rolled into place before all the key points in the city—the TV and radio stations, the newspaper offices, and the White House.

Yeltsin arrived at the White House at about 10 A.M. There he established the democratic resistance, ordered up a barricade, and began communicating with the outside world in any way he could. He also called the Russian parliament into nonstop session. Just after noon Yeltsin walked down the front steps of the White House and clambered up on one of the rebels' T-72 tanks. As a small knot of demonstrators and reporters crowded around, his voice boomed out: "Citizens of Russia. . . . The legally elected president of the USSR has been removed from power. . . . We are dealing with a right-wing, reactionary, anti-constitutional coup d'état. . . . Accordingly, we proclaim all decisions and decrees of this committee to be illegal. . . . We appeal to citizens of Russia to give an appropriate rebuff to the putschists and demand a return of the country to normal constitutional development." He went on the makeshift radio inside the building and said the same thing.

Muscovites began streaming to the White House, first a few thousand, then 10,000. By the end of the day 25,000 demonstrators were outside the building protesting the putsch. Many of the military began siding with the government and defecting from the coup. The next morning Yeltsin, without sleep—he would not sleep for three full days—looked out the White House windows and saw 10,000 protestors still there. They were Yeltsin's army, the only power he really had—the stubborn will of the people. As the morning passed, the crowd began to thicken again, and by ten-thirty, the time Yeltsin called for a demonstration, there were about 100,000 people massed around the building.

Gorbachev, meanwhile, continued under house arrest in the Crimea, listening to his transistor radio and demanding in vain that his captors free him to address the people.

So far, the White House had not been stormed. But there was a feeling it could happen any moment. Nobody knew why it hadn't happened already. Indeed, plans were afoot, and as David Remnick says in his excellent first-person account in *Lenin's Tomb,* the plans were brutally simple. The storming was to be called Operation Thunder. One group would rush the parliament building, blasting through the doors with grenade launchers, moving from there to the fifth floor to arrest, or kill, Yeltsin. Troops working with KGB agents would arrest the other Russian leaders. The tanks would fire shells to deafen and stun defenders of the White House, and helicopter gunships would support the operation and storm the roof and balconies.

But by now allegiances were muddled at best. Many of the officers and soldiers no longer had any heart for the coup. It was beginning to unravel.

On the morning of August 21, thousands awoke on the barricades relieved to still be alive, still there, and still not attacked.

The tanks had not moved. In fact, the coup had already collapsed. Remnick tells us that a combination of confusion, stupidity, drunkenness, lack of will, miscalculation, rain, and hap-
penstance had all conspired against the coup leaders. The tanks
began turning around near Red Square at eleven in the morning.
By one in the afternoon convoys were rolling along the main
arteries out of the city back toward the barracks and glad to be
leaving. The coup had fizzled.

Most Muscovites were relieved. "That's not the way to do a
coup," one said. "You remember how it was in Chile: fast and
energetic. Ours was a thick porridge, a Russian idiocy." Another
said: "Did these guys really think they could get away with this?
. . . What can you expect from seventy years of communism."

Gorbachev flew back that day from the Crimea. But for him
the coup was the end. Yeltsin–the hero of the resistance and now
the major figure in the land–had saved Gorbachev's job, but his
power was gone, and the party was dead. Within days he had
resigned as general secretary, dissolved the Central Committee
and, in essence, ended the seven decades of the Bolshevik era.

Four months later, on Christmas Day, 1991, he announced on
television that he was giving up trying to hold the Soviet Union
together. "I hereby discontinue my activities at the post of president of the Union of Soviet Socialist Republics," he said. He was
out of a job and one of the world's two great superpowers was
out of business. At 7:32 P.M. the red hammer and sickle, which
had flown over the Kremlin for most of this century, was lowered
for good, and the red, white, and blue flag of the Russian Federation rose in its place.

What was left in the wreckage were fifteen separate national
states in an uncertain association and with an undefined future.
A state council was cobbled together to act in the place of the
Supreme Soviet. The coup de grace had come on December 8
when without warning the heads of the three Slavic states, Russia, Belarus, and the Ukraine–the heartland of the old Soviet
Union–announced in Minsk that the old order had ceased to exist
and that they had formed a new Commonwealth of Independent
States. On December 21, eight other republics joined the first

three in proclaiming the end of the Soviet Union and united under the commonwealth banner.

THE DISINTEGRATION OF the Soviet Union was by no means a planned event. Nobody knew, least of all Gorbachev, that *he* would turn out to be "the gravedigger of communism," presiding over the virtual dismantling of the Communist order. Without intending to, as one Russian has said, he had played his great role on the world stage by "yanking the stopper from the bottle."

Somebody had to do it. The Soviet system had simply never worked right. It had never met its people's needs. It had never kept pace with the capitalism it was bent on replacing. In exchange for a rigid, tightly controlled political, economic, and military system, the Russian people had been promised a stable and decent living from the cradle to the grave. In the end the government could not deliver. The cumbersome centralized system run by bureaucrats was unable to adapt to shifting needs. It could not keep pace with the technological revolution sweeping the world. It could not nourish high-tech industries based on computers, semiconductors, satellites, innovation, and risk-taking. Only Western-style, free-market economies with privately owned companies—in short, the despised capitalism—could do that.

The economic historian Robert Heilbroner put it this way: "No government, anywhere, has the manpower or the skill to ride a complex, modern economy all the way down to the corner grocery store, anticipating people's preferences and requirements. The markets do this better." The Communist governments clearly showed they did not possess such skill. Moreover, to make their system work—in effect, to cram it down their people's throats and make it stick—the Communist nations had to be repressive. And that turned out to be their Achilles' heel.

Nicolas Berdyaev, a Russian-born philosopher who has written widely on his native land, has said that one thing Lenin didn't foresee—nor Marx nor Engels—was that class oppression comes in more than a capitalist guise. The dictatorship of the proletariat developed a colossal bureaucracy that spread like a dense fog over the whole country and subjugated everything to itself. It became more powerful and at least as despotic as the hated tsarist regime, and like any other despotic state, used the same methods of falsehood and violence. It created a privileged class that exploited the masses just as pitilessly. Socialism, Berdyaev wrote, wasn't realized in Russia; state capitalism was. In the end, it was not the interests of the workers, not the value of a person, and not the worth of human labor that were recognized as the supreme values, but the state itself and its economic and political power.

Russia never possessed an abundance of goods and services. Scarcity, which Soviet Russia did have in abundance, breeds inequality. In the upheaval of the 1917 revolution and its aftermath, the little industry that did exist collapsed into ruin. Economically, the nation was thrown backward. In this situation a single-party system—a dictatorship—became a temporary expedient that soon became the norm, and in the end guaranteed its own failure.

This outcome was not what Marx and Engels and Lenin, the great troika of world communism, expected, of course. Marx believed in happy endings. But the triumph of democracy was not the happy ending he had in mind. It is clear that the utopian classless state he envisioned can never be. There will always be conflict, and the first objective of government should be to keep the conflict from careening out of control and destroying people. There is no way to solve humanity's problems once and for all time. The idea of the Marxist society goes so much against the human grain that it is simply unworkable.

That is why communism was doomed from the beginning. Anatoli Sobchak, the former mayor of St. Petersburg, a sturdy champion of reform, had it right when he said, by way of epitaph to the Gorbachev era: "Our great mistake during those six years had been to try to reform what was unreformable."

Ultimately, what is important about Gorbachev is neither his many strengths nor his inevitable weaknesses. Rather, it is that at a crucial time in history, he helped free his country from an evil, totalitarian system and set it on a path to a better, democratic future. In so doing, he induced the final collapse of communism as an effective ideology. For that his place in history is secure.

Gorbachev, and communism, renewed democracy in another way. They reminded us of the strength and wisdom of a free people. Wherever human beings seek to govern themselves, there will be those who believe the governing situation should favor them over those who disagree. That is not peculiar to the Communist Party or the Russian people. It is a fact of human nature, universal in its reach. But no ideology or government that exists only to legitimize the interests of a particular group will maintain its hold over the people for very long.

The Soviets discovered, in the course of more than seventy painful and costly years, that policies designed to protect an elite against the mass of the people could not gain the allegiance or the support of the people, even when enforced by secret police and closed trials, even when rhetorically presented in the broadest and blandest terms of the greater public good.

It will be the final service of communism to democracy if its failure can stand as the practical proof of that fact.

For the West, learning to deal with this new Russia would be a strange and novel experience. New worries replaced old. What would become of the Cold War and the arms buildups? What would our relationship with Russia be? And what would we find when the Iron Curtain was raised?

Part 2

THE

LEGACY

Chapter 11

INNOCENTS

AT HOME

IN 1913, ANDREW CARNEGIE, the American steel tycoon, wrote an article titled "The Baseless Fear of War." In it he asked rhetorically, "Has there ever been danger of war between Germany and ourselves, members of the same Teutonic race? Never has it even been imagined."

A year later the unimaginable happened.

Soon after the First World War, France created the Maginot Line, the defensive strip of fortresses separating the French homeland from Germany. It was intended to prevent, ever again, a German invasion of French territory.

Fifteen years later German troops overran France.

Wishful thinking is a powerful seducer.

For Americans the temptation to engage in wishful thinking has been strongest in the arena of foreign policy. Foreign affairs do not often arouse and hold the passions of the American public. That fact is reflected in our politics.

The 1960 Sino-Soviet split marked the end of Soviet military assistance to China and with it the end of "monolithic" communism. Yet five years later Americans were battling "monolithic" communism in Vietnam.

Most Americans failed to grasp the significance of Soviet behavior in April 1986 when an accident in a nuclear reactor released radioactive materials over the Russian city of Chernobyl. It was the first time the Soviets ever openly acknowledged such a disaster. We likewise little understood what was happening when Gorbachev announced that Soviet troops would be withdrawn from Afghanistan.

In the fall of 1984 the committee funding the reelection campaign of President Reagan broadcast a television advertisement that showed a large bear lumbering through a forest as a male voice-over intoned ominously: "Some people say the bear is tame. Some say it's vicious. Some say there's no bear." As the Soviet Union neared collapse, many Americans were being persuaded, by a candidate for president, of the mortal threat it posed to our safety and security. The message of the ad was inaccurate. But in one respect it was literally true: there was no bear.

The failure to foresee the collapse of communism should not have come as a surprise. There had been other signals that our leaders failed to recognize throughout postwar history.

Why is that?

The American people have usually made domestic issues, such as jobs and wages, the center of their political concern. We've enjoyed the luxury of doing so safely because we are a vast and wealthy country separated from Europe and Asia by the world's widest oceans.

The other side of this coin is that Americans don't treat seriously policies they don't see as important. Absent an immediate crisis, the political management of foreign policy has proven to be easier than the day-to-day management of domestic issues. Domestic politics involves making and changing policies on crime, jobs, drug abuse, health care, defense bases, food stamps, Social Security, schools, and the many other matters that directly affect people's lives. Americans can and often do vote against those who raise their taxes or cut their benefits, so political leaders pay attention.

By contrast, presidents often know that the consequences of

their foreign policies may not be known until they are out of office. President Truman was only half joking when he defined a statesman as a politician who has been dead forty years.

For the half century following the Second World War, we concentrated our foreign policy on the containment of communism. We spent trillions of dollars on weapons, armies, aid, wars, and treaties to assure our security, to protect our allies, to woo neutrals, and to discourage adversaries.

Then, suddenly, the enterprise against which we had spent those trillions of dollars collapsed.

Why didn't we see it coming?

In retrospect, it is clear that we authorized and financed a costly and elaborate national intelligence apparatus that failed to give adequate warning of the coming collapse. We paid for studies by Kremlinologists who pored over organizational charts of the Presidium of the Supreme Soviet but failed to recognize the most elementary facts about the Soviet economy. We financed consultants on Politburo struggles. Specialists published monographs and books by the dozens. Yet few experts, let alone ordinary citizens, were prepared for the sudden Soviet disintegration, or understood how and why it happened.

From the beginning our perception of the Soviet Union reflected both wishful thinking and willful self-deception. We kept hoping they would turn out to be "just like us," and we kept fearing that they were really much more powerful. As a result, Soviet propaganda claims were treated in America with both derision and delusion.

After the Second World War, Americans saw themselves as the undisputed military, economic, and scientific masters of the world. So for Americans, the launch of the Soviet Sputnik in October 1957 was a psychological bombshell. It had never occurred to us that the Russians could beat us at anything, least of all in space.

Sputnik had an immense impact on our schools, our transportation system, and, of course, on our military and space programs. It was the first major propaganda victory the Russians incontestably won, and they won it on a worldwide stage. There was no longer any doubt that Soviet science had come of age. It could no longer be called backward. Jokes about Russian inventions suddenly didn't seem so funny.

That spectacular first victory in space ushered in a period when Soviet claims had to be taken seriously. And they were, inside the Soviet Union and here. When Khrushchev announced at the Twenty-second Party Congress in 1961 that communism would dominate the world in our lifetime, that it would bury us, he was heard around the world. Not only had the Soviet Union beat America into space, but the first person to orbit the earth, in April 1961, was a Russian, Yuri Gagarin.

For Russians, whose sufferings in what Stalin called the Great Patriotic War had been so terrible, life had been getting steadily better. Their newspapers and radios told them, day after day, the many ways their lives had improved. But they didn't need the propaganda. Everyone could remember or had family members who could recall the terrible postwar years of purge and starvation.

Voices of dissent were there, but muted. Khrushchev began to free them. In 1962, overriding the Presidium, Khrushchev authorized the publication, in Russia, of *One Day in the Life of Ivan Denisovich,* by Aleksandr Solzhenitysn. For Russians this was a mobilizing event almost on a par with the impact of Sputnik on Americans. The book burst like a bombshell on educated Soviet society.

For the first time, the truth was being told about Stalin's camps, to Russians, by a Russian, inside Russia. It wasn't coming from Radio Liberty or the BBC. It wasn't purveyed by foreigners whose motives were automatically suspect. It was, many Russians felt, the dawn of a new era in which the hard work of building socialism would go hand in hand with the development of a decent society, a society without lies, without censorship, without secret police.

There were other signs of enlightenment and progress within the Soviet Union in those days. Science cities were constructed, housing thousands of researchers and scientists whose work was beginning to bear fruit—work, citizens were told, for the good of the whole society. Russians were proud to have educated and employed almost 1.25 million scientists, more than any other country in the world.

The Virgin Lands program promised to put under the plow a million square miles of Siberian steppe—an area one-quarter the size of the United States—to create enormous factories for food that would dwarf anything the Americans could produce. The "hero" projects—enormous construction works such as the Bratsk hydroelectric dam in Siberia, built by free workers earning premium wages—were a sign that the country was succeeding. It seemed that the ideals for which so many had suffered and died in the 1930s were vibrant and meaningful, that the future was going to be a Soviet future in which they and their children would be leaders, not followers or supplicants.

Apartment buildings rose and Russians moved out of overcrowded dormitories and communal apartments where they shared kitchens and bathrooms with strangers. People, at least in some cities, could see and feel real change in their lives.

The U.S. engagement in the Vietnam War, a subject of relentless domestic Soviet criticism, was a signal for many that Western societies were not immune to terrible errors. For others it was confirmation that everything their leaders had told them about America was true. Their own country had indisputably become a world power to be reckoned with. Moscow's universities were filled with students from Africa and Asia, who had come to learn how to build the society of the future.

The policy of détente with the United States that marked the post-Stalin years reassured people that never again could anything as devastating as the Great Patriotic War happen on Russian soil. If there was ever a time in the sad history of Soviet communism that people had reason to believe again, this was the time. Many millions did believe.

It is easy, in hindsight, to disparage their belief in these accomplishments. But at the time they felt real to the Soviet people. And compared with what had gone before, they were real enough.

Conditions of life that most Americans would not tolerate were to Russians major improvements, and there was the promise of more to come.

But there was not more to come. The era of hope was soon over. For many Soviet citizens, it ended with the 1968 invasion of Czechoslovakia. By 1974 readers in the United States could buy books by American journalists such as Hedrick Smith and Robert Kaiser, who covered Moscow and traveled to the open cities of the country. They interviewed dissidents and ordinary Russians. They visited the republics and reported on the treatment to which they were subjected.

Their reports and those of other Americans increasingly reflected pervasive public cynicism within the USSR. "We pretend to work and they pretend to pay us," was a Soviet joke that became common in the West. Later the jokes became more bitter: "Capitalism is the exploitation of man by man. And communism is the exact opposite." "If the countries of Saharan Africa went Communist, in five years' time they'd be importing sand." "The capitalist world is on a precipice so they can get a better look at us down here."

These American observers reported the "hidden inflation"–the practice by which a product at one price would vanish from shelves to be replaced by an almost identical product at a higher price. The pervasive shortage of consumer goods in the Soviet Union became a staple of American news reports: there was a hunger for jeans, a demand for Western music. There was also a yearning to travel outside the borders of the USSR. Stories of official chauffeurs moonlighting as taxi drivers, and the importance of removing windshield wipers from parked cars lest they be stolen, were staples of Western news reports. Russians acknowledged that without a bribe of some kind, "free" medical care could mean no care; that without a barter economy side by side with the ruble economy, no one could live. The existence of a dual system of stores and services, one for common citizens and one for the ruling caste, became well known.

These were all warning signals of a society in economic decline.

During the 1970s, statistics indicated that it was only a matter of time before Russians would be a minority within their own country. Russian birth rates were falling and those of the Muslim republics were rising. The military included more and more recruits from Central Asian countries who could not speak fluent Russian. Ninety-five percent of officers were Russian while an increasing majority of their troops were ethnic minorities. That fact was reflected in growing ethnic tension.

The appalling incidence of alcoholism, the shortcomings of the health care system, and the demographic data all pointed to a *decline* in life expectancy in the late 1970s. No advanced nation had ever experienced a decline in life expectancy, yet statistics showed that male Russians could expect to live fewer years in the 1970s, when communism was supposedly coming into its own, than they could in the early 1960s.

So the Soviets stopped publishing the statistics.

The recognition by Russians themselves that Khrushchev's promise wasn't being kept, that the Soviet economy had not over-taken the West, proved to be one of the most corrosive elements in what came to be called the "period of stagnation" under Brezhnev. Hope vanished, and cynicism and despair enveloped the country like a heavy, unyielding fog.

It wasn't necessary for Brezhnev in 1981 to announce that the promise of reaching full communism had been put on permanent hold. Everyone with eyes could see that it was a promise that could not be kept. All his statement did was confirm that the leadership had no intention of keeping it either, something most Soviet people knew by then.

In the West, we had access to materials that could not be published inside the USSR itself, for the brief Khrushchev "thaw" had by that time turned again to ice. The expulsion of Solzhenitsyn and the publication in the West of the three volumes of his *Gulag Archipelago,* the defection of talent, and the crush of Jews begging to leave the Soviet Union sent more signals that something was terribly wrong.

Yet, during these same years, American intelligence was concluding that the Russian economy was showing real growth, that the Soviet threat was not diminishing, that East Germans had reached parity with West Germans in their per capita income. All of these conclusions were wrong. The signs of decay in the Soviet Union were widespread, even undeniable. But American policy was based on a strong and threatening Soviet Union. And so intelligence was molded to fit policy. Inconvenient facts were ignored. When Ronald Reagan took the oath of office as president in 1981, he almost immediately announced an *increased threat* of an expansionist Soviet Union, which he insisted American tax dollars must pay to counteract.

Some of his supporters contend that it was President Reagan's military buildup that caused the collapse of the Soviet Union. Without that buildup, which forced them to spend themselves into bankruptcy—that argument goes—the Soviet Union would still be there, a menacing presence, threatening us with nuclear war.

The U.S. military buildup was a factor, but was not decisive in the collapse of the Soviet Union. But the argument is serious enough to warrant a response.

If the Reagan military buildup didn't kill communism, then what did? The answer, simply put, is: communism itself, along with democratic capitalism, with which communism could not successfully compete.

Human beings act in their own self-interest. Communism contradicted that reality and failed. Democratic capitalism is based upon that reality and is succeeding.

The failure of communism was inevitable. Its structure and its rigidity guaranteed that. But the success of democratic capitalism was not inevitable. Its flexibility, especially its capacity to change under pressure, made its survival possible.

Sixty years ago the opposite seemed likely. The Western world was locked in a depression and capitalism itself tottered on the brink of collapse. Fascist governments imposed state control on the economies of Germany and Italy, with apparent success. And in Russia, communism seemed to offer the hope of a more prosperous and humane future.

What happened? Why? And how was it that so many people believed in a system that, in retrospect, was so brutal, unfair, and built on a foundation of cynicism and lies?

To answer that question we must go back once again to the early days of communism in Russia, from 1918 to 1921–the years of War Communism–when the system promised that the enormous mobilization of resources and manpower that had previously been mustered only for war would in the future be harnessed to build a better life for the people. Instead of resources being wasted in incompetence or squandered on extravagance while peasants and workers froze and starved, communism–for the first time, in the experience of most Russians–held out the hope of an equitable share for all. The hope proved illusory, but the will to believe was fueled by years of hardship and privation, by the growing realization that another kind of life was possible, and by the absence of compelling alternative visions.

Russia emerged from World War I having lost valuable territories–Poland, the Baltic littoral, parts of the Caucasus–and with its new revolutionary government facing foreign intervention and civil war. By 1921, with their civil war ending, Russians were ready to rebuild.

Successive five-year plans–the first beginning in 1928–turned a primitive agricultural economy into an industrial and military power in just two decades. The entire Soviet society was encouraged, prodded, coerced, and bludgeoned to meet that goal. "Shock workers" and "heroes" of Soviet labor and agriculture were trumpeted. Heroic feats of childbearing by Soviet women were honored with medals. City workers were required to spend their summer weekends harvesting potatoes. Massive (but useless) projects such as the White Sea Canal were proudly shown to visiting foreigners, as if to prove that no project, no matter how large, was beyond the capacity of scientific socialism.

Propaganda within and outside Russia tirelessly reiterated the giant advances in engineering, industrialization, output, and growth that were taking place in Socialism in One Country. Production and harvest figures were manufactured to fit the regime's propaganda needs. Repetition did for those fake figures what

Hitler's Big Lie accomplished a decade later: Russians and foreigners alike accepted them.

Russia was, after all, the nation of the Potemkin Villages, temporarily erected cottages full of temporarily imported peasants
that lined the route of Catherine the Great, the eighteenth-century
empress of all the Russias, to convince her that the work of col-
onizing the southern steppes was moving forward. The Soviet
five-year plans were twentieth-century Potemkin Statistics
designed to convince Russians and the world that the Soviet system was moving forward. But just as the southern steppes *were*
ultimately populated, so the five-year-plans, despite enormous
waste and human hardship, did move the lumbering giant into
the twentieth century.

In an early book about the Soviets, a disillusioned Western emi-
grant who returned home wrote: "Ever since 1931 or thereabouts
the Soviet Union has been at war . . . people were wounded and
killed, women and children froze to death, millions starved, thousands were court-martialed and shot in the campaigns of collectivization and industrialization. I would wager that Russia's battle of metallurgy alone involved more casualties than the battle
of the Marne."

During the years between the world wars, millions around the
world, in this country, and in the Soviet Union itself, saw this great
heaving mass of humanity pushing itself into the twentieth century as a heroic and admirable enterprise.

In the depths of the Great Depression, when 15 million unemployed Americans were looking for jobs that did not exist, the
chimera of an activist, engaged, and working Soviet Union
attracted many. Will Rogers said, "Those rascals in Russia . . .
have got some mighty good ideas . . . just think of everybody in
a country going to work."

At a time when the economic future of the West and the social
organization of democracies seemed to be crumbling, when the
certainties of religion and traditional society were being called
into question, the contrast to an organized, purposeful, and ener-
gized Soviet system struck many observers as significant.

What did communism promise that made so many people so eager to believe?

The answer to that question lies in the contradictions that exist within every human being and in the constant tension between good and evil. People want to be, and they believe it is possible to be, good. But in their daily lives they see much behavior that is bad.

Every system of religious or moral belief embodies some version of the precepts so well expressed by the Christian Beatitudes: a belief that the last shall be first, that the poor are not destined to suffer needlessly and endlessly, that there can be a just and fair outcome for all. But much of human experience contradicts that vision, so religious doctrine tends to focus instead on a more just and pleasant life after death.

Communism promised to make that vision a reality, and to make it a reality in *this* world. It was a promise that held great hope because it appealed to people on an elemental level. The material plenty brought by the industrial revolution offered the great mass of humanity the hope for the first time of physical comfort and sufficiency, and an end to the scarcity that had been the lot of most of humanity for most of history. Yet for more than a generation, the fruits of the industrial revolution remained tantalizingly beyond the reach of millions. In fact, the disparity between plenty and poverty became even more marked.

The attraction of communism was the hope it held out as a scientifically certain path to the goal that had eluded people from the very beginning of human societies: how to organize society so no one need go hungry, no one need suffer pointlessly, no one need be deprived—a society where there is true justice and equality for all.

However, in the Soviet Union, communism didn't deliver on its promises. Not only can we now see clearly that it was doomed to fail; we know it was, in fact, a cynical ruse to impose a totalitarian system to perpetuate the power and privilege of a small elite at the expense of everyone else. It was founded on a big lie and nourished by many small lies. For when the real world contradicted the ideology, the real world had to be changed—by rewriting history, by falsifying statistics, by more and more lies—rather than change the ideology. In time the gap between what communism was supposed to be and what it in reality was became too great. And what so many once believed was no longer believed by anyone, and communism fell.

Chapter 12

THE SATELLITES

SPIN AWAY

THE TWENTIETH-CENTURY RIVALRY between communism and democracy was in part economic. It quickly developed into a military rivalry and a nuclear standoff. It was brought to an end in part by economics.

In 1988 an earthquake in Armenia showed the poverty of Soviet life. The Soviets were forced to appeal abroad for the most elementary assistance—blankets, tents, medicines, basic construction machinery—products often in short supply in Third World nations, but not—supposedly—in the world's second-greatest superpower.

Gorbachev visited the United States in December 1988 and addressed the United Nations General Assembly. He said that "all of us, and primarily the stronger of us, must . . . rule out any outward-oriented use of force." His announcement of a unilateral cut of 50,000 Soviet troops and 5,000 tanks from Central Europe by 1991 was unprecedented.

Americans welcomed Gorbachev as they would a rock music superstar. He was greeted by outthrust hands, cheers, and welcoming smiles when he walked the streets of New York and Washington.

We had reason to hope from his words and his acts that the Cold War had taken a different and more favorable turn. But many in America were wary. For seven decades Soviet arms and influence had moved outward, not inward. Within our lifetimes, Soviet troops had crushed revolts in East Germany, Hungary, Czechoslovakia, and Poland.

Americans had risked and lost their lives in the outbreaks of violence that characterized the Cold War era. American taxes had paid the high price of the Cold War. People were weary of the nuclear standoff, the persistent demand that more and more of our wealth be sunk into costly nuclear weapons for a confrontation that by now few believed would ever take place.

In Moscow and other Soviet cities by the end of 1988, the concern of ordinary people was simple survival. The *Washington Post* quoted a Moscow woman as saying, "I'm glad we're talking with the Americans. Maybe they can send us some food."

The great illusion of economic and military dominance by the Communist system was over. It was finished in the East European satellite nations as well, as the events of the following year clearly demonstrated.

The expansion of world trade and the acceleration in the movement of goods and services, together with the exploding productive force of the industrial revolution in the nineteenth century, changed forever the human relationship to economics. It is a change we've been struggling to understand throughout this century. It was the Stock Market Crash of 1929 that helped precipitate the Great Depression. It was the worldwide depression of the 1930s that helped buoy the fortunes of a minor German political party, the National Socialists, and its leader, Adolf Hitler.

As part of the sweeping changes made by Roosevelt, the Securities and Exchange Commission was created to regulate the financial markets and to prevent some of the unsound practices that had contributed to the crash of 1929. In addition, construction began on what came to be known as a social "safety net," an organized effort to build a floor below which no American would fall. As it turned out, the safety net was unsafe for many Americans; it proved to be full of holes through which many individuals did fall. But there was enough redistribution of income to assure that aggregate purchasing power did not decline too sharply in times of economic downturn. Therefore, the recession of 1981 did not become the Depression of 1982; the stock market drop in October of 1987 did not become the Stock Market Crash of 1988. Instead of devastating our economy, the 23 percent drop in the stock market of 1987 had its most serious impact on other nations, including those in Eastern Europe. For them, as for other debtor nations, American credit dried up and loan repayments were pressed. The leaders in those countries reacted in the only way command economies *can* react: they reduced the availability of consumer goods and raised prices.

There is a link between the diminution of Western credit for faltering Eastern economies and the dramatic open flight to Western Europe that took place twenty months later.

In Poland, the resurgence of the decade-old Solidarity movement was fed by the acceleration of economic disaster. Poland's path to modernization during the 1980s had been to rely on massive overseas aid and loans. By the end of the decade Poland's international debt was $35 billion. But her command economy was no more able to use the borrowed capital for economic growth than her leaders were able to win the loyalty of the Polish people or prevent the resurgence of religious faith. By the end of the decade, the Poles moved to salvage what they could of their economy, and midyear elections brought in a government dominated by reformers.

Hungary during the 1980s tried to develop a mixed economic system, or "goulash" communism. It was intended to supply consumer wants without stripping too much of the economy from the hands of the apparatchiks. The failure of "goulash" communism to move the country forward led in part to intraparty disputes between reformers and adherents of more radical economic innovation during 1989.

Against the background of glasnost and perestroika in the Soviet Union, Hungary's leaders felt secure enough to resign from the Communist Party, rename themselves socialists, and make a commitment to multiparty democracy. Elections were held in March and April 1990; the center-right Democratic Forum and its allies won nearly 60 percent of the seats in parliament and agreed to form a conservative coalition government.

In Czechoslovakia, the experience of the "Prague Spring" of 1968, which was suppressed by Russian tanks, made reformers more cautious and the Communists much less open to reform. Little more than two decades later, the Velvet Revolution won for Czechs in ten days what the Polish Solidarity Union had taken almost ten years to accomplish. But it was unable to hold the country together. A peaceful separation between the Czech Republic and what is now Slovakia became official on January 1, 1993.

Glasnost in the Soviet Union, the announcement of unilateral troop cuts, and all the other changes of that momentous time had already set in motion the march of people voting with their feet. About 200,000 ethnic Germans had come "home" to Germany by the beginning of 1989. West Germany found itself welcoming Germans who spoke not a word of the German language, people whose ancestors had lived along the Volga River for more than two hundred years, and some who had not actually lived in Germany for seven centuries.

In a spring thaw, a small crack in the winter ice lets a little trickle of water run; it becomes a stream and causes more cracks, from each of which water pours in a torrent that carries the broken ice along until it overruns the riverbanks and floods all in its path.

So it seemed in Eastern Europe. By the summer of 1989, what had been a trickle became a flood. Before the floodwaters receded, the Iron Curtain had been swept away.

Hungary cracked the ice when it made the decision to open its border with Austria in May 1989. The barbed wire was cut, rolled up, and removed; the plowed strip of land was left to spring growth. People began to cross, tentatively and secretively at first, often at night. But they crossed with increasing boldness when they saw that the border was not being guarded, shots were not being fired, dogs were not chasing them.

By summer, East Europeans were streaming into West German embassies in Budapest and Prague. They simply ignored laws that said they could not leave. All over the East, people were on the move. Young couples flung their belongings over embassy fences and vaulted after them to secure a place in the line issuing visas to the West. Television, as always, captured a large part of this spectacle. We saw parents saying farewell to their sons and daughters at dilapidated railway stations, worried they would never see them again. We saw families plotting to smuggle their small children to freedom. We saw young men and women, married couples, with infants and without them, searching for a way, any way, to the West.

All of Eastern Europe was in motion and turmoil. Finally, the authorities were forced to give way. The beleaguered embassies decided they could no longer handle the waves of refugees individually. The government of West Germany decided it would simply accept all those coming west. A train was chartered for a load of East Germans who could not be accommodated in any other way. The East German government was forced to let them go.

An earlier generation saw the Berlin Wall being built. Although it was an outrage against human sensibility, the West became numb to its existence. The terrible toll of human life lost to the bullets of East German guards enforcing its brutal purpose stood as damning proof of the bankruptcy of communism. No moral authority can justify a regime that needs a wall topped with barbed wire and broken glass embedded in cement, as well as patrol dogs and armed guards, to enforce its will. Yet the Berlin Wall stood for almost thirty years. It stood as a symbol—a testament to the imprisonment of the human mind and the human spirit. It survived because it is possible to terrorize people if you are willing to kill enough of them. It fell when its enforcers were no longer willing to kill to sustain their authority.

By the late summer of 1989, as people from the East crossed borders forbidden to them since the end of the Second World War, it was as though an invisible chain had snapped. Fear of the border guards, fear of the Stalinist system, the fear of fear itself had cracked. A spirit moved through millions of people elevating them to a new consciousness, into a new way of living—into freedom.

By fall the disintegration had continued so long that American television stopped carrying the stories. There was nothing newsworthy any longer about hundreds of thousands of people fleeing to freedom. There was nothing left to say, no pictures left to show that hadn't been seen before. The story faded.

On November 10, 1989, East Berliners began to punch holes through the Berlin Wall from their side. By November 14, several new entry points were established, and East Berliners streamed into the streets and stores of West Berlin for the first time in three decades.

A month later the Velvet Revolution in Czechoslovakia ended the Communist Party's monopoly on political power and paved the way for the re-creation of a civil society and for democratic elections in 1990.

The sounds of breaking ice spread still farther, to the Balkans and the lands of the lower Danube. The people of Rumania rose up against the regime of Nicolae Ceauşescu, one of the most repulsive Communist dictatorships in all of Eastern Europe. While the Velvet Revolution in Czechoslovakia evoked images of the beautiful bridge spanning the river in Prague, crowded with peaceful people armed only with moral force, the pictures from Bucharest were very different: gunfire in the streets against the hated security police, violence in the countryside, and ethnic score-settling among Hungarians, Rumanians, and Gypsies. The half-finished Stalinist boulevard leading to the massive palace on which Ceauşescu had lavished so much of his nation's scanty resources was the image of a wholly corrupt system.

In Bulgaria, mounting protests and rising ethnic tensions preceded the period of democratization. In November, Todor Zhivkov, Bulgaria's leader since 1954, was forced to resign. His successor survived him only six months before being forced out in turn. Efforts to form a coalition government to replace the one-party Communist system failed. Until the Bulgarians took steps to adopt a new constitution setting up elections in July 1990, the crisis continued. Adopted in July 1991, their democratic constitution, based on the separation of powers, was the first of its kind in Eastern Europe. Elections followed in October 1991.

Finally, in March 1992, the collapse of communism in Eastern Europe was completed when Albania elected its first non-Communist government. In the national elections in March, the Albanian Democratic Party routed the Socialist (formerly Communist) Party, winning 62 percent of the vote to only 25 percent for the Socialists.

THE ECONOMIC AND political transitions have been difficult in these countries. Decades of repression and government-imposed censorship left people wholly out of touch with the free competition of ideas essential to a democracy. Often, what Americans see as competitive political debate is seen by East Europeans as disloyalty or provocation to be censored or crushed.

The total failure of centralized command economies to raise the living standards of working people has left a legacy of widespread poverty in virtually all these nations. It is the lack of economic growth that creates the greatest strains on society. When unemployment and food prices rise, while real income for work declines, a society is vulnerable to demagogues—to Mussolinis and Hitlers.

And nations whose borders were artificially drawn to resolve a political problem, not to encompass a homogeneous group, are open to the temptations of extreme nationalistic and ethnic passions.

Since communism fell, ethnic hatreds have erupted: German skinheads attack Turkish workers in what had been West Germany and Vietnamese workers in the former East Germany. Hungarian politicians repeatedly insist that the 5 million ethnic Hungarians living outside the country's political borders have a claim on her protection and patronage.

With the breakup of the Soviet Union the reemergence of ethnic rivalries and hatreds has been a harsh reminder that human societies and human passions are not affected only by economics.

Even before the formal dissolution of the Soviet Union in December 1991, fighting between Armenians and Azerbaijanis had erupted, tensions were rising between Georgians and Ossetians in the Caucasus, and the Catholic Ukrainians of the west were seeking autonomy for their faith against the claims of the Ukrainian Uniates and Orthodox in the east. In the Russian Republic, antisemitism and bigotry against the peoples of the Caucasus were expressed openly.

Ethnic tensions among non-Russians were first explained as pent-up resentment against the Soviet system, reflecting the same dissatisfaction with economic hardship that Russians were expressing. While a few pessimists may have thought civil unrest would lead to localized civil wars, few predicted the eruption of violence where it did erupt—in the Balkan state of Yugoslavia.

IN AUGUST 1992, I stood in a square in the center of Pakrac, a small town in Croatia where 8,500 people lived until 1991. The mayor of Pakrac, Vladimir Delac, a thirty-eight-year-old Croat, pointed to a roadblock in the street less than two hundred yards away.

"Right down there," he said, "are the Serbs."

On this side of the roadblock about 1,500 Croats lived. On the other side, Serbs lived; Delac didn't know how many. Until 1991, Serbs and Croats lived side by side. They went to school together and worked together, even though they didn't socialize much. Then the war of "ethnic cleansing" hit Pakrac.

One Sunday in August 1991, almost all the Serbs left. Many of them returned the next day, armed and accompanied by tanks and soldiers of the Yugoslav Federal Army. For five months war raged in Pakrac. Thousands fought. Hundreds died, at least 120 of them inhabitants of the town. Many more, from other places in Croatia and Serbia, came to fight and die. All around where we stood were damaged buildings, some completely destroyed. A few, however, stood untouched. A nearby village was less fortunate. There, every building was destroyed. First, the Serbs won control and leveled every Croatian house. Then the Croats regained control and retaliated against every Serbian dwelling.

Walking along the uneven, unpaved village street, passing the broken shells of one ruined house after another, it was hard to tell who had won.

"How long will it be before Serbs and Croats can again live together?" I asked the mayor of Pakrac. Before he could answer, a man standing next to him shouted, "Never!"

The mayor thought a while, then answered softly, "We will repair our buildings long before we repair our souls."

WHAT HAD BROUGHT this about? The final breakup of the Turkish Empire, which was completed by the end of the First World War, did not resolve questions of national status in the Balkans any more than the 1919 Treaty of Versailles created permanent peace in Western Europe. It is now clear that the breakup of the Soviet Union has not resolved those questions either.

The history of the region is illuminating. Briefly, the industrial revolution, which began in Great Britain and spread south through Europe, never reached the Balkan peninsula. Economic growth and modernization changed societies in much more important ways than simply introducing machinery and systems for manufacturing goods. It dramatically altered the relationships among people. For peasants a modern economy replaced forced labor and introduced money wages. It secularized church property, as all sources of capital were tapped for economic expansion. It encouraged the legal emancipation of Jews and other disenfranchised minorities so that the society could take full advantage of the abilities of all people. A modern economy cannot flourish in a tribal society. By the same token, tribal loyalties remain strong where there is no economic growth and little mobility.

But the people of the Balkan peninsula were the subjects of two of the oldest and least-developed empires that lasted into the twentieth century—the Hapsburg and the Ottoman. The Balkans had few large cities, and beyond primary products had only limited trade. One of the conflicts in one of the Balkan crises of this century is called the War of the Pigs, because it erupted over Austria's refusal to permit Serbia's main export to be imported.

The towns and villages of the Balkans were multiethnic communities where people of different faiths lived side by side in a clan structure that lasted far longer than in most of Western Europe. Few large, modernizing institutions, such as universities, developed in the Balkans as they did in Prague, Cracow, and Vienna.

The recent and limited modernization Yugoslavia enjoyed under Tito preserved instead of diluting ethnic identity, because under Tito, civil rights were apportioned by national grouping. The people of Serbia and Croatia are ethnically similar; their languages are virtually identical. But the Serbs are mostly Eastern Orthodox Christian, the Croats mostly Roman Catholics. Many Serbs fought with the Russians during the Second World War, many Croats with the Germans.

It's important not to fall into the trap of assuming that every ethnic difference is an inevitable prelude to a shooting war. Ethnic differences exist all over Europe but they do not all lead to violence or war. The Czechs and the Slovaks agreed peacefully to their national "divorce" after independence. The new nation of Slovakia came into existence on January 1, 1993, without bullets being fired.

Every nation's history is different. What may encourage a safe and peaceful outlet for ethnic pride in one place may be highly divisive in another. The ethnic differences between Welsh, Cornish, and Scots in Great Britain aren't a cause of national instability or potential war. But in other places, tribalism becomes a destructive force when it is a primary focus of people's energies. When the efforts of influential people are directed toward dividing the population into ethnic or caste groupings, that energy and talent are lost to activities that can reduce differences, such as economic enterprise.

The "minority rights" constitutions, which many of the new nations of Eastern Europe are adopting, have not worked out over the longer term. They paper over differences but do nothing to advance broadly based economic growth, which is the principal solvent of tribal loyalties.

The differences in how the peoples of the former Soviet bloc have come to terms with their new independence reflect much more clearly their pre-Soviet histories than the influence of the more recent Communist rule. If we ignore those older histories, we will continue to be surprised by eruptions of ethnic, national, or religious fervor.

I believe that the world of the twenty-first century will be far more confusing than the Cold War world of this century. In the last half of this century the threat of nuclear holocaust was sufficient to keep lesser rivalries in abeyance. But the disappearance of the two-power conflict has given space and opportunity for smaller, older, and often far more savage rivalries to reassert themselves.

Chapter 13

THE CATASTROPHE

BEHIND THE

CURTAIN

WHEN THE IRON CURTAIN FINALLY LIFTED, the most shocking sight for many of us was the stunning extent of the environmental damage it had hidden for so long.

The observations of dissident writers had prepared us for the moral poverty of communism. We understood that societies that encouraged children to denounce their own parents, that denied workers the fruits of their labor, and that forced people to become state-defined "black market criminals" just to buy the necessities of life, were sick societies. And so they turned out to be.

What Americans didn't know was how *physically* sick the people in those societies were.

When the curtain lifted, the reality was hard to believe.

"The forest began to die about ten years ago," Andrzej Piotrowski, a Polish Green Party leader, told a Reuters reporter in 1991, "but every effort to speak about it was silenced by officials."

He was talking about the "black triangle," which covers about seven hundred square miles of Central Europe from the German-Polish border through the northern Czech Republic and Slovakia into Poland and Rumania—an area two-thirds the size of

Rhode Island. Three-fourths of the forests in the "black triangle" have been killed by acid rain. Skeletal tree trunks now stand on what were once thickly forested mountain ranges. Surface mines scar the landscape. A miasmic air pollution threatens the forests of Western Europe. Life expectancy along this swath of land is fifteen years lower than in other parts of the region.

In Central and Eastern Europe, the great Silesian Coal Basin, stretching from Leipzig in Germany to Cracow in Poland, is today a man-made lunar landscape, caked with decades of soot, its air impermeable to sunlight in many places. The huge forests of Central and Eastern Europe, the green lungs of the continent, are damaged. Rivers and lakes throughout the region are contaminated, well beyond being simply unpotable or dangerous for swimming. Some are unusable even by industry because the water is so contaminated it destroys pipes.

After the curtain lifted, we learned that in widespread areas of Europe, future generations of Poles, Czechs, Russians, Ukrainians, Latvians, Estonians, Hungarians, Bulgarians, and others have been deprived of a healthy environment. Hundreds of thousands of people will watch their children grow up in a contaminated natural world—the physical counterpart of the suffocating spiritual death caused by communism.

The West first began to see signs of it in an automobile—the little Trabant. The Trabant, produced in East Germany, was the car of the masses. When the Berlin Wall fell, the crowds that streamed through on foot were followed each weekend by thousands of determined East Germans packed into Trabis, rolling west to look and buy.

For a time the car became something of a celebrity. A German movie was made about the epic voyage of a Trabi to France. But the Trabis' quaintness soon wore thin. They began to irritate West Germans as their plodding progress blocked the paths of swift BMWs, Porsches, and Mercedes. The car was soon the butt of Western jokes: a Trabi's value could be doubled by filling its gas tank; its most valued accessory was a map of West Germany; it was constructed by two persons, one of whom folded while the other stapled. *Time* magazine noted that the little Communist-built vehicle outclassed the average lawn tractor by having a trunk and passenger space, but not much more. The jokes were well meant, born of immense sympathy with the people of eastern Germany in their flight west to participate in the marvels of a capitalist economy.

What we Westerners didn't know then was that each Trabi also emitted eight times as many hydrocarbons into the air as a Western car, and a hundred times as much carbon monoxide as a car with a catalytic converter. Cities choked with these two-stroke engines burning leaded fuel forced their citizens to breathe in nine times as much pollution, twice as much lead—indeed, to breathe air that was the equivalent in lung damage to long-term cigarette smoking.

The Sachsenring enterprise, after building more than 3 million Trabis, ceased production in 1991. Despite enormous West German investment in improved auto production facilities for East Germany, including a major Volkswagen factory in Mosel, where the Trabis were built, many thousands of those vehicles still belch smoke throughout eastern Germany.

The little Trabi was just the tip of the iceberg. Beneath it, across all of Central and Eastern Europe and European Russia, was an ecological nightmare. As the full extent of the devastation became known, the Trabi jokes lost their humor.

Russia alone, a country covering close to 6 percent of the earth's surface, has seen vast forests clear-cut and the soil left to wash or blow away. Russian industry has poisoned some of the earth's greatest rivers. Overuse of chemicals has polluted some of the richest farming soil in the world. Intensive overgrazing has created Europe's first sand desert. An irrigated cotton monoculture in Central Asia has partially evaporated the fourth-largest inland sea in the world, the Aral.

Russian scientists' system of environmental mapping has isolated 290 areas where pollution and contamination directly imperil the health of human beings. These 290 areas comprise 16 percent of the land area of the former Soviet Union, equaling all of Western Europe in size. One Russian scientist says a fifth of the Russian population lives in ecological disaster areas and another third or more live in areas of environmental stress. Moscow's chief geneticist told the national daily newspaper *Izvestia* in November 1996 that congenital defects in Russia's newborns had increased by 30 percent in the past fifteen years.

The southern Urals city of Chelyabinsk, called the most radioactive city in Russia, is where Kyshtym-57, the main Soviet nuclear research center, was built in 1947. It had no waste-treatment facilities at first. Wastes were dumped raw into Lake Karachai and local reservoirs. These waters now contain radiation equal to 140 Hiroshima-size bombs. The lakes are spring-fed and in wet seasons threaten to overflow their banks into nearby rivers. During the droughts of 1967 and 1972, natural evaporation lowered water levels so much that surrounding regions were radioactively contaminated. Meanwhile, half the young men of Chelyabinsk are considered physically unfit to serve in the Russian armed forces.

In late 1988 children living in the Ukrainian city of Chernovtsy began to lose their hair, probably due to heavy metal contamination of the water supply and locally grown food. Similar problems have occurred in other parts of Russia and the former republics.

In 1989 an epidemic of hair loss among children in Sillamae, a town of 21,000 in northeastern Estonia, was traced to radioactivity—in some cases several hundred times higher than safe levels. Sillamae has a fifty-year-old uranium enrichment plant. Processed radioactive ore was bulldozed into pits and spread on the local beaches like sand. The materials contain small bright beads of ores that local children pick up and play with. The children's hair loss was ultimately traced to the fact that their kindergarten was built atop an old quarry filled with processed ore waste from the enrichment plant. Contamination levels there and in surrounding streets were equivalent to those around Chernobyl after the nuclear reactor accident.

In 1989 President Gorbachev stopped all nuclear testing. But for the people living near test regions like Semipalatinsk, Karaganda, and Pavlodar, it was too late. Five years after the fall of communism, the people of Kazakhstan have found that the effects of long-term exposure to gamma radiation and internal radiation due to ingestion of contaminated food, water, and air are comparable to those suffered by some survivors of Hiroshima. Every third child is born dead or with mental or physical defects. Cancer deaths in Semipalatinsk rose sevenfold between 1975 and 1986; cases of severe anemia rose sixfold; 50 percent of the population suffer damage to the immune system.

Nonradioactive contamination is even more rampant. The Russian environmental agency says that only 23 percent of Russian children can be judged "practically healthy." Allergies, respiratory problems, nervous disorders, and intestinal complaints have doubled since the 1970s. In Armenia air pollution is blamed for a rise in infant mortality and birth defects in newborns. The capital, Yerevan, has seen leukemia rates increase many times over in the last fifteen years. In the south, in Volgograd, air pollution has been linked to high miscarriage rates and skin and intestinal disorders. Lung diseases caused by air pollution have been found in Ukrainian industrial cities, in the Kola Peninsula in the North, in Karabash in the Urals. Inhabitants of the Kuzbass industrial region have disproportionately high lung cancer rates.

Official reports note that 50 million people living in 103 different cities face air pollution levels ten times the official safety limits. In sixteen of those cities, air pollution is fifty times higher. To take a single example, air pollution deposits thirteen tons of emissions per year for each inhabitant in the city of Norilsk. It is difficult for human lungs to stand up against an assault as heavy as that.

Lake Baikal in Siberia is the world's deepest freshwater lake and one of the largest. It holds a fifth of the earth's entire freshwater supply. It is home to a variety of unique biological life forms, an evolutionary laboratory matching the Galápagos Islands in the Pacific. Soviet-era emphasis on heavy industry at all costs is threatening the lake. Forty industrial plants line its shores, dumping wastes directly into it. The paper mills have been equipped in recent years with pollution controls, but Russians say these are only turned on when foreigners visit.

All major Russian rivers and lakes are tainted by heavy pollution and a combination of fertilizers and industrial and household wastes. Only 30 percent of household wastes in Russia are treated before release into the water supply. St. Petersburg, a city built on canals, has virtually no sewage treatment facilities. Nor do many other large cities.

The Black Sea is the world's largest landlocked ocean. Pollutants from the Danube, Dnieper, and Don Rivers over the past thirty years have cut its fish harvest from 900,000 to 100,000 tons. The surface waters of the sea, once rich fish-spawning grounds, are now 90 percent dead. Many famed Black Sea resorts, where Communist elites and workers alike passed their summer holidays, are now closed to swimming. In places the Black Sea is a green soup that kills fish and shrouds the entire area in noxious odors.

Recently, the six countries bordering the Black Sea and the thirteen nations that use the rivers that pollute the sea agreed on an action plan to combat the pollution. But the plan still requires funding. An earlier effort in 1995 to clean up the Danube–a major source of pollution of the Black Sea–has foundered because of the lack of funds.

Soviet concentration on centralized heavy industry created a demand for water for industrial sites often far from water sources. Conversely, drier inland regions were earmarked for crops that needed intensive irrigation. The result has been the redistribution of water for industry and irrigation. Huge dams and reservoirs not only swamp their immediate surroundings but also reduce river flow, preventing the waters from flushing out the pollutants dumped in them. A drop of Volga River water, which once would have flowed down the length of the river in a month and a half, today needs a year and a half to complete its journey because of the diversion of the river's waters. One outcome is a concentration of toxins in rivers. Another is the contamination of fish; in 1989, 70 percent of the fish taken from the Volga were contaminated with mercury.

The Volga flows into the Caspian Sea, a vast inland body of water which, along with the Black Sea, once accounted for 90 percent of the sturgeon catch, the source of Russia's famous delicacy, caviar. Today the sturgeon are gone, and their survival as a species is in doubt. The Caspian receives fully 40 percent of Russia's wastewater, and is also dying.

The Aral Sea, the fourth-largest inland water body in the world, 26,000 square miles in size, has been destroyed. Diverting water from the flow that fed the Aral to the surrounding monoculture cotton crop has caused the sea to shrink by almost two-thirds. Its main fishing port, Aralsk, once produced a tenth of the Soviet fish catch. Today the town sits in the middle of a desert, forty miles from the water. The sea itself is surrounded by a lunar landscape of dried, salt-covered flats that were once a sea bed. In the high winds common to central Russia, the salts are carried throughout the region, making other soils saline.

Meanwhile, the cotton crop itself has dealt enormous health damage to the people of Uzbekistan. The working conditions of women and their preschool children—who accompany their mothers into the fields—are appalling. Women work in the fields for nine hours at a time without food, exposed to high levels of chemical pesticides. Health conditions of cotton workers are comparable to those found in Bangladesh, one of the world's poorest nations.

The government of Kazakhstan found that 90 percent of the children in the Aral Sea region suffer from pollution-related illnesses. Two-thirds of them have three or more medical conditions, ranging from respiratory problems to neurological pathologies. Half of them are anemic and two-thirds of those past the age of three months have excess salt levels in their bodies. Lead levels in people exposed to the Aral region's environment are two to thirty-two times the norm. The economic problems in this republic have further complicated the health problems because it lacks the funds to replace Soviet-era free medicines and food supplements for its people.

In the lands of the Kalmucks, between the Caspian Sea and Gorbachev's native Stavropol to the west, sheep herds twenty times too large for the carrying capacity of the land have grazed the pasture past the point of recovery, creating a sand desert. And it is spreading—by about 10 percent a year. It will reach the southern Ukraine by the end of the century.

Even worse problems abound. Salination from overirrigation has made some soils unusable. Around the heavy industrial centers, pollution has contaminated soil so thoroughly that food grown on it should not be eaten by human beings. In some regions, that's not a danger because the soil won't support growth at all. Around Magnitogorsk in the Urals, uncontrolled pollution since 1932 has created a dead zone about twelve miles wide.

In the Russian Far North and Far East, the search for oil, gas, gold, and other minerals has damaged the fragile ecology of the arctic and subarctic tundra and northern forests. Obsolete and aging equipment leaks an estimated 1 million tons of oil onto the tundra each year. Heavy equipment tears up and destroys vegetation in one of earth's slowest-regenerating regions.

It's estimated that as much as 7.5 million square miles of reindeer grazing land have been destroyed. The toll on the peoples native to the Far North has been devastating. Those who lose their reindeer grazing lands are reduced to penury. These populations now are plagued by unemployment, alcoholism, and violence. Their death rate is two to three times higher than among European Russians; half of all deaths are caused by accident, murder, or suicide. One of these Siberian native groups, the Evenks, has a life expectancy of only thirty-two years.

The massive assault on the environment has in turn caused even more problems. In Central Asia, where diversion has turned the Amu Darya and the Syr Darya Rivers into meager streams, Uzbeks and Turkmens in neighboring republics send raiding parties across the Amu Darya to blow up competing pumping stations and destroy the canals that divert the precious water. Upstream, the Kirghiz and Tadzhik people threaten to impose charges for the water they pass on downstream.

Overall, Russia has made little progress in halting environmental degradation. A Duma deputy, Tamara Zlotnikova, said in November 1996, "The extermination of an entire people is taking place before the world's eyes and the world is silent." She asserted that Russia is the only country that has abolished its environmental ministry in the face of severe ecological problems. The man in charge of the one-room environmental "interdepartmental commission," Alexei Yablokov, has tried to monitor the problems that Russia faces. He documented a decline of 330,000 in Russia's population in 1995, despite half a million immigrants returning from former Soviet territories. Men are dying at four times the rate of women; on average Russian men now die at age 58–two years before they are eligible for pension.

The damage is not to Russia alone but to the Central and Eastern European states as well, and the full extent of the harm to the environment and to people's health is still being calculated. To start with, acid rain and other pollutants have already damaged about half of Central and Eastern Europe's forests. Just to stop the damage now and to stabilize it at current levels, estimates suggest, sulphur dioxide emissions in the region would have to be reduced by 70 percent by the year 2000. But reaching that target will cost $10 billion a year. In fact, emissions will more likely drop only 3 percent a year by the end of the century. By then and at that rate, the forest areas afflicted by acid rain will have doubled.

Hungary spends twice as much energy per unit of production as West European countries. Hungarian apartments, like those in Russia and other parts of the East, have no individual thermostats; they were cheaper to build that way. So apartment heat is regulated by opening windows, the most wasteful method known. The country's environmental ministry has found "pathological changes" in children exposed to high pollution levels in Budapest. An estimated 400,000 Hungarians drink water with high arsenic content.

The government of Václav Havel in the Czech Republic estimated that about seventy-two tons of pollutants fall every year on each square mile of Czech land, compared with a Swedish rate of 0.7 tons. More than 30 percent of the land, including Prague, the capital, is ecologically damaged. Nearly 60 percent of forests are stricken; about a fifth of Slovakia's forests are damaged. Seventy percent of the country's rivers are unfit for drinking or fishing.

The lignite mines in Bohemia, huge open pits stretching for miles, have swallowed an estimated 150 villages and towns since the end of World War II. The town of Most, a thirteenth-century Gothic village, is one of those casualties. Where it once stood, a huge open-pit mine now scars the earth. A newly built Most of concrete slabs was constructed nearby. The only part of the original ancient medieval city that still exists is its old church, a sixteenth-century structure that now stands next to a factory at the edge of the mine pit. An orange-gray smog shrouds Most. When a smog alert is sounded, some workers send their families out of the region altogether, away from the pollution. Children in Most are issued gas masks.

The town of Chomutov in a valley south of the Erzgebirge Mountains in northern Bohemia, not far from Most, may be the most polluted in the Czech Republic. Seven power plants in the area burn lignite, the region's soft ash-laden brown coal. The earth is scarred by hundreds of square miles of strip mines from which the sulphurous fuel is scoured. Several times a year an atmospheric inversion sends fire engines racing through Chomutov streets, broadcasting warnings to the citizens to get inside, out of the air pollution. Children aren't allowed out of classrooms or homes during these inversions. All windows are kept closed.

Workers are paid an annual additional bonus of 2,000 Czech crowns (about $100) to compensate for the dangerous conditions. They call it "coffin money." Workers also receive free coal to heat their homes. That only worsens the situation, because low-stack emissions from home and apartment chimneys keep the ash, sulphurous discharges, and other noxious output nearer the ground, where it adds to the pollutant load.

This region is about 5 percent of Czech territory, but it produces 40 percent of its electricity and over half its sulphur dioxide. The pollution is pervasive, thick, and low-lying. In Chomutov, four of five children admitted to the hospital have respiratory illnesses, allergies, asthma, and bronchitis. From December to February the wards are filled with babies and toddlers, as the region's weather and wind patterns intensify the low-lying pollution. Fully one-third of all children in the area suffer respiratory problems.

A geneticist who has studied a nearby town, Teplice, found that the incidence of allergies, mental illness, birth defects, and premature births is about twice the normal rate for the country. He sees indications of other serious damage as well, including immunological defects, a lowering of the immune response similar to AIDS, but from chronic exposure to levels of pollutants human lungs are not equipped to handle. Sulphur dioxide levels, which the World Health Organization says shouldn't exceed 50 micrograms per cubic meter, routinely run 100 to 170 micrograms and can reach 1,000. Infant mortality rates are 60 percent above Western levels, and rising.

The forest on the surrounding Erzgebirge Mountains is dying. The grass is a sickly yellowish brown, and miles of skeletal tree trunks stretch to the German border. Trees planted to revive the forest are stunted and brown.

Czechs estimate that cleanup of the soft-coal-burning region will cost not less than $24 billion over the next fifteen years. So the Czech Republic is forced to continue to rely on nuclear power, including plants with the troubled Soviet design known as VVER. The Czech Republic is Eastern Europe's largest producer of nuclear plants, and derives almost a third of its own energy from nuclear power.

But how safe is Soviet technology? In 1975 a four-unit nuclear complex at the Baltic Sea town of Greifswald in the former East Germany barely avoided an accident when fire cut off the power to eleven of the twelve cooling pumps. A Chernobyl-size catastrophe could easily have occurred.

Other reports of nuclear accidents at current plants, together with the existence of as many as twenty-four suspect VVER-model reactors in Eastern Europe, have accelerated safety inspections by the International Atomic Energy Agency.

The Slovakian Bohunice nuclear plant, a VVER model located less than fifty miles from Vienna, has been nicknamed "Chernobyl at the Gates" by Viennese, after the time when the Turks were "at the gates" of Europe and were stopped by Viennese resistance in 1683. Prague's Atomic Power Commission registered 360 safety incidents at the station in 1989 alone, and teams of inspectors from other countries have recommended its shutdown. Similar worries face other nations in the region, whose choices are limited to the polluting soft lignite from Silesia or the dangerous Soviet-era nuclear plants.

The former East Germany was also badly polluted. East Germany industry emitted five times as much sulphur dioxide as West Germany, twice as much as Poland. One-fifth of the water was too polluted for any use, and one-third of all animal and plant life was at risk of extinction.

Bitterfeld, about 110 miles south of Berlin, was the most polluted town in what its residents bitterly called the world's most polluted country. At the heart of East Germany's chemical industry, Bitterfeld's plants once emitted fifteen times as much sulphur dioxides and airborne particulates as anyplace else in the country. One local chemical plant dumped forty-four pounds of mercury into the Saale River every day—ten times as much as West Germany's giant chemical producer BASF pumps into the Rhine each year.

In Bitterfeld children often became sick shortly after birth. Life expectancy was five years below the national average for men, eight years for women. The pollution was so thick it blocked out the sunshine. Rivers flowed red from steel mill wastes, drinking water carried many times the European limit for heavy metals, and the air killed three-quarters of the trees in the area.

East Germans who tried to make their government respond to these and other problems under the old regime were harassed. Scientists were told to develop trees resistant to pollution, as though it were possible to develop a living plant that thrives on poison.

Since reunification in 1990, the changes in East Germany have been dramatic. New shopping centers, clean power plants, better roads, and modern factories and workplaces have brought former East Germans some of the benefits of Western economies that other Central and Eastern Europeans can still only dream about.

Environmental change has begun. At Bitterfeld many chemical plants closed in the face of competition from more modern, more efficient plants in the West. In the coal mining regions of Saxony and Brandenburg, 245,000 acres of land are slowly being converted to parks and recreation areas.

But the financial and social costs have been enormous. Since 1990 the citizens of the former West Germany have paid additional taxes of $100 billion a year to achieve the transformation. No other region of Central or Eastern Europe or of the former Soviet Union has seen, or can hope to see, any comparable effort.

Many East Europeans envy the former East Germany's relatively easy move into the orbit of the West. But there have been severe difficulties there as well. Birth and marriage rates in the East German states have fallen by more than half since 1990. Unemployment would be close to 40 percent were it not for make-work government projects. Eighty percent of working people have been forced to change jobs or to move to other regions to find work. The East Germans have made a good start at regeneration of the natural environment, but it will take much longer for the human effects of communism to be reversed.

The pollution behind the Iron Curtain spared none of the Eastern bloc nations. In Rumania the town of Copsa-Mica sits in the center of a fifteen-mile-wide area of caked soot from its own factories.

Bulgaria is a country of fertile soils and moderate climate, with many of its streams and rivers running into the Black Sea; only six of them can still be fished. Under the postwar Communist regime, Stalin turned the region adjoining the annexed land of Morava into the breadbasket of the entire region. Bulgaria exported two-thirds of the food it grew to other countries in the Soviet bloc. Then, in the 1950s, industry started to arrive.

In a valley north of the Balkan Range lies the town of Srednogorie. Thirty years ago the valley grew acres of roses whose petals were pressed for medicines and perfume oils. When the first copper factory arrived in Srednogorie, the community believed its higher-paying jobs would lead to a better life for everyone. What they did not know was that for the next thirty years emissions from the factory would douse their bodies, land, and water with a continuous outpouring of arsenic and lead. Arsenic has been found as far as twenty-five miles from the plant. An accidental spill of two hundred tons of arsenic in 1988 killed cattle and sheep and contaminated the farmland; residents weren't told what happened. Meanwhile, secret government documents showed that arsenic, lead, and copper levels in the town's dust exceeded the officially permitted rate by at least seventy times.

In 1988, when workers found cracks in the walls of the plant's waste-containment reservoir, the government covertly decided to let water out of the reservoir to reduce the pressure on its retaining walls. The sludge released into the nearby Pirdopska River was a toxic, highly concentrated brew of arsenic, lead, and other residues that remain when copper, silver, and gold are extracted from raw ores. After the sludge was released, some fields irrigated with the contaminated water registered concentrations of arsenic four thousand times higher than the permissible level. Throughout the summer of 1989, the authorities continued to allow the people to swim and fish in the contaminated rivers. In one affected village, farmers reported that their sheep were aborting instead of lambing and that their cows were going mad.

It wasn't until nine months later that protests forced the authorities to impose a five-year ban on swimming and fishing in the contaminated river and irrigating with its water. But 150,000 acres of contaminated agricultural land were still growing food people were not warned against eating. Twice in 1989, when the plant's controls failed, it gave off clouds of gas so poisonous that children were evacuated from the town.

The local hospital sees a frightening number of babies born with deformities, and adults with cancer and chronic mouth and lung diseases. Infant mortality is almost three times the rate elsewhere in Bulgaria.

Srednogorie is said to be Bulgaria's most dangerous town, but at least ten others are struggling with similar threats of pollution. Sofia, the capital, once known for its clear mountain air, loses a third of its water to a giant steel plant nearby, while that plant and another annually dump 20,000 tons of grime on the city's center.

By 1995 the number of automobiles on Sofia's streets had increased. But of 2.5 million autos in all of Bulgaria, only about 15,000 have catalytic converters. In southern Bulgaria a large lead and zinc smelter operates in Plovdiv. Lead concentrations in the bodies of people in the region are up. In the nearby village of Kuklen, children have so much lead in their blood that in the United States they would be candidates for detoxification in a hospital.

Tragically, a country that once exported two-thirds of its produce to help feed its Communist neighbors was by the end of the 1980s forced to import food itself, in part because almost two-thirds of its own land was so badly damaged by industrial fallout and chemical overuse.

In 1983, the Communist regime of Poland, under prodding from the Polish Ecological Club and others, issued a preliminary finding that eleven regions of the country suffered severe pollution. Those regions are concentrated in the Silesian Coal Belt, where over a third of the Polish people live.

Adam Urbanek, chairman of the Man and Environment Committee in the Polish Academy of Science, told a Western reporter in 1989: "We were all convinced that a planned economy created a real chance for effective environmental protection and that socialist countries having that kind of economy would have an advantage over Western countries. But that hope proved totally unfulfilled. Priorities were neglected, because the only priority under our system turned out to be heavy industry."

Marec Paszucha, the deputy mayor of Cracow, told another Western reporter that same year: "They wanted to break up bourgeois society and mix it with the working classes. They succeeded, and the results were catastrophic for the social structure and the ecology."

Those two comments reflect stark differences in the assumptions of each speaker. One was hopeful that communism would help his country avoid the mistakes of the capitalist West. The other was mistrustful of Communist motives from the beginning. But both acknowledge that communism has been a disaster for Poland's environment. The country has estimated that its environmental cleanup and abatement bill for the next two to three decades will run to $260 billion in 1993 dollars, a debt the next generation of Poles, as well as this one, must pay.

In 1996 opposition political leaders claimed that the costs of environmental cleanup accounted for 10 to 20 percent of the nation's Gross Domestic Product. A large amount of measurable property damage is from corrosion. The Institute of Precision Mechanics at Warsaw found that a huge portion of the cost results from the accelerated corrosion of the infrastructure—everything from bridges to paint.

An example is Cracow, once one of Europe's cultural treasures. A medieval city, it was once the seat of the kings of Lithuania-Poland, and boasts the Jagellonian University and the thousand-year-old Wawel Castle. Throughout its history it has had strong ties to Austria and France. At the end of World War II it had a population one-third greater than it has today. The city was saved from destruction in the Nazi retreat and today eight hundred of its historic buildings have been repaired and reconstructed. But the postwar domination by the Soviet Union and the Communist governments of Poland has done more damage to Cracow than the Nazis did.

In the early 1950s, the giant Lenin steel complex was built just outside the city. It is a network of power plants, foundries, apartment complexes, and public halls. It was designed to employ 40,000 people. When communism collapsed, its foundries still used open-hearth technology that existed nowhere in Western Europe. It had none of the scrubbers or advanced filtering systems that are common in steel plants in the Western world. The location of the Lenin Steelworks worsens the climate inversions that gave Cracow the world's most polluted urban air. The complex dumped 500,000 tons of air pollutants on the city every year.

The damage is visible everywhere in the city. The ancient red brick of the university is black with soot. The carvings on Wawel Castle are being turned to unrecognizable clumps of stone. Tapestries inside closed homes are blighted, and windows preserved from medieval times are being ruined.

The damage is outpacing the restoration. It is evident in the lives of the workers as well. Eighty percent of the Lenin Steelworks labor force retires prematurely on disability pensions; only 12 percent make it to normal retirement age. In 1994 frustrated workers threatened a hunger strike. That finally led to changes. The plant was renamed after Tadeusz Sendzimir, a Polish metallurgist who invented a steel-making process. Substantial changes were made as well. Continuous casting technologies have replaced open-hearth furnace production. Polish officials hope that the nationwide modernization of the industry will be complete by the year 2002.

The kind of degradation that is concentrated in Cracow can also be found across enormous stretches of the Polish countryside. The government in 1983 acknowledged that 11 percent of the land was damaged: that is 13,500 square miles on which 13 million people live.

Ninety-five percent of Poland's rivers and lakes are polluted. One survey found that 65 percent of the water was so contaminated by salts, mercury, cyanide, and human waste that industries were reluctant to use it at all. Poland began classifying water into three grades: fit to drink, fit for agriculture, and fit for industry. It has been forced to add a fourth category, which is "beyond categories"—in other words, unfit for any use.

Much of the farmland is overly acidic, and around industrial sites such as Katowice, average soil lead content exceeds the safety levels fivefold. Cadmium, another toxic metal, has infested some farms at four times safe concentrations—and in some places fifty times. Forty-one species of animals and birds have become extinct in Poland, and much of the remaining wildlife is at risk.

Life expectancy for men surviving infancy is lower than it was twenty years ago. For men aged forty to sixty, it is at 1952 levels. In the Silesian region, where the coal is mined and burned to produce electricity, circulatory disease levels are 15 percent higher than in the rest of the country, cancer rates are 30 percent higher, and respiratory diseases are almost 50 percent higher. A quarter of pregnancies have medical complications. Elevated lead levels have caused an alarming increase in the numbers of retarded children.

In 1989 the last five houses in the village of Wroblin, near the city of Glogo, were waiting to be bulldozed on government orders. What had once been a village of fifty-five homes, a church, a tavern, and a coffee shop became rubble. Ironically, the reason the government ordered Wroblin bulldozed was that it had been designated—together with several nearby villages—as a "protected zone."

For an American a "protected zone" conjures up the idea of a national park or wilderness area. In Poland under the Communists, a "protected zone" was exactly the opposite. What was being "protected" wasn't the safety of the environment, but the right of a polluting copper plant to continue polluting. The plant had to be protected, so the people had to be moved and their homes destroyed.

This illustrates an important difference between communism and democracy. Communism subordinates everything to its ideology and to whatever that ideology dictates, no matter how inhumane. Democracy takes steps dictated by the choices of the people, however imperfect. Under communism mistakes cannot be admitted because the ideology doesn't admit that mistakes can be made. Under democracy, correcting mistakes is what the system is supposed to do—and indeed does allow. That is why communism is dying and democracy is flourishing.

In America environmentalists are often accused of being extreme, of seeking to frighten people with doomsday scenarios and worst-case projections. Of course, some claims for the environmental cause are overstated. But so are some claims for the safety of industry and the benevolence of development in general. In a free society the right to speak out creates the possibility that some on both sides of every issue will speak intemperately and sometimes misleadingly.

But there can be few more graphic demonstrations of the larger truth about our natural environment than what has been revealed behind the Iron Curtain. A disregard for human dignity goes hand in hand with a disregard for the world we all inhabit. The habit of thinking that human beings are cogs in an economic machine leads directly to the habit of thinking that nature is nothing but a resource to be exploited for the same economic machine.

The natural world responds unforgivingly to exploitation, whether it is capitalist or Communist. Rivers don't know if the waste dumped in them comes from Communist or capitalist industry. The water is just as filthy in either case.

The natural world has its own laws and its own imperatives. Human beings disregard these natural laws at their own peril, whatever political or economic theories they choose to follow. That is the lesson that governments all over the world, under whatever system, democratic or otherwise, must repeatedly learn.

Chapter 14

THE COMING

WORLD CHALLENGE

THE TWENTIETH CENTURY has been one of innovation, horror, and drama. Early on, the United States became a powerful international economic and military force. Now, as we approach the millennium, America has emerged as *the* dominant world power—economically, militarily, and culturally.

Two great world wars were fought in this century. In both, Germany was the aggressor—and the loser. Yet both times from the ashes of defeat she emerged, phoenixlike, larger and stronger than ever. At the dawn of the twenty-first century, Germany is again the preeminent economy of Europe.

Man's capacity for evil found new and ominous outlets in this century. Fifty million people died in the Second World War, 20 million of them Russians. But it was the systematic murder by the Nazis of 6 million human beings, most of them Jews, that remains the most haunting memory of that conflict.

However, no event had greater meaning for the future than the triumph of democracy and the collapse of communism. This has left the United States in a position of unparalleled military dominance. That, combined with our moral status, will present exceptional challenges in the years ahead.

There have been dominant military powers throughout history. But such powers have usually been viewed with hostility by their neighbors and by those they sought to control. The Romans, the Ottoman Turks, the Hapsburgs, the British at the peak of empire, the French under the Bourbons and Napoleon—all fought and were feared by their neighbors and a succession of enemies. They had to force their way onto the soils of other nations and states. They maintained control by force or the threat of force.

The United States has no territorial ambitions. We do not seek to conquer other lands or to control other peoples. Others know that. They do not fear military conquest by the United States. To the contrary. Not only does America not have to force her way into other countries, she has difficulty disengaging.

Over the past few years I have met and talked with leaders in almost every country in Europe. I have asked each of them this question: Now that the Soviet Union no longer exists and her forces have been withdrawn from Eastern Europe, do you believe that the United States should withdraw her military forces from Western Europe?

Without exception, the answer has been no. There has not been one yes. Not even a maybe. European leaders—British, French, German, Scandinavian, Austrian, Italian, Czech, Slovakian, Hungarian, Polish, Russian, Ukrainian, and others—all want the United States to maintain a military presence in Europe. Most don't merely want it; they insist on it, fearing a dangerous instability should the Americans leave. Some who do not have U.S. forces on their soil want them sent there, as a short-term economic boost and long-term political insurance policy.

This extraordinary confluence—a dominant military power possessing a high level of moral authority—would alone place a heavy burden of leadership on the United States in the coming century. When combined with other pressures—population growth, Islamic fundamentalism, nationalism—it will no doubt present this country with an increasing number of requests to intervene in and resolve conflicts in every part of the world. Those added pressures, some of which overlap and intersect, will alter the shape of our world and the challenges our children will face.

POPULATION GROWTH

The continuing growth of world population will influence all efforts to gain access to trade, raw materials, technologies, and skills—in short, to all the tools of human survival and prosperity.

The United Nations announced in the late 1970s that the population growth rate had peaked and was beginning to decline. That was widely construed to mean that rapid population growth was over. That was not true. Population growth rates do not stop and start abruptly. When a car on a highway slows from a hundred miles an hour to sixty, we don't say it's stopped. It's still moving very fast. Global population is still rising, although a little more slowly than in recent years.

A survey by the United Nations, the preliminary results of which were made public in November 1996, confirms a modest slowing in the rapid rate of growth of the past half century. Between 1990 and 1995, population growth worldwide was 1.48 percent, down from the 1.57 percent projected in 1994; fertility declined from a previously projected average of 3.1 children per woman to 2.96. As a result, it is now estimated that in the year 2025 the earth's population will be 8 billion, down from the 8.5 billion projected in 1994.

To put these figures into context, it is helpful to look at the number of years it has taken (and in the future is expected to take) for 1 billion people to be added to the population. The 1 billion figure was first reached in 1804, eighteen centuries after the birth of Christ. It then took 123 years to add another billion, then thirty-three, fourteen, and thirteen years; by 1999, after just twelve years, another billion will bring the total to 6 billion.

The pace is expected to slow and stabilize in the next century: twelve, fourteen, thirty, then thirty-five years to reach 10 billion. This is good news but hardly cause for complacency.

Rates of population expansion are uneven among countries and continents. Between 1960 and 1990, U.S. population grew almost 40 percent, from 180 million to 250 million. In that same time span Europe's population of 425 million rose almost 20 percent, to 497 million. By contrast, the population in Africa—281 million in 1960—more than doubled, to 647 million. The overall Asian population has mushroomed from 1.66 billion to 3.1 billion in the same thirty years. Most of the 2.3 billion people who will be born between now and 2025 will live in the underdeveloped countries of Latin America, Asia, and Africa.

The shift in relative world makeup is notable. From about 1900 to 1950, the peoples of the developed nations comprised about one-third of humanity. Today they comprise about one-fifth, and by 2025 will make up less than one-sixth.

Nations face the enormous task of feeding, housing, educating, and employing these billions in some of the most marginal regions of the world. The task is complicated by the fact that much of this population growth is expected to occur in urban areas. Even now African cities are experiencing a growth rate of 5 percent per year, placing an intolerable strain on sanitation services, drinking-water supplies, housing, electricity, job availability, and food distribution systems. Asian cities, with a growth rate of over 3 percent, face similar strains.

Population growth also puts enormous pressure on the natural environment—freshwater use, waste disposal, croplands—as well as creating huge demand for other resources of all kinds, from energy to health care. The developed Western countries, including the United States and the nations of Western Europe, use about half of the world's primary energy production. The developing countries use less than 20 percent. The world's seven largest economies burn about 43 percent of the world's fossil fuels. Each American uses thirty-three times as much energy as each Indian. But it is in the least-developed countries that energy demand is growing fastest. In Southeast Asia, energy use is rising by more than 11 percent a year. Much of that energy demand is fueled by economic growth and the demand for better transportation.

The world's supply of light vehicles is estimated at half a billion. About a third of them are American, another third European. But the growth rate of light vehicles is outpacing population growth, even in parts of Asia and Latin America. At current rates, the world vehicle fleet could reach 1 billion by the year 2030, generating enormous demands for energy. The U.S. Energy Department has estimated that almost all increases in oil demand for the next twenty years will come from fleet growth alone.

The pressures on medicine worldwide are just as daunting. Despite impressive advances in medical science, major debilitating diseases are making frightening inroads. Even diseases once believed stamped out are making a comeback, while new scourges such as AIDS confront some of the world's most resource-poor nations with crises they cannot handle. About half of the world's AIDS cases are in Africa; by the year 2000, that will mean several million cases.

The high price of disease control and medical services, along with the economic drain diseases create, put an enormous strain on the poorest countries, where an average of less than $2 per capita is spent on health care each year. Access to medical services is wildly disproportionate among the developed and undeveloped nations. For example, the United States, with 260 million people, has more than 500,000 physicians. Bangladesh, a nation of 115 million people, has only 15,000 doctors. As population and urban crowding multiply in the coming decades, Third World countries such as Bangladesh face increasingly unmeetable demands for health care services.

As populations continue to rise, freshwater becomes more and more precious. Data about drinking-water access are notoriously hard to verify. The World Health Organization defines "access" as the existence of a public water supply within two hundred meters of a dwelling. Even by that standard the Congo, Mali, Mozambique, and Uganda cannot supply half their urban populations. In Bangladesh, with an urban growth rate of over 6 percent, barely a quarter of city dwellers have access to safe drinking water. Overall, it is estimated that 1.5 billion of the world's people are without safe drinking water.

These contrasts illustrate the huge differences in material well-being that already exist in the world, and point to the strains we can expect in the future. Combined with the inevitable political conflicts that governments have with one another, the pressures on the world's poorest half–and the "haves" as well–are likely to grow.

Political conflicts have always forced people from their homes and across borders into neighboring countries. According to the United Nations, about 18 million persons are currently displaced by famine, war, political conflict, natural disaster, or a combination of these. Within some countries enormous numbers of persons are homeless. More than 2 million people, almost 10 percent of the total population of the former Yugoslavia, were dislocated by the war there; another 650,000 may have become refugees in other European countries. The number of persons seeking asylum in the United States rose to just over 147,000 in 1993. We face a backlog of over 325,000 cases, persons whose right to be here is in doubt, but who are in the meantime working and may end up remaining illegally. Germany in 1992 had almost half a million non-German refugees seeking asylum, a far greater burden on an already densely populated country with an unemployment rate above 10 percent. The other countries of Western Europe, combined, received almost a quarter million refugees.

The growing resistance of Europeans and Americans to immigrants who are seen as competing for jobs, as well as for social welfare services they do not pay for, is but the tip of the iceberg internationally. In Germany neo-Nazi attacks on "foreign-appearing" persons have become common. Public demand forced the government in June 1993 to sharply curtail generous refugee laws. The large numbers of displaced persons, many of them homeless, the growing disparity in wealth among nations, and the rapid increase in population in undeveloped and less-developed countries have all contributed to making immigration an explosive political issue, conjuring up negative images, provoking intense feelings, and sparking debate as do few others. In the contest for the Republican presidential nomination in 1996, Pat Buchanan invoked immigrants as a cause of economic anxiety for Americans, riding the issue to victories in Louisiana and New Hampshire and to headlines everywhere. In 1994, Californians voted for a referendum to deny illegal immigrants access to education and every other public service except emergency medical treatment.

My mother was an immigrant, my father the orphan son of immigrants. I believe deeply that the United States should maintain a policy of accepting some legal immigrants. But that should not preclude a review of both current policy and its underlying assumptions. Although only Australia, New Zealand, and Canada, along with the United States, maintain large-scale immigration programs, while the majority of the world's nations effectively bar immigration, we should not join the majority. Migrants have contributed hugely to the richness and depth of American culture; our willingness to accept some new citizens will serve us as well in the future as it has in the past.

We should, however, step up our efforts to prevent illegal immigration. Half of all illegals *enter* the country legally but *remain* illegally. The number of illegals can be substantially reduced through better enforcement at the borders and, with improved technology, much more effective monitoring of those who enter legally. Ultimately, we can best discourage illegal immigration by encouraging economic growth and job creation in the home countries of illegals. Free trade, with all its short-term costs and dislocations, remains a powerful engine of economic growth.

Meanwhile, the gap between the world's richest economies and its poorest is increasing.

The U.S. economy annually produces $21,100 worth of goods and services per American. The Canadian and Japanese economies both produce more than $19,000 per capita. Fourteen of the twenty-six European countries produce more than $10,000 for each of their citizens, and the majority of the remainder produce national wealth well above the world average. There's every reason to believe the newly freed East European nations will catch up with West European economic growth early in the next century.

It is a different picture in other parts of the world. Egypt's economy generates just $630 per capita, and Egypt is one of the world's largest foreign-aid recipients. Many other countries are even poorer: Nigeria's economy generates $250 per person, Bolivia's $600, Haiti's $400, Kenya's $380. Bangladesh and Ethiopia have per capita production rates of $180.

The impact of these disparities and the worldwide struggle for a share of the planet's resources are likely to generate conflicts in trade, immigration, investment, and job growth that will challenge the world for decades to come.

ISLAMIC FUNDAMENTALISM AND NATIONALISM

Throughout the twentieth century, relative wealth and poverty, and the lust for power, fueled most of the conflicts within and among nations. The labels of communism, fascism, colonialism, and capitalism reflect the preoccupation of our century with political ideologies.

Two ideologies that have reemerged following the demise of Western colonial power in the Middle East and Communist hegemony in the European East are Islamic fundamentalism and nationalism. Some fear that these ideologies may come to play as large a role in the world as communism has for the past seventy years.

Terrorism directed at the West has been an element of the Islamic fundamentalist movement in the Middle East for several decades. The victory of the Ayatollah Khomeini over the Shah of Iran in 1979 seemed to endow fundamentalist Islam with a potency and power against which many feared that Western pragmatism might founder. But nearly two decades later, Islamic fundamentalism seems to be but one of several ideological movements, not markedly different in its ability to inspire supporters nor more successful in winning official government support.

When the OPEC nations, led by Arab oil producers, first wielded the oil price weapon twenty years ago, substantial oil funds were channeled to support Islam, both against socialistic governments in the Arab world itself and against what were seen as permissive Westernizing practices.

Oil money helped ferry millions of believers to Mecca for the annual pilgrimage, fueling movements across Arab lands to ban alcohol, to insist on the subservience of women, and to oppose Westernizing culture and modernity as an evil force.

But throughout the decade of the 1980s, countervailing signs appeared as well. Although the Ayatollah damned the United States as the "Great Satan," Iran found itself fighting in Afghanistan on the same side as the West—against an atheistic Soviet Union.

Iran and Iraq found themselves at war with each other. Syrian soldiers and PLO terrorist groups battled in Lebanon. In 1990 the Islamic world was split by the invasion of Kuwait by Iraq, an invasion reversed by Western power, led by the United States.

Although Muslims comprise a fifth of the world's population, the most populous Islamic states, Indonesia and Bangladesh, have not partaken of the fundamentalist extremes. While Islamic believers and others in India have clashed repeatedly throughout the last couple of decades, it was usually over local religious and economic issues, not the ambitious internationalist agenda promoted by the fundamentalist states of the Middle East. Despite its large Hindu majority, India is thought to have a larger Islamic population than neighboring Pakistan. But its Islamic population seems more concerned about getting its share of Indian economic growth than in confronting the West.

Within Islam, fundamentalism is primarily the province of the Shia, the minority among Islamic believers. It has failed to attract broad support among the majority Sunni believers. When Islamic fundamentalists seized a holy shrine in Mecca by force in 1979, they were ejected by Sunnis after a week of fighting. In 1987 a riot of 155,000 Iranian pilgrims to Mecca was ended by Saudi soldiers. The Iran-Iraq War ended without a victory for the Iranian Shia against the secular Iraqi state whose war effort, in turn, was funded by the conservative Sunni-majority Gulf oil states.

The diversity among Islamic countries makes it unlikely that a Pan-Islamic movement could unite them in an anti-Western crusade. Islamic movements frequently reflect causes and conditions in the individual countries where they are located, much as do Western political parties. Political parties can range from democratic to religiously inspired advocacy to extreme national authoritarianism. Islam, too, has more than one face.

NATIONALISM AS AN ideology is a product of nineteenth-century Europe. The industrial revolution more dramatically and more quickly altered the Western world for its inhabitants than anything comparable in known history. Theories such as Marxism, anarchism, utilitarianism, and nationalism flourished as people tried to explain what *was* happening and to predict what *would* happen.

In our century communism has been regarded as the most influential of these theories. But with the collapse of communism in Europe and Russia, nationalism and ethnic rivalries loom larger.

Both world wars included explicitly national and ethnic aspects. World War I resulted in part from Pan-Slavic Russian support of the South Slavs of Serbia. Germany's entry into the war in part reflected ethnic support of the Germanic Austro-Hungarian Empire. Hitler's 1938 Anschluss with Austria was also ethnic. The destruction of Czechoslovakia was fueled, he claimed, by the ethnic drive to regain the Sudetenland—11,000 square miles of territory inhabited by 800,000 Czechs and 2.8 million Germans.

Because of the horrors of Hitler's regime, the postwar world focused on German racism, virtually overlooking the strong Pan-Slavic movement. With the Balkan eruption and the Zhirinovsky phenomenon in Russia, that is changing. Nationalism and ethnic identity are both stronger and less predictable than Americans had anticipated.

Throughout human history, most people have lived in societies dominated by tradition: hierarchical societies governed by authorities, whether religious or secular, where each individual's life was largely determined by existing conditions, not by what the individual chose to do. It is this structure that the industrial revolution changed.

In Great Britain the process took place over several generations, while nations on the periphery of Europe, in regions such as the Balkans and the Caucasus, remained traditional societies much longer. Most of the Islamic states of the Middle East emerged as nations only in this century.

The idea of the nation-state was born amid the emerging modern industrial economy and reflected a moment of optimism in human history. Many people believed that wars would not be necessary if every nationality had its own state. They thought that people of similar ethnic origin, who spoke the same language and shared the same history, made up a more natural and therefore superior community than the combinations of peoples forced to live within a political entity such as the Ottoman Empire.

Independence and self-determination for each nationality was the most influential idea that President Woodrow Wilson took to Versailles after World War I. It appealed to Wilson's principles of "justice to all peoples and nationalities and their right to live on equal terms of liberty and safety with one another, whether they be weak or strong."

Nationalism is the principle on which postwar and postcolonial political settlements have been based ever since. It is reflected in the United Nations charter.

After the terrible religious conflict known as the Thirty Years' War left Central Europe devastated in the seventeenth century, it was long believed that war could only be avoided if religious status ran with state boundaries, a belief that has persisted in some Islamic countries to this day. Full civil rights were denied to those of minority religious faiths in Europe until the nineteenth—and in some cases even the twentieth—century.

With the development of modern economies and the natural sciences, the national group began to displace the religious group among more and more peoples. Today it takes precedence for most. In the Balkans, history has further complicated matters:

Croats, Serbs, and Slavic Muslims were separated politically between the Austro-Hungarian and Ottoman Empires and thus between Catholicism, Orthodox Christianity, and Islam.

The practical problems created by national states became clear after World War I.

Sir Lewis Namier described how, after the defeat of both Germany and Russia in the First World War made the existence of an independent Poland a possibility, a Polish diplomat "expounded to me the very extensive (and mutually contradictory) territorial claims of his country, and I enquired on what principle they were based, he replied with rare frankness: 'On the historical principle, corrected by the linguistic wherever it works in our favor.' "

In other words, a "national" territory can be defined by whatever theory grants a particular group the land area it wants. The Serbs today assert that a Serbian battle against the Turks that took place in the year 1389 gives them control of Kosovo, although the region is now about 95 percent Albanian.

Tomáš Masaryk used a similar combination of principles to create Czechoslovakia, which included Slovaks, who are not Czechs, and also incorporated much of German-speaking Bohemia. This in turn gave Hitler his pretext for biting off the Sudetenland in 1938 and led to the extinction of Czechoslovakia until its postwar reappearance. It is now gone again.

Hungary today contains 10 million Hungarians, but another 5 million live outside its borders in Rumania, Croatia, and Slovakia. Interwar Poland had a 14 percent Ukrainian population and a 10 percent Jewish one, along with German, Byelorussian, Masurian, and Ruthenian minorities.

In the post–World War II period, forced removals settled some national boundaries. When the boundaries of European nations were set in 1945 and 1946, the Germans lost all of East Prussia, which went to Poland. The western Polish border moved about 70 miles into German territory and the Soviet border moved about 150 miles west into Polish territory. Expulsions forced people to conform to borders. The Poles expelled Germans and moved Poles from eastern Poland into the vacated area. Stalin then moved Russians into the areas of eastern Poland that had been vacated by the Poles. Today's ethnic cleansing and territorial demands reflect a European tradition, not an innovation.

The problem of borders will exist wherever there are nation-states. Before twentieth-century cartography, national boundaries were less precise. There is no "natural" suprapolitical way to establish borders that can withstand valid challenge wherever a mixed population exists. A major problem for the nation as a state is the treatment of nonnationals living within it. One of two things happens to them. They either have a status, such as Jews had in interwar Central Europe, under which they suffer legal disabilities, and are vulnerable to legal and physical assault. Or they are made minorities, existing on the majority's sufferance but without the capacity to win better treatment on their own.

Wilson's error in 1919, repeated by others since, was to confuse the essentially American concept of self-determination with the European concept of national self-determination. The words are similar, but the ideas are very different.

For Americans, self-determination or self-government is a concept that assumes representative democratic institutions. It does not require an affinity of ancestry, history, or religion. But to a Hitler or a Zhirinovsky, self-determination has nothing to do with representative institutions. It has everything to do with ancestry, history, and religion. It is a description of a people's national destiny.

If the goal of nation-state self-determination is peace, it has not worked. A world of nation-states in this century has not proven more peaceful than the world of empires and colonies in earlier centuries.

The Marxist theory was that nationalism was an expression of the bourgeois period of history through which the world would pass, but that it would wither away because it was a product of "false consciousness." Marx was wrong about this, too. We are in danger of making the same error as Marx if we take nationalism as a universal phenomenon.

It is easy to mistake the beliefs of one's own time for universal truths. For hundreds of years, it was a "universal" truth that the largest problem facing human societies was the problem of growing enough food to keep everyone well fed. Today we know that's not the case. The problem of food and hunger is a problem of distribution and organization—a political problem.

Nationalism as a doctrine arose in and from a specific set of circumstances and conditions, and it reflects a set of ideas about society, politics, and human beings that are *not* universal. Like all ideologically driven principles, nationalism, as Namier said, can be adapted to the goals of whoever is invoking it. Hitler did it when he talked of the German nation and demanded that any territory occupied by German-speaking people must become German. Today, Vladimir Zhirinovsky is asserting a claim of Russian supremacy over bordering lands based on the historical relationship between those territories and the Russian Empire.

It is an error to assume that nationalism is powerful because it speaks to something so strong in human nature that it will find its way to the surface regardless of the political conditions in which a person lives. There is not much evidence in history to support that claim. Nationalism does not seem to have been a feeling that all persons in all places have felt as central to their lives. Greeks born into the Roman Empire wanted Roman citizenship but always considered themselves Greeks—and somewhat superior to the ruling Romans, for that matter.

Citizens of America, Canada, Australia, and New Zealand, all modern multiethnic societies, seem to be relatively untroubled by ethnicity. They join ethnic clubs and form anti-defamation societies, and they have preferences in food and traditions in holiday celebrations. But there's no serious evidence that second- or third-generation Polish-Americans, for example, harbor innate ethnic hatred for newly arrived Russian immigrants.

A situation such as now exists in the Balkans, where people have seen their relatives murdered in cold blood, fuels enmity. But whether it is fair to characterize those as national enmities, ethnic enmities, or blood feuds should remain an open question until we know a good deal more about conditions there. War reports by journalists, no matter how vivid and compelling, are not a good basis for making judgments about societies.

Where there are no perceptible threats and no perceptible enemies, ethnicity isn't a much stronger tie than any other. It exists, but determines fewer of a person's choices and activities than many other, more immediate pressures. It is only in an absence of alternatives that ethnicity tends to fill the void. This is when people become willing to kill each other because of the way they spell their names.

Nationalism is also a tool that has been cynically and effectively manipulated by elites. Miloš Vasić, the editor of *Vreme,* an independent newspaper in Belgrade, wrote in *The New Yorker* that the war in the Balkans was caused by precisely that misuse of ethnic identity: "It's an artificial war, produced by TV. All it took was a few years of fierce, reckless, chauvinistic, intolerant, expansionist, war-mongering propaganda to create enough hate to start the fighting among people who had lived together peacefully. You must imagine a United States with every TV station everywhere taking exactly the same editorial line—a line dictated by David Duke. You, too, would have war in five years."

THE IDEOLOGIES OF ISLAMIC fundamentalism and nationalism are manifestations of the same drives for security that have fueled conflicts since human history began. The international challenge facing the elected leaders of the United States in the next century will be to effectively exercise the power that flows from the United States' unique status as a moral and military power, without succumbing to the temptation to regard every problem in the world as one that requires an American solution. More simply put, it will be to know when it's appropriate to say yes and when it's necessary to say no.

Chapter 15

INTO THE

AMERICAN CENTURY

WE HAVE JUST COMPLETED a half century of military mobilization to defend the West against the former Soviet Union. While not abandoning our commitments abroad, I believe we must now mobilize with the same energy and commitment to confront the serious problems here at home that have been too long neglected. Violent crime is making many of our inner cities uninhabitable. Too many of our schools aren't preparing our children for the next century. Health care costs more and serves fewer people. The American dream drifts steadily further out of the reach of more and more Americans.

An immediate challenge is to continuously adjust our military establishment to meet the constantly changing threats to our security. A large national economy cannot be turned suddenly. Just as Russians and other East Europeans are discovering that it isn't possible to reverse the economic arrangements of seven decades without pain, Americans are finding that our own economic conversion isn't painless or cost-free either. Communities that have grown up around defense bases are looking for alternative ways to use those bases as the shape of our military changes. They wonder where the jobs will come from when the Pentagon stops buying.

Not surprisingly, the states that enjoyed the most robust economic growth because of defense contracts are now feeling the most painful contractions. When a community loses its economic mainstay, the contraction doesn't stop with the workers in a single plant or the people who worked on the military base. It affects every person in the town. Real estate loses value. Families lose equity in homes for which they have worked a lifetime. Small businesses find their customer base smaller, sometimes so much smaller that there's no way to keep going. Fewer people are left to pay higher taxes to maintain local services.

Conversion is difficult and painful. It is, in fact, a major economic and social shift, and its impact will be felt in many lives for many years to come. In some localities, the effect is similar to the contraction of purchasing power the whole country experienced during the Great Depression. That it is happening on a smaller and more local scale is of little comfort to the people it affects. We should recognize the similarities and take the steps necessary to prevent an already difficult transition from becoming more difficult still.

It has often been said by economic historians that in the end it wasn't so much what President Roosevelt did that ended the Depression, but World War II. That's partly true.

Before the war, conditions were improving modestly. But the Depression was far from over. By 1937, those modest signs of recovery persuaded some economists that it was time to return to the "sound principles" of governmental noninterference. Those "sound" principles stopped the recovery in its tracks. The recession-within-the-Depression of 1937 gave both Roosevelt and his opponents a shock.

For the United States, World War II turned out to be the most massive government spending program in its history. The budget doubled and redoubled, and the country went back to work. In the 1980s, when deficits were spiraling upward, we spent a trillion dollars to buy ever more sophisticated defense equipment. Each cycle increased overall economic activity.

It would be foolish to ignore the hard-won economic experience of the past. We learned during the 1930s, and particularly in 1937, that it's possible for an economy with great productive capacity to reach equilibrium at a much lower point than full production and full employment.

The best course is to stick with the one set by President Clinton in 1993: a steady, downward pressure on the deficit to bring the budget into balance. It has already produced steady economic growth and, for the first time in many years, a lower federal deficit four years in a row.

Economic policy in the post–Cold War era will not be easier to manage; indeed, in some ways it will be harder. The automation of manufacturing processes and in the service industries, with more functions performed by robots and computers, has reduced the demand for semiskilled labor.

At the same time, immigration to industrialized countries and the spread of low-tech manufacturing worldwide has widened the supply of less-skilled and lower-paid workers. There is now a global worker pool. When credit-card billing operations can be performed as reliably in the Philippines as in Nebraska, American workers must compete with an enormously expanded pool of lower-paid workers.

The new global economy also demands high-level skills. Those who can develop and manipulate the systems of modern production and processing will be in greater demand and command higher incomes.

These changes—increased automation in manufacturing and services and the widening of the pool of low-income workers—combined with other factors in recent decades to deepen income inequalities. By the end of the 1980s, reflecting a trend in all advanced economies, income disparity in the United States was the greatest it had been since 1939. Countries such as France, which sought by aggressive increases in minimum wages and unionized wage demands to preserve income growth for lower-skilled workers, were forced to compensate with higher levels of unemployment. We must recognize these factors and the global economy of which ours is a part and respond with better education and training to provide American workers with the skills that command high incomes.

One of the lessons we should learn from the end of communism is that without replenishing investment in equipment and people, economic stagnation is inevitable. The command economies of the Communist bloc didn't allow free play to consumer demand, so the producers of goods weren't warned by declining sales and profits when their products were undesirable. When the Iron Curtain lifted, we found that behind it the machinery was practically rusted through. There had been no incentive for factory managers to modernize, for workers to innovate, or for central planners to boost productivity. The result in some of those countries has been an educated workforce stuck with yesterday's technology. Their products will be unable to compete with those of the West until production processes and facilities are modernized and market feedback prods managers and workers to produce goods that satisfy people rather than the paper goals of a five-year plan.

Despite the strains of shifting to postindustrial production, the American economy remains an engine of job creation and growth. Ours is an economy that generates jobs, that creates markets for new products, and that will continue to be a source of innovation and growth.

Innovation and growth must go hand in hand with maintenance. Our nation has some of the best transportation, energy, sanitation, and public service infrastructures in the world. These are all elements of a modern society built on the investments our parents made. It is now our turn and our obligation to maintain those investments to sustain the free-enterprise system that makes possible our prosperity.

Our largest cities have aging water supply and treatment systems. The cost of replacement and renovation will be high. Yet the cost of neglect could be higher, and the health threats from malfunctioning sanitary systems cannot be tolerated. Old bridges and unsafe dams have to be rebuilt. Highway capacity and airports have to keep pace with transportation demands. New high-speed rail and mass transit systems are needed to relieve congestion. Crumbling schools must be reconstructed. Older ports must be modernized. Fiber-optic and other up-to-date communications systems must be built.

All of these are immense projects. All will demand workers and resources. And all are important to our future prosperity.

Most important, we must invest in people. In the post–World War II period and after the Korean War, the GI Bill made higher education available to millions of Americans who would not otherwise have had that opportunity. (I was one of them. After graduating from Bowdoin College in 1954, I served for two years in the U.S. Army. The GI Bill's benefits, when combined with the income from a full-time job, enabled me to attend evening classes at the Georgetown University Law Center, from which I graduated in 1960.) The costs of the GI Bill in direct taxpayer dollars were repaid many times over in higher incomes, higher living standards, and higher revenues to government. The GI Bill, like the land-grant colleges of the nineteenth century, was a great American innovation, one in which we should take pride and that should serve as a model for future action.

Educating our children for the future workplace is essential. More flexible training and retraining for today's workers is equally important. Most of all, we must develop better ways of blending the demands of a family life that is good for children with the need for two-income households. The future of the country depends on the environment in which today's children are raised. Children who grow up without an understanding of the liberties, rights, and obligations that are at the core of American life, who are exposed only to the economic benefits of living in an industrialized country and not to the responsibilities, may not understand that the driving engine of our prosperity is human freedom. Children who grow up in poverty, without skills or hope, in homes without parents or with parents who fail to provide nurture and direction, in streets where jobless adults hang around aimlessly—these children can become expensive burdens on society: through lives of crime, or through premature maternity or welfare dependency. And when their numbers are large and their behavior aggressive, they can fray the cohesion of our society by seeming to repudiate the values that sustain most American families. They can cause violence and divisions that not only ruin lives but undermine our future prosperity. I believe that the values of discipline, self-control, delayed gratification, and the work ethic are central to achievement in human life. But unless those values are grounded in the broader value of individual liberty and other American ideals, they can as easily produce a disciplined and successful criminal as they can a law-abiding citizen.

We ban some drugs not because we oppose the sense of well-being that certain chemicals can create in our brains, but because we know that euphoria unmoored from values is ultimately destructive, as are rewards unrelated to work. Some of the greatest pleasures of being human—mastering a skill, the intense satisfaction that comes from creative work or the enjoyment of great art, the deep and powerful response to spiritual experiences—require personal effort: study, practice, the acquiring of expertise. These are what our Founders meant by the "pursuit of happiness."

The chief crime the Communist system imposed on its people is that it barred them from the pursuit of happiness, in the process depriving them of their right to feel human. It made them into little more than creatures for the satisfaction of economic needs.

This is also a lesson of communism: an economic system is not an end in itself. James Madison described the purpose of government two hundred years ago as well as it has ever been described: "Justice is the end of government. It is the end of civil society. It ever has been and ever will be pursued until it be obtained, or until liberty be lost in the pursuit."

For a good part of this century, the American economic system and government were on the defensive. We faced problems at home that were widely known, because we have a free press. We read in our newspapers what other nations' critics said about our shortcomings. Privately, many Americans agreed with them.

During the Depression, many Americans marveled at Hitler's ability to give German citizens work. We were told that in Mussolini's Italy and Hitler's Germany the trains ran on time, with the clearly implied criticism that if our system couldn't even produce accurate railway timetables we should be ready to scrap it and try something else.

Although efforts to improve the conditions of life for working people here seemed painfully slow and inadequate in the 1930s, nonetheless the American system was able to abolish child labor; create minimum-wage and maximum-hour standards for workers; adopt fair labor standards; create the world's most efficient and broad-based credit system, which enabled people to buy homes, cars, refrigerators, and other large consumer goods they had never owned before; and create a social safety net that began with Social Security, and with the additions of Medicare, Supplemental Security Income, and other programs, has created an elderly generation with the lowest level of poverty and hardship in our history.

These actions helped more people participate actively in our free enterprise system, thereby unleashing the full human potential of our society. These are all genuine achievements. In recent years, as we have confronted the difficult tasks facing a modern society, it has become fashionable to sneer that government isn't the solution but the problem. It's a lot more revealing to ask what would have happened with child labor, workplace conditions, home ownership, illness, and old age without government action.

What is needed is a free-market economy with limited action by government to prevent the excesses inherent in an unrestrained free market from destabilizing the society. As we enter the twenty-first century, the United States appears to have achieved roughly the proper balance between private and public action. It requires constant refinement, of course, and that will be the subject of unending political struggle and experiment. But the principal economic lesson of the twentieth century is that a state-controlled economy cannot function efficiently. Clearly, the most efficient form of economic organization is the free market—with just enough regulation to prevent the social fabric from disintegrating.

That principle has been widely accepted in the United States. There is a broad consensus that the government has an indispensable role in establishing the political and economic stability necessary for the effective functioning of a civil society.

Thus, no mainstream political figure—not even the most conservative Republican—calls for the abolition of the Securities and Exchange Commission, or the repeal of insurance of bank deposits, or the unemployment insurance system, or the regulation of the financial, banking, and insurance systems, child labor and fair labor laws, the control of water and air pollution, or a whole host of comparable restraints. There *is* vigorous debate over how much or how little restraint there should be. But the basic premise stands unchallenged.

Government's role is important but limited. For example, there is insufficient private benefit to any one corporation in building a good highway between two cities. But there's clearly a benefit to all companies and all people when good highways are built and maintained by the government.

The stagnation of most incomes in this country has been well documented. It has helped lead to a situation where one wage earner with an average income can no longer make enough money to support a spouse, two children, and a mortgage payment. It has meant that millions of mothers of young children have been forced to enter the paid workplace to make a decent living for themselves and their families.

This has changed the childhood experiences of millions of Americans, and seldom for the better. By itself this would create strains in our society. Combined with other stresses, it has, for many, replaced hope with despair. Unfortunately, those most vocal about the breakdown in family values have had little to say about the economic forces that compel families to devote most of their waking hours to income production instead of child-rearing.

If there is one thing that is plain about the American experience, it is that leaders who inspire hope and give us the imagery to believe in ourselves win the loyalty of Americans. Leaders who seek to divide and conquer by turning Americans into a good "us" and an unworthy "them" ultimately fail.

FDR inspired people with the reassurance that their ingenuity and efforts could lift the miasma of failure that had crippled their hopes. Father Coughlin, the popular "radio priest" of the 1930s, had an audience of 10 million Americans, relatively as large an audience as Rush Limbaugh has today. He is an almost forgotten figure now, his fulminations against bankers, Communists, and Jews a discredited and minor footnote of history.

America responds to inspiration, and over time rejects divisiveness. Senator McCarthy today is not a revered figure, although in his time he roused millions to frenzies of fear and witchhunting. By contrast, Ronald Reagan won the votes and the allegiance of Americans because of his optimism and confidence in our national future.

Many Republicans have claimed that in November 1994, American voters repudiated the New Deal and all that it stands for–particularly the role that government plays in American society. The Republicans' "Contract with America"–which called for deregulation of an overly regulated economy, downsizing government, "devolutionizing" duties to states and cities and away from the federal government, privatizing tasks that government now does, term limits, a balanced-budget amendment to the Constitution, and reducing Medicare spending, even as more Americans become eligible–was effectively marketed as something the American people wanted enacted into law. That is how it was reported in the media before and after the 1994 elections. The Associated Press reported that "only issues supported by more than 60 percent of the public made it into the Contract." The *New York Times* said, "The Contract's provisions were tested in polls before the document was adopted, and a majority of Americans approve of them." The *Washington Post* reported that "[Frank] Luntz [the Republican pollster] market tested the Contract like a breakfast cereal."

It seemed to be a persuasive argument: the American people overwhelmingly support the provisions of the Contract so they should be enacted into law. Wholly apart from the wisdom of legislating by public opinion poll, the assertions of support for the Contract were untrue. The falsity of the assertions was exposed by an enterprising reporter named Frank Greve, who works for the Knight-Ridder chain of newspapers. Luntz initially told Greve that only "his client," the Republican National Committee, could release the backup material. RNC officials, upon being asked, said they had never seen the poll. Luntz then said he had done the survey "for himself" and that the materials were "private information," and he refused to let the reporter see them. Confronted with the code of ethics of the American Association for Public Opinion Research, which obliges a pollster who reports results to also disclose his questions and research methods, Luntz acknowledged that he had only tested campaign slogans. For example, he counted people as supporting tort law reform if they agreed with the statement that "we should stop excessive legal claims, frivolous lawsuits, and overzealous lawyers." Pollsters from the Roper Center for Public Opinion Research and Princeton Survey Research Associates said it is impossible to seriously judge public opinion with such leading questions.

At this point the RNC said there was *no* polling to develop the Contract. "We did what we did because it was good policy, not because it was popular," said Chuck Greener, communications director for the RNC. Barry Jackson, chief of staff to the House Republican Conference, added, "What Luntz has said about extensively testing the content is simply untrue."

This story appeared in Knight-Ridder newspapers on November 10, 1995. It was not picked up or followed up by the Associated Press, the *New York Times,* or the *Washington Post,* even though they had all carried the initially misleading stories.

While there is an undeniable streak of antigovernment hostility in our society, I believe that most Americans do not share that hostility. As trust declines—trust in neighbors and friends, trust in police and other legal symbols of authority, trust in our basic institutions—so also does trust in our government decline. But what the American people want is better and more effective government, not its elimination or evisceration. President Reagan said the government is not the solution, it's the problem. In 1994 a Republican candidate for the U.S. Senate said he wanted a federal government that does nothing. While these statements, and others like them, may draw applause from the faithful, they do not represent the considered view of the majority.

We should not confuse novelty with change. Republican majority rule in the Congress is a novelty, in that it has been four decades since that occurred. But true change alters the conditions of daily life for people so as to alter their expectations, their hopes, their plans, and their behavior.

Roosevelt brought about true change when he provided a degree of stability to the lives of ordinary citizens. Instead of destitution after a job loss, Americans could count on unemployment insurance to help tide them over. Instead of an old age of indigence and loss of self-respect, Americans could build on the base that Social Security assured them.

Nothing in the Contract carried similar assurances. Nothing in the Contract altered the relationship of today's working families with the economy, with their workplaces, with their status in our society. And to the degree that some elements of the Contract threatened to reduce the scope of the social safety net, it represented a threat to families' economic security. By targeting laws and regulations that protect our health and safety, the Contract revealed its desire to reestablish conditions that earlier generations repudiated. But in the end, it was the Contract itself that was repudiated.

We are passing through a period when, for political purposes, enemies must be created in the absence of real ones. A decade ago it was Soviet power. Today it's government itself.

That's not surprising. No one has easy answers for the problems ahead. It's important to remember that, to his contemporaries, Roosevelt's answers didn't seem persuasive and weren't seen as solutions.

In such circumstances those with the loudest voices, the most insistent public relations staffs, and the most relentless claims are often given attention over those with more meaningful ideas but who don't stoop to clamor.

There are still many Americans struggling to obtain the basics—food, shelter, economic security, a decent education for their children, health care. These Americans will respond to policies that promise to fulfill what they regard as their birthright, a decent life and the promise of a better one for their children.

The problems our economy and our society face are likely to be social and economic pressures that create change against which individuals can do little, but for which the society doesn't have an immediate or well-planned response.

One such problem the modern economy faced early on was efficiency and the assembly line. The tolerance of human beings for machines that moved the work under their hands and forced them to repeat the same motions over and over became the subject of intensive study. Solutions involving both technology and human relations were found.

Surprisingly enough, our system has adapted to major changes in the workplace and in such institutions as the human family with little organized outcry. Yet change in public policy, one of the least influential factors in a human being's life, is greeted with huge, well-financed mobilizations of interests opposed to change.

That's what happened in 1994 to health care reform. In the past the same thing happened with Medicare, Social Security, the right of working men and women to organize and bargain collectively. The same opposition said many of the same things. Opposition has marked every major social advance in this century. And all our nation's gains in growth and well-being have come despite the gloom-and-doom–sayers, who announce with predictable consistency that every social advance will lead, inevitably, to economic downfall. On the contrary, social advances lead to economic uplift. The reason for that should be obvious. Economies are the result of human activity. Improved human conditions lead to improved economies. The reason the Communist commissars failed was that they lacked faith in human beings. They placed their faith, instead, in theories of historical inevitability. Historical inevitability turned out not to be inevitable.

The same lack of confidence in people animates most of those who oppose social advance today, as it has throughout our history. Social Security, regulation of banking, labor laws, pure food and drug laws, universal education, Medicare—the list is endless; most of these ideas were condemned in their time as the work of socialists, Communists, and worse.

With the possible exception of Abraham Lincoln, Franklin Roosevelt was the most vilified president in U.S. history. Today, as we confront change as momentous as that over which FDR presided, it's well worth remembering that the human ability to predict the future is limited. Those who today are convinced that nothing government does can succeed may be as wrong as those who thought the opposite in Roosevelt's time.

Still, I feel safe in saying that one fear, once so pervasive in this country, is unlikely to be revived. That is the fear of communism. Throughout the McCarthy witch hunts of the 1950s, the argument was not only that spies and traitors in our midst were selling military secrets to the Russians, but that our way of life was being subverted. It was this fear that made so many Americans ready to give McCarthy the benefit of the doubt. Yet then and now, despite the many voices warning us against "creeping socialism," socialism remains unappealing to most Americans.

One of the reasons Americans can hope and strive for a better life is that the government's role isn't to guarantee success. It's to help create the conditions that give each individual a fair chance to succeed.

Ours isn't a perfect system. No human system is. But for more than two hundred years, Americans have enjoyed an unsurpassed degree of individual liberty combined with broadly shared material prosperity. Our system works because it is based on the understanding that while human beings seek financial security and physical comfort, they also have a larger destiny. That destiny, along with financial security and physical comfort, can best be achieved where everyone has a fair chance to succeed; where men and women know that reward is related to effort; where there is no limit to how far and how high one can go if one is willing to work hard.

That's the good news. The even better news is that our greatest years lie ahead of us, in the twenty-first century, a century I predict will be described by future historians as the American Century.

Selected Bibliography

Arbatov, Georgi. *The System: An Insider's Life in Soviet Politics*. New York: Times Books, 1992.

Beer, Max. *Fifty Years of International Socialism*. London: George Allen & Unwin, 1935.

Berdyaev, Nicolas. *The Origin of Russian Communism*. Ann Arbor: University of Michigan Press, 1969.

Berlin, Isaiah. *The Crooked Timber of Humanity: Chapters in the History of Ideas*. Edited by Henry Hardy. New York: Knopf, 1990.

——. *Karl Marx: His Life and Environment*. 4th ed. Oxford: Oxford University Press, 1978.

Bernstein, Irving. *The Lean Years: A History of the American Worker, 1920–1933*. Boston: Houghton Mifflin, 1960.

Beschloss, Michael R. *Mayday*. New York: Harper & Row, 1986.

Bialer, Seweryn, and Michael Mandelbaum. *The Global Rivals*. New York: Knopf, 1988.

Binyon, Michael. *Life in Russia*. New York: Berkley Books, 1985.

Blumenberg, Werner. *Karl Marx*. London: NLB, 1972.

Blumenthal, Sidney. *Our Long National Daydream*. New York: Harper & Row, 1988.

Browder, Earl. *Marx and America*. 1958. Reprint, Westport, Conn.: Greenwood Press, 1974.

Bullock, Alan. *Hitler and Stalin: Parallel Lives.* New York: Knopf, 1992.
———. *Hitler: A Study in Tyranny.* New York: Harper & Row, 1964.
Burns, James MacGregor. *The American Experiment.* 3 vols. New York: Knopf, 1989.
Caplan, Richard, and John Feffer, eds. *State of the Union 1994.* Boulder, Colo.: Westview Press, 1994.
Carr, Edward Hallett. *The Bolshevik Revolution, 1917–1923.* 3 vols. New York: Macmillan, 1950–1953.
Chamberlain, William Henry. *The Russian Revolution, 1917–1921.* 2 vols. New York: Macmillan, 1952.
Cole, G. D. H. *A History of Socialist Thought.* 5 vols. London: Macmillan, 1953–1960.
Conquest, Robert M. *The Great Terror: A Reassessment.* New York: Oxford University Press, 1990.
D'Encasse, Helene Carrere. *Decline of an Empire: The Soviet Socialist Republics in Revolt.* New York: Newsday Books, 1979.
Deutscher, Isaac. *Stalin: A Political Biography.* London: Oxford University Press, 1949.
———. *The Unfinished Revolution: Russia, 1917–1967.* Oxford: Oxford University Press, 1967.
Doder, Dusko, and Louise Branson. *Gorbachev: Heretic in the Kremlin.* New York: Penguin, 1991.
Eastman, Max. *Marx, Lenin and the Science of Revolution.* Westport, Conn.: Hyperion Press, 1973.
Engels, Friedrich. *The Condition of the Working-Class in England.* In vol. 4 of *Karl Marx and Friedrich Engels: Collected Works.* London: Lawrence & Wishart, 1975.
Florinsky, Michael T. *Fascism and National Socialism: A Study of the Economic and Social Policies of the Totalitarian State.* New York: Macmillan, 1936.
———. *World Revolution and the USSR.* New York: Macmillan, 1933.
Fontaine, André. *History of the Cold War.* 2 vols. New York: Vintage, 1970.
Freidel, Frank. *Franklin D. Roosevelt: Launching the New Deal.* Boston: Little, Brown, 1973.
———. *Franklin D. Roosevelt: A Rendezvous with Destiny.* Boston: Little, Brown, 1990.
Friedrich, Carl J., and Zbigniew K. Brzezinski. *Totalitarian Dictatorship and Autocracy.* 2d ed. Cambridge: Harvard University Press, 1965.

Gardner, Lloyd C., Arthur Schlesinger, Jr., and Hans J. Morgenthau. *The Origins of the Cold War*. Waltham, Mass.: Ginn-Blaisdell, 1970.

Goldman, Eric F. *The Crucial Decade: America, 1945–1955*. New York: Knopf, 1956.

Gorbachev, Mikhail. *The August Coup: The Truth and the Lessons*. New York: Harper Perennial, 1991.

Gwertzman, Bernard, and Michael T. Kaufman, eds. *The Decline and Fall of the Soviet Empire*. New York: Times Books, 1992.

Halle, Louis J. *The Cold War as History*. New York: Harper & Row, 1967.

Hazen, Baruch A. *Gorbachev and His Enemies: The Struggle for Perestroika*. Boulder, Colo.: Westview Press, 1990.

Hofstadter, Richard. *The American Political Tradition and the Men Who Made It*. New York: Vintage, 1973.

Holborn, Hajo. *The Political Collapse of Europe*. New York: Knopf, 1951.

Hollander, Paul. *Political Pilgrims*. New York: Harper Colophon, 1983.

Hook, Sidney. *Towards the Understanding of Karl Marx: A Revolutionary Interpretation*. London: Victor Gollancz, 1933.

Hough, Jerry F. *Russia and the West: Gorbachev and the Politics of Reform*. New York: Simon & Schuster, 1988.

Hyde, Montgomery H. *Stalin: The History of a Dictator*. New York: Farrar, Straus & Giroux, 1971.

Johnson, Paul. *Modern Times*. New York: HarperCollins, 1991.

Kaiser, Robert G. *Russia: The People and the Power*. New York: Pocket Books, 1976.

Khedourie, Elie. *Nationalism*. Oxford: Blackwell, 1993.

Kilroy-Silk, Robert. *Socialism Since Marx*. New York: Taplinger, 1972.

Laski, Harold J. *Karl Marx: An Essay*. In *Karl Marx: An Essay by Harold J. Laski, with the Communist Manifesto by Karl Marx and Friedrich Engels*. New York: League for Industrial Democracy, 1933.

Lefever, Ernest W., and E. Stephen Hunt, eds. *The Apocalyptic Premise: Nuclear Arms Debated*. Washington, D.C.: Ethics and Public Policy Center, 1982.

Leighton, Isabel, ed. *The Aspirin Age, 1919–1941*. New York: Simon & Schuster, 1949.

Lerche, Charles O., Jr. *The Cold War . . . and After*. Englewood Cliffs, N.J.: Prentice-Hall, 1965.

Leuchtenburg, William E. *Franklin D. Roosevelt and the New Deal, 1932–1940*. New York: Harper & Row, 1963.

——. *The Perils of Prosperity, 1914–32.* Chicago: University of Chicago Press, 1958.

——, ed. *The New Deal: A Documentary History.* New York: Harper & Row, 1968.

Lewin, Moshe. *The Gorbachev Phenomenon: A Historical Interpretation.* Expanded ed. Berkeley: University of California Press, 1991.

Lichtheim, George. *Marxism: An Historical and Critical Study.* 2d ed. rev. New York: Praeger, 1965.

Luxemburg, Rosa. *The Russian Revolution* and *Leninism or Marxism?* Ann Arbor: University of Michigan Press, 1961.

——. *Selected Political Writings of Rosa Luxemburg.* Edited by Dick Howard. New York: Monthly Review Press, 1971.

Maier, Charles S., ed. *The Origins of the Cold War and Contemporary Europe.* New York: New Viewpoints, 1978.

Manchester, William. *The Glory and the Dream.* Boston: Little, Brown, 1973.

Marx, Karl, and Friedrich Engels. *The Communist Manifesto* and *Address of the Central Authority to the League, March 1850.* In *Karl Marx and Friedrich Engels: Collected Works.* London: Lawrence & Wishart, 1978.

McLellan, David. *Karl Marx: His Life and Thought.* New York: Harper & Row, 1973.

——. *Marxism after Marx: An Introduction.* New York: Harper & Row, 1979.

Meyer, Alfred G. *Marxism: The Unity of Theory and Practice.* Cambridge: Harvard University Press, 1954.

Millett, Allan R., ed. *A Short History of the Vietnam War.* Bloomington: Indiana University Press, 1978.

Mills, C. Wright. *The Marxists.* New York: Dell, 1962.

Morgan, Ted. *FDR: A Biography.* New York: Simon & Schuster, 1985.

Morrison, John. *Boris Yeltsin: From Bolshevik to Democrat.* New York: Dutton, 1991.

Moynihan, Daniel Patrick. *Loyalties.* New York: Harcourt Brace Jovanovich, 1984.

——. *Pandaemonium.* New York: Oxford University Press, 1993.

Namier, Lewis. *1848: The Revolution of the Intellectuals.* Garden City, N.Y.: Anchor, 1964.

Nettl, J. P. *The Soviet Achievement.* London: Thames & Hudson, 1967.

Perkins, Frances. *The Roosevelt I Knew.* New York: Viking, 1946.

Pethybridge, Roger, ed. *Witnesses to the Russian Revolution.* London: George Allen & Unwin, 1964.

Pfaff, William. *The Wrath of Nations.* New York: Simon & Schuster, 1993.

Plamenatz, John. *German Marxism and Russian Communism.* London: Longmans, Green, 1954.

Raushenbush, Stephen. *The March of Fascism.* New Haven: Yale University Press, 1939.

Reed, John. *Ten Days that Shook the World.* Edited by Bertram D. Wolfe. New York: Vintage Books, 1960.

Reiss, Curt, ed. *They Were There: The Story of World War 2 and How It Came About, by America's Foremost Correspondents.* Garden City, N.Y.: Garden City Publishing Co., 1945.

Reminiscences of Marx and Engels. Moscow: Foreign Languages Publishing House, n.d.

Remnick, David. *Lenin's Tomb: The Last Days of the Soviet Empire.* New York: Random House, 1993.

Revel, Jean-François. *Democracy Against Itself: The Future of the Democratic Impulse.* New York: Free Press, 1993.

Rossiter, Clinton L. *Marxism: The View from America.* New York: Harcourt, Brace & World, 1960.

Rubel, Maximilien, and Margaret Manale. *Marx Without Myth: A Chronological Study of His Life and Work.* New York: Harper Torchbooks, 1976.

Ryazanoff, D., ed. *Karl Marx: Man, Thinker, and Revolutionist.* London: Martin Lawrence, 1927.

Schapiro, Leonard, and Peter Reddaway, eds. *Lenin: The Man, the Theorist, the Leader: A Reappraisal.* New York: Praeger, 1967.

Schlesinger, Arthur M., Jr. *The Age of Roosevelt.* 3 vols. Boston: Houghton Mifflin, 1958.

Seton-Watson, Hugh. *From Lenin to Khrushchev: The History of World Communism.* New York: Praeger, 1960.

Sheehan, Michael. *The Arms Race.* Oxford: Martin Robertson, 1983.

Shirer, William L. *The Rise and Fall of the Third Reich: A History of Nazi Germany.* New York: Simon & Schuster, 1960.

Smith, Hedrick. *The New Russians.* New York: Random House, 1990.

——. *The Russians.* New York: Quadrangle/New York Times Book Co., 1976.

Smith, Page. *America Enters the World: A People's History of the Progressive Era and World War I.* New York: McGraw-Hill, 1985.

——. *Redeeming the Time: A People's History of the 1920s and the New Deal.* New York: McGraw-Hill, 1987.

Snyder, Louis L. *The War: A Concise History, 1939–1945*. New York: Julian Messner, 1960.

Solzhenitsyn, Aleksandr I. *The Gulag Archipelago*. New York: Harper & Row, 1978.

——. *The Oak and the Calf.* New York: Harper & Row, 1979.

Toland, John. *Adolf Hitler*. Garden City, N.Y.: Doubleday, 1976.

Trotsky, Leon. *Lenin*. New York: Blue Ribbon Books, 1925.

——. *The Revolution Betrayed: What Is the Soviet Union and Where Is It Going?* Translated by Max Eastman. Garden City, N.Y.: Doubleday, Doran, 1937.

——. *The Russian Revolution: The Overthrow of Tzarism and the Triumph of the Soviets*. Selected and edited by F. W. Dupee. Garden City, N.Y.: Doubleday/Anchor, 1959.

——. *Stalin: An Appraisal of the Man and His Influence*. London: Harper & Brothers, 1941.

Ulam, Adam B. *The Communists: The Story of Power and Lost Illusions, 1948–1991*. New York: Charles Scribner's Sons, 1992.

——. *Lenin and the Bolsheviks: The Intellectual and Political History of the Triumph of Communism in Russia*. London: Secker & Warburg, 1966.

Ward, Geoffrey C. *A First Class Temperament: The Emergence of Franklin Roosevelt*. New York: Harper & Row, 1989.

Weiss, John, ed. *Nazis and Fascists in Europe, 1918–1945*. Chicago: Quadrangle Books, 1969.

Wildman, Allan K. *The Making of the Workers' Revolution: Russian Social Democracy, 1891–1903*. Chicago: University of Chicago Press, 1967.

George Mitchell was born in Waterville, Maine, in 1933. He began his political career in the 1960s as an advisor to Maine Senator Edmund Muskie. A lawyer by training, Mitchell was appointed to a federal judgeship by President Carter in 1979. After Muskie was appointed Secretary of State by Carter in 1980, Mitchell was named to complete the unexpired Senate term. In 1982 Mitchell was elected to a full Senate term in a stunning come-from-behind victory. After trailing in polls by 36 points, Mitchell rallied to win the election with 61% of the votes cast. In 1988 he retained his seat with 81% of the vote (to this day, a record for a Maine officeholder). He retired from the Senate in 1995 as the Senate Majority Leader, a position he had held since 1989.

Mitchell's work in the Senate led to the enactment of nursing home standards in 1987. In 1990 he led the successful reauthorization of the Clean Air Act, including new controls on acid rain. He was the principal author of the Low-Income Housing Tax Credit Program and he was instrumental in passage of the Americans with Disabilities Act.

After Mitchell's retirement from the Senate, President Clinton named him as his Special Advisor on Economic Initiatives in Northern Ireland. In the same year, at the invitation of the British and Irish governments, he was named Chairman of the International Commission on Disarmament in Northern Ireland and Chairman of the Peace Talks in Northern Ireland. In addition, Mitchell serves as Chairman of the International Crisis Group, a nonprofit group dedicated to the prevention of crises in international affairs. George Mitchell is also the author of *Men of Zeal: The Iran-Contra Hearings* (coauthored with then Senator, now Defense Secretary, William Cohen) and *World on Fire: Saving an Endangered Earth.*